GODDESS LAKṢMĪ :

ORIGIN AND DEVELOPMENT

GODDESS LAKṢMĪ :

ORIGIN AND DEVELOPMENT

Dr. UPEṆDRA NATH DHAL

M.A. (Sanskrit & Oriya), B.ED., PH.D.,
Formerly Head, Post Graduate Department of Sanskrit,
Utkal University, Bhubaneswar (ORRISA)

EASTERN BOOK LINKERS

DELHI : : INDIA

Publishers :

EASTERN BOOK LINKERS

H. O.: 5825/7, New Chandrawal,
Jawahar Nagar, Delhi-110007
Ph.: 9811232913

Show Room: 4806/24, Bharat Ram Road,
Darya-Ganj, New Delhi-110002
Ph. 45797575, 9718887575
e-mail: eblindology@gmail.com
ebl.info76@gmail.com
Website: www.eblindology.com

Edition: 2024

Rs.: ₹ 550.00

ISBN: 978-81-86339-07-7

GODDESS LAKSMI: ORIGIN AND DEVELOPMENT

By **UPENDRA NATH DHAL**

TO

PROFESSOR ANAM CHARAN SWAIN

FOREWORD

The benevolent and beautiful goddess Lakşmī has for three millenniums been among the most popular of Indian divinities. The spouse or śakti of the high god Viṣṇu, she has not generally received the same devotion as that accorded to her Śaivite counterpart, Pārvatī or Durgā, and few temples have been established in her honour. Yet she remains an important element in the religious life of Hinduism, and her images and pictures are to be found in many Hindu homes; for she is the bringer of good fortune in all practical enteprises, the bestower of health and security on her worshippers. Though in the past, like Durgā, she was sometimes worshipped in terrible forms, she is now-a-days looked on as altogether benevolent, a mother goddess without the awsome power of Durgā, but with no terrifying aspects, a goddess to be loved rather than feared.

Dr. U.N. Dhal has asked me to write a few words of introduction to his monograph on the origin of this beautiful and lovable divinity, and I am very glad to do so, not only because the cult of Lakṣmī is an important feature of Hindu religious life which has not been given as much attention as it deserves, but also because the work is one of much merit.

What impresses me strongly about this study is the way in which, in quite a small monograph, the author has succeeded in compressing an enormous amount of knowledge and information drawn from sources ranging from the Vedas to reports on contemporary or near contemporary popular Hindu rituals. In its admirable conciseness this book contrasts strongly with many similar ones, which consume much ink and paper and a great deal of the reader's time on unnecessary detail or peripheral matters which are scarcely relevant. In Dr. Dhal's study every sentence is important. This scholarly monograph forms an important contribution to the elucidation of Indian religious history, and it should be read by all students of the subject.

A. L. Basham
Australian National University,
Canberra.

January, 1976.

PREFACE

In the later half of the nineteenth century Hindu religion was studied by some western scholars with a view to prove their erroneousness. The religious bigotry and racial prejudice of these scholars led them to present a distorted picture of Hindu religion and Hindu divinities. Scholars and Indologists like H. H. Wilson and M. Monier-Williams who were pioneers in the field of historical study of Hindu cults were not free from such blemishes. Unlike Wilson and Monier-Williams, in 1882 A. Barth in his *The Religions of India* tried to give a faithful and realistic picture of Hindu religion in which he has not only traced in detail the growth and development of religious cults of India but has discussed them in a masterly way. After Barth's treatise *The Religions of India* by E. W. Hopkins appeared in 1894 in which the author has explained the religions of India in an orderly succession. He has made a study of Hindu religion "with the purpose to know the manner in which the religious and theistic ideas arose and developed among the people and the light these shed on the origin and development of such ideas elsewhere".[1] The same unbiased and objective approach to the study of Hindu religion was found in F. Max Muller who undertook the translation and edition of the *Sacred Books of the East* with the aim of helping philosophers and historians in evaluating correctly the real development of the early religious thought.[2] In these volumes he has tried to study the religions "on a

1. E.W. Hopkins, *The religions of India*, pp. 564-5.
2. F. Max Muller, *Sacred Books of thc East*, Vol. I, Preface, p. XX.

more real and sound, on a more truly historical basis".[3] In 1897 A.A. Macdonell brought out his pioneering work *Vedic Mythology* where he has made an exhaustive study of the different Vedic deities and the myths connected with them. The comparative and critical approach of Macdonell is evident in his introduction to *Lectures on Comparative Religion* where he says that the purpose of his study was to remove the prejudice and like a judge he wanted to take into consideration the merits and demerits of the religions without being biased by them.[4]

In the early part of the twentieth century scholars came to the field who took up the study of some particular aspects of Hindu religion or some particular Hindu divinity. R. G. Bhandarkar's monograph *Vaiṣṇavism, Śaivism and Minor Religious systems* published in 1913 is an outstanding work of this type. Bhandarkar has tried to study the deities of Vaiṣṇavism, Śaivism and other religious sects in a general way. Like Hopkins and Macdonell he did not confine his attention to a particular period but traced the development of the Vedic Religion or a divinity from the Vedic times onwards ending in Purāṇa literature.

Since then much has been written in general on Hindu religion and on particular Hindu divinities. In 1957 Tarapada Battacharyya brought out a monograph entitled *The cult of Brahmā*. *Materials for the Study of the Early History of the Vaiṣṇava Sect* written by H. C. Raychaudhury in 1920 describes the historical development of the Vaiṣṇava Sect. In 1954 J. Gonda published *Aspects of Early Viṣṇuism* where he has shed new light on Viṣṇu, the God of fertility and his relation with Indra.

The Śaiva sect and the divinity Śiva also attracted the attention of scholars. Mention may be made of the works like *The Śaiva School of Hinduism* (1934) by S. Shivapada

3. *Ibid*, Preface, p. IX.

4. A. A. Macdonell, *Lectures on the Comparative religions*, pp. 6-7, Calcutta, 1925.

Sundaram, *Origin and Early History of Śaivism in South India* (*1936*) by C.V.N. Ayyar, and *Śaivamata* by Yaduvaṁśī.

Besides these three principal divinities of the Hindu religion, considerable work has also been done on Gaṇeśa. Alice Getty's monograph Gaṇeśa (1927) and Haridas Mitra's book *Gaṇapati* throw much light on this important Hindu deity. The book *The Cult of Skanda-Kārttikeya in Ancient India* by Asim Kumar Chatterjee is a study on the same line.

A number of works has also come out on Mother Goddess in general. R. Briffault's *The Mothers* in three volumes is an outstanding work in this field. *Mother Goddess* by S.K. Dikshit and *Indian Mother Goddess* by N.N. Bhattacharya are the other important works on the subject. For the first time A.K. Coomaraswamy made a detailed study of the mother goddess Lakṣmī in his paper Early Indian Iconography II, Śrī-Lakṣmī in 1929. After him it was Gerda Hartmann [5] who wrote a treatise on Lakṣmī entitled *Beitrage zur Geschichte der Gottin Lakṣmī*. The authoress has discussed in her work the origin of the divinity, different purāṇic myths related to her and her relation with Mother Goddess Durgā ; but the book written far back in 1933 lacks a systematic treatment of the subject. The other treatise *Prācīna Bhārat me Lakṣmī pratimā* (Lakṣmī Images in Ancient India) limits itself to the discussion of images.

There are various aspects from which a study can be made on Lakṣmī the most popular divinity of the Hindu pantheon. There is a large number of images of Lakṣmī spread over both North and South India. An interesting study of the Goddess can be made from iconographical standpoint. The importance of Lakṣmī in pāñcarātra sect is another subject of research where one can trace the rise of Lakṣmī to supreme importance under the influence of the

5. I am thankful to Prof. K. Brurn, Frier University, Berlin for so kindly lending me a copy of Gerda Hartmann's work for my reference.

principle of Śakti. In the past, during the days of India's cultural hegemony the worship of Lakṣmī had spread to other parts of the East like Java, Bāli, Borneo, Indonesia etc., popularly known as the countries of Greater India. A number of hymns in honour of Lakṣmī find place in Sylvain Levi's *Sanskrit Texts from Bali.* A study on the subject will be both fascinating and rewarding. This deity is no less popular in Jainism and Mahāyāna Buddhism. A study of her role in these two religions will be no less interesting.

In the present study I have tried to present a picture of Lakṣmī as she appears in Sanskrit texts. In the first Chapter I have shown the origin of the concepts like Śrī and Lakṣmī and their gradual development into two divinities in the Vedic literature. The distinct features of these two divinities are made clear in the Śri-Sūkta which is appended to the ṚgVeda as a Khila; so a separate chapter has been devoted for this. The Purāṇapañcalakṣaṇa texts which constitute the urkern of the Purāṇas was formed even before the epic stories were finalised. So I have tried to show the development of the goddess as depicted in the Purāṇapañcalakṣaṇa texts in the third Chapter. In the chapter dealing with materials from the epics and the Purāṇas, an attempt has been made to describe the development of the divinity in a systematic manner with the help of different purāṇic legends. Due to the merger of Lakṣmī with Śrī, the inauspicious aspect of Lakṣmī formed a separate divinity namely Alakṣmī ; so the origin and the development of Alakṣmī has been discussed in Chapter five. When the Goddess became popular, various religious observances were formed in her honour ; the sixth Chapter deals with the festivities in honour of the divinity. Lastly, the growing importance of Lakṣmī in the Pāñcarātra sect has been mentioned in a general way.

I am deeply indebted to Dr. A. C. Swain, Professor and Head of the Department of Sanskrit, Utkal University Bhubaneswar, for his scholarly advice and encouragement in completing this work. There are many others to whom I wish to acknowledge my indebtedness. Dr. K. Brurn, Professor

fessor of Indology, Freie University, Berlin and Dr. J. Gonda, Professor of Oriental Languages, University of Utrecht, Netherlands were kind and prompt enough in sending some rare reference meterials to me on request. Dr. R. N. Dandekar, the former Director, Centre of Advanced Study in Sanskrit, University of Poona has ungrudgingly helped me with his valuable advice and suggestions whenever I had had the occasion to approach him. My thanks are due to them all.

I had the occasion to meet the eminent scholar and Indologist Professor A. L. Basham, Department of Asian Civilizations, Australian National University, Canberra, when he came to India last year on a lecture-tour. I am thankful to him for going through the book and writing the foreword.

My thanks are also due to Shri Inderjeet Sharma of Messrs. Oriental Publishers and Distributors, New-Delhi, for taking all possible care in printing and publishing this treatise.

VANI-VIHAR **Upendra Nath Dhal**

10th October, 1977.

CONTENTS

ABBREVIATIONS

A.A.	Aitareya- Āraṇyaka
A.B.	Aiterya-Brāhmaṇa
A.B.O.R.I.	Annals of the Bhandarkar Oriental Research Institute
Ap.Sr.S.	Āpastamba-Śrauta-Sūtra
A.S.S.	Ānandāśrama Sanskrit Series
Asv. Gr. S.	Āśvalāyana-Gṛhya-Sūtra
A.V.	Atharva Veda
Bar.Up.	Bṛhadāraṇyaka-Upaniṣad
Baudh. Dh. S.	Baudhāyana-Dharma-Sūtra
Baudh. Sr. S.	Baudhāyana-Śrauta-Sūtra
Ed. P.	Brahmāṇḍa Purāṇa
Bhag.	Bhāgavata
Br.P.	Brahma Purāṇa
Dbh.	Devībhāgavata
E.R.E.	Encyclopaedia of Religion and Ethics
Ga.P.	Garuḍa Purāṇa
G.B.	Gopatha-Brāhmaṇa
G. Gr. S.	Gobhila-Gṛhya-Sūtra
Hvm.	Harivaṁśa
H.O.S.	Harvard Oriental Series
Hir.Gr.S.	Hiraṇyakeśī Gṛhya-Sūtra
I.A.	Indian Antiquary
I.H.Q.	Indian Historical Quarterly
J.A.S.	Journal of the Asaiatic Society of Bengal
J.A.O.S.	Journal of American Oriental Society
J.B.	Jaiminīya-Brāhmaṇa
J.R.A.S.	Journal of the Royal Asiatic Society Great Britain and Ireland
Kath. Gr. S.	Kāṭhaka-Gṛhya-Sūtra
Kath. S.	Kāṭhaka-Saṁhitā

L.P.	Liṅga Purāṇa
Mark. P.	Mārkaṇḍeya Purāṇa
Mbh.	Mahābhārata
M.Gr.S.	Mānava-Gṛhya-Sūtra
M.S.	
(Maitr. S.)	Maitrāyaṇī-Saṁhitā
Mt. P.	Matsya Purāṇa
Par. Gr. S.	Pāraskar-Gṛhya-Sūtra
P.B.	Pañcaviṁśa-Brāhmaṇa
Pd. P.	Padma Purāṇa
PPL	Purāṇa-pañca-lakṣaṇam
Ram.	Rāmāyaṇa
R.V.	ṚgVeda
S.B.E.	Sacred Books of the East
S.B.	Śatapatha-Brāhmaṇa
Sk. P.	Skanda Purāṇa
T.A.	Taittirīya-Āraṇyaka
T.B.	Taittirīya-Brāhmaṇa
T.S.	Taittirīya-Saṁhitā
Va.P.	Vāyu Purāṇa
Vam. P.	Vāmana Purāṇa
V.S.	Vājasaneyī Saṁhitā
Var. P.	Varāha Purāṇa
Vidh. P.	Viṣṇudharmottara Purāṇa
Vi. P.	Viṣṇu-Purāṇa
Z.D.M.G.	Zeitschrift der Deutschen Morgentandischen Gesellschaft, Leipzig, Wiesbaden.

CHAPTER I

Sri-Laksmi in Vedic Literature

Indian Culture is a synthesis of Aryan and non-Aryan elements. In the process of subjugating the aboriginal population, the Aryans have adopted and encouraged a three-fold policy of conquering, colonizing and civilising the people. The non-Aryans who were possessors of an advanced material civilisation have to a greater extent influenced the Indian Culture which is noted for its power of assimilation. This is the case of a captor, who, in course of time, was himself captured and captivated. The Aryan element gave the newly formed Indian culture form and unity, discipline and order, but it was mainly the pre-Aryan Dravidian element on which the superstructure of the Indian culture is erected. In the general way three-fourth of our Indian culture is of non-Aryan origin. So it is expected that in order to trace the origin of our culture one has to go back to those non-Aryan sources. Unfortunately there is no written record of these non-Aryan traditions. So for tracing the evolution of any concept in our religion and philosophy, there is no other way for us but to begin with the Vedas, the earliest written records of the religion and civilisation of India.

The Vedic religion is characterised by the pre-eminence of male gods where female divinities may be said to be almost conspicuous by their absence or unimportance. The anthropologists and sociologists say that this is mainly due to the then prevailing patriarchal system in Indo-Aryan society. The female deities who make their appearance and are given secondary place are mainly Aditi, Pṛthivī, Sarasvatī and Rātri. Unlike all these female deities traced in the ṚgVeda, the goddess Śrī or Lakṣmī is mentioned not in the ṚgVeda.

proper, but in the fifteen verses appended to the regular collection of hymns of the fifth book of the ṚgVeda. So postponing the discussion of this appended hymn (Khila Sūkta) to a later section, we shall first take up the analysis of the terms like *śrī* and *lakṣmī*, the most common designations of our goddess as they appear in the ṚgVeda.

The passages in the ṚgVeda where *śrī* refers to benefit, advantage, riches, prosperity, well-being :

Three female divinities—Bhāratī, Ilā and Sarasvati are invoked—

ता नश्चोदयत श्रिये । (1, 188, 8)

"excite, inspire us for the increase of well-being."

अस्य श्रिये समिधानस्य वृष्णो । (4, 5, 15)

The bull (Agni) enkindled for the benefit of the sacrificer.

श्रीणामुदारो धरुणो रयीणां । (10, 45, 5)

Agni is a keeper of riches, and gives liberally various kinds of prosperity.

देवैरुत श्रिया । (6, 48, 19)

Pūṣan is equal with other gods in bestowing wealth and prosperity.

युवोर्विश्वा अधि श्रियः पृक्षश्च । (1, 139, 3)

The Aśvins are in possession of all *śriyaḥ*-benefit, prosperity, refreshment or nourishment[1].

वृषणं सश्चत श्रिये । (1, 64, 12)

Cleave to the impetuous vigorous Maruts for prosperity (*śrī*).

वर्धस इंद्र विश्वा अभि श्रियः । (3, 44, 2)

1. Goṇda justifies this interpretation in his book—*Aspects of early Viṣnuism*, p. 177.

Oh Indra, do thou increase upon us all sorts of prosperity (*śriyaḥ*)

यस्मिन् विश्वा अधि श्रियो रणंति । (8, 92, 20)

We are inviting that Indra to Soma drink in whom are embedded all benefits and prosperity.

श्रिये जातः । (9, 94, 4)

Soma, the king of plants and the drink of immortality is born in order to enhance well-being or prosperity.

श्रिय आ निरियाय । (9, 94, 4)

Soma has come forth for prosperity.

श्रियं वयो जरितृभ्यो दधाति । (9, 94, 4)

Soma bestows prosperity and vigour upon the invokers.

श्रियं वसाना अमृतत्वमायन् । (9, 94, 4)

The invokers have clothed themselves with prosperity or well-being.

जज्ञानं सप्त मातरो वेधमशासत श्रिये । (9, 102, 4)

When Soma was born, the seven mothers instructed him like a sage for the benefit and well-being (of the sacrificer)

श्रिये ते पादा दुव आ मिमिक्षुर् । (6, 29, 3)

The invokers offer adorations at your (Indra's) feet for prosperity.

श्रिये मनांसि देवासो अक्रन् । (6, 44, 8)

The gods turn their mind for bestowing benefits and prosperity.

तव श्रिये व्यजिहीत पर्वतो । (2, 23, 18)

Oh Bṛhaspati, for your benefit the mountain opened up the herd of kine it had concealed.

उप स्तोमान्तुरस्य दर्शथः श्रिये। (8, 26,4)

Oh Aśvins, do thou take note of the hymns of praise of the devout worshipper for his benefit.

इषुर्न श्रिये इषुधेर्। (10, 95, 3)

As an arrow goes out of the quiver attaining *śrī*—the distinctive prize of hitting the target, Urvaśī has gone out not to return again.

श्रिया त्वग्निमतिथिं जनानां। (10, 1, 5)

We invoke Agni, the guest of men for benefit.

अस्मे सोम श्रियमधि नि धेहि। (1, 43, 7)

Soma, grant us *śrī* which consists of a hundred men and great renown.

श्रिये ते पृश्निरुपसेचनी भूत् श्रिये दर्विररेपाः। (10, 105, 10)

May the spotted milch cow (refers to the Soma plant) bring you prosperity, may the flawless ladle bring you prosperity.

सुश्रियो दामन्वन्तः सुरातयः। (5, 79, 4)

Patrons with gifts, givers of rich presents are called *suśriyaḥ*—"blessed with fortune."

कृतं नः सुश्रियो नरेमा। (8, 8, 17)

Aśvins are addressed—Oh lords, make us blessed with fortune.

राजा हि कं भुवनानामभिश्रीः। (1, 98, 1)

Agni who leads all beings to *śrī*—prosperity.

श्रिये दिवो दुहितुर्जायमानः। (7, 67, 2)

The sun, the banner of the Dawn, the daughter of heaven is perceived rising in order to bring prosperity.

One of the main functions of the Maruts is to shed rain. They dispel the darkness, and their singing strengthens Indra in slaying Vṛtra. So it is said :

श्रिये चिदा प्रतरं वावृधुर्नरः । (5, 55, 3)

The strong and powerful Maruts have grown for prosperity.

श्रिये छंदो न स्मयते विभाती । (1, 92, 6)

Whenever Uśas shines, like a seducer she smiles for prosperity.

श्रिये सुदृशो वपुरस्य सर्गाः । (4, 23, 6)

The efforts of shining Indra are for the happiness of all.

उदु श्रिय उषसो रोचमाना । (6, 64, 1)

The morning Dawns have gone up shining for our prosperity.

पवमान विदा रयिमस्मभ्यं सोम सुश्रियं । (9, 43, 4)

Oh Soma Pavamāna, find out for us splendid wealth.

प्रातर्दनिः क्षत्रश्रीः । (6, 26, 8)

The son of Pratardana is endowed with the *śrī* of ruling power. Here *śrī* may be translated as welfare or prosperity (material power).

आसुते सिंचत श्रियं रोदस्योरभिश्रियं ।
रसा दधीत वृषभं । (8, 72, 13)

Milk and water are the two ingredients added to Soma juice. With reference to the milk it is said—pour the splendour (*śrī*) upon the pressed out Soma juice. For sweetening and invigorating (enriching) the Soma juice milk was added to it. With reference to this admixture of milk with Soma, it is said—Here pouring out of *śrī* upon Soma juice can only mean sweetening and enriching the Soma juice.

In Some passages meaning like splendour, beauty and glory can be justified. The Maruts are heroes of vigour endowed with mighty arms, their bows and arrows are strong; so according to the poet—

अनीकेषु अधिश्रियः । (8, 20, 12)

Beauty and splendour are embedded in all their faces.

The Maruts have spears on their shoulders, strength and energy are seated in their arms, the weapons in their cars, courage is in their heads, thus all splendour is assembled in their limbs—

विश्वा वः श्रीरधि तनूषु पिपिशे । (5, 57, 6)
अनु श्रिया तन्वमुक्षमाणाः । (6, 66, 4)

The Maruts manifesting their bodies with beauty and splendour are watering the earth.

शुभ्रा व्यंजत श्रिये । (8, 7, 25)

The bright celestial Maruts have decked their bodies for beauty.

श्रिये श्रेयांसः·········महांसि चक्रिरे । (5, 60, 4)

The Maruts put all splendour for display of their glory.

श्रिये कं वो अधि तनूषु वाशीः । (1, 88, 3)

The Maruts have swords upon their bodies for exhibiting their power and supremacy.

श्रिये मर्यासो अंजीन्रकृण्वत । (10, 77, 2)

The young Maruts have put on their ornaments for enhancing their beauty.

अधि श्रियो दधिरे पृश्निमातरः । (1, 85, 2)

Maruts, the sons of Pṛśnī, have put on splendour.

येषां श्रियाधि रोदसी विभ्राजंते । (5, 61, 12)

The Maruts shine in their chariots like golden sun shining above in heaven, both the worlds are over-spread by the splendour of Maruts.

गवामिव श्रियसे शृंगमुत्तमं । (5, 59, 3)

Like the horns of the cows, the horn of the Maruts is exalted for glory.

श्रियसे कं भानुभि: सं मिमिक्षिरे । (1, 87, 6)

The Maruts united with light and rays obtained splendour for glory.

श्रिया संमिश्ला ओजोभिरुग्रा: । (7, 56, 6)

The Maruts invested with beauty are terrible by their strength.

तव श्रिये मरुतो मर्जयंत । (5, 3, 3)

The Maruts have adorned themselves for the glory (*śrī*) of Agni.

Indra with the help of Maruts attains victory in his fight with Vṛtra and Sambara.

रुद्रास: सक्षत श्रियं । (8, 13, 28)

Maruts called sons of Rudra help Indra in the attainment of *śrī*. So helping Indra in the attainment of *śrī* would mean—helping in attainment of glory, pre-eminence, importance, greatness.

In tha ṚgVeda there are many instances where *śrī* just cannot be translated as 'beauty'. *Srī* refers to the totality of many elements which endow a man with *śrī*.

The Maruts have many good things on their arms; there are golden ornaments on their chests ; white garlands hang on their shoulders; their weapons are sharp. After describing these different features on the Maruts the poet says—

अधि वयो न पक्षान् व्यनु श्रियो धिरे । (1, 166, 10)

Like birds spreading out their wings, the Maruts spread out their *śrī*. Here *śrī* constitutes all the different elements like sharp arrows, beautiful garlands etc. which the Maruts possess.

वशानां भवथा सह श्रिया । (3, 60, 4)

By coming to the Soma drink in company with Indra, the Ṛbhus attained the *śrī* of all desires. Geldner[2] takes it to mean—'der krone (aller) Wunsche', which according to him would mean—immortality and divine rank.

मर्या इव श्रियसे चेतथा नरः । (5, 59, 3)

Think of glory like manly youths.[3]

समिद्धस्य प्रमहसोऽग्ने वन्दे तव श्रियं । (5, 28, 4)

Oh Agni, I praise thy *śrī* when thou art kindled and exalted in the strength. Here *śrī* does not refer to the beauty of Agni, rather the epithet—*samiddhasya* and pramahasaḥ make it clear that here *śrī* would mean 'glory and greatness.'

श्रिये रुक्मो न रोचत उपाके । (4, 10, 5)

Like a gold ornament in the vicinity Agni shines beautifully.

तव श्रिया सुदृशो देव देवाः । (5, 3, 4)

Oh Agni, the gods gained immortal life through thy splendour.

The glory and splendour of Agni when he glows in front of sacrifice are enviable to look at.

स्पार्हया यस्य श्रियो दृशे । (7, 15, 5)

Like the wealth of a man endowed with heroic sons the *śrī* of Agni when it glows in front of sacrifice is enviable to look at. Here *śrī* cannot be rendered as 'beauty'. The wealth of a man, having no sons, does not add to the glory of a man. But the same wealth of a man endowed with heroic sons brings glory and pre-eminence to its possessor. So *śrī* would mean 'glory, pre-eminence'.

2. K. F. Geldner, Der *Rig Veda* Erster Teil, p. 408.
3. F. MaxMuller, *S. B. E.*, Vol. 32, p. 347.

दृशानो रुक्म······दुर्मर्षमायुः श्रिये रुचानः । (10, 45, 8)

Like a gold ornament Agni shines imperishable life for well-being.

स दर्शतश्रीरतिथिर्गृहेगृहे । (10, 91, 2)

Agni, a guest in every home when kindled, his glory and splendour become manifest.

श्रियं वसानो अमृतो विचेता । (2, 10, 1)

Agni, the wise immortal when kindled upon the altar is invested with beauty and splendour.

अयं विश्वा अभि श्रियोऽग्निर्देवेषु पत्यते । (8, 102, 9)

Of all the gods this Agni alone possesses all glory and splendour.

Agni is called Adhvaryu : without him there can be no sacrifice. He causes the oblations to reach the gods. In this sense *Śrī*[4] of Agni consists in his glory and power, rank and position among the gods :

य उ श्रिया दमेस्वा दोषोपसि प्रशस्यते । (2, 8, 3)

For this glory and pre-eminence Agni is extolled in our homes both in the morning and evening.

शोचिर्वसानाः पर्यायुरपां श्रियोमिमीते बृहतीरनूनाः । (3, 1, 5)

Arraying himself in radiance and in the vitality of the waters, Agni displays his substantial and complete *Śrī*. If we take into consideration R. V. 1, 1, 3. here *Śrī* would mean glory, pre-eminence, capability.

तव स्पार्हे वर्णे आ संदृशि श्रियः । (2, 1, 12)

4. Gonda cites different instances from Ṛg Veda and proves that '*śrī*' was at least not always of an aesthetic or preponderantly aesthetic order. *Op. Cit.*, p. 180.

In the delightful colour of Agni can be found all beauty assembled.

अधि श्रियं नि दधुश्चारुमस्मिन् । (1, 72, 10)

The gods placed the beauteous splendour in Agni.

तव श्रियो वर्ष्यस्येव विद्युतः । (10, 91, 5)

The beauty of Agni is like the lightning of the rain-cloud.

श्रिये सुदृशी रुपरस्य याः । (5, 44, 2)

The rays of the sun beneath (Agni) present a lovely appearance in beauty and splendour.

विश्वा अधि श्रियो दधे । (2, 8, 5)

Agni is possessed of all glory.

इह सुश्रियं दधुः । (3, 3, 5)

Gods have established Agni in great splendour. This particular stanza makes it clear that *śrī* cannot refer to beauty alone, but to preeminent position. The bright Agni, his bright chariot, his residence in waters, his all pervasive attribute, his energy etc.—all these make Agni *suśrīḥ*

Aśvins invited to the morning libation of Soma are addressed as such...

युवोरुषा अनु श्रियं । (1, 46, 14)

— Dawn follows the beauty and splendour of your path.

युवं श्रियमश्विना·········वनथः शचीभिः । (4, 44, 2)

Oh Aśvins, you have enjoyed that beauty (refers to *Sūryā*) by your actions.

युवं श्रीभिर्दर्शताभिः·········सूर्यायाः । (6, 63, 6)

Oh Aśvins, with your ostentation of splendours you have brought rich gifts for Sūryā.

स्पार्हया श्रिया तन्वा शुभाना । (7, 12, 1)

The Aśvins look handsome with your enviable glory (*spārhayā śriyā*).

समु श्रिया नासत्या सचेथे ।। (1, 116, 17)

By attaining Sūryā the Aśvins were united with *śrī*. Here *śrī* would mean not beauty but pre-eminence, glory.

सह श्रिया नासत्यावृणीत । (1, 117, 13)

The daughter of Savitā chose your car along with your *śrī* (with reference to *Sūryā's* marriage with the Aśvins).

श्रिये पूषान्निपुकृतेव देवा । (1, 184, 3)

The Aśvins came to the wedding of Sūryā for attainment of *śrī*—pre-eminence, glory distinction.

युवोः श्रियं परि योषावृणीत । (7, 69, 4)

The maiden, the daughter of Sūrya made choice of *śrī* of the Aśvins, Aśvins are the two husbands of *Sūryā*. She chose them because of their *śrī*. Here 'beauty' cannot be taken to be the only meaning of *śrī* rather here '*śrī*' would mean—their 'superiority', 'pre-eminence'.

सूर्यस्य श्रिया सुदृशी हिरण्यैः । (1, 122, 2)

Bedecked with golden ornaments the Dawn is beautiful with the splendour of the Sun.

अधि श्रिये दुहिता सूर्यस्य । (6, 63, 5)

Uṣas, the daughter of Sūrya has mounted the chariot for displaying her beauty.

श्रिये परुष्णीमुषमाण ऊर्णां । (4, 22, 2)

Like waves of the river Parūṣṇī Indra is represented as clothing himself in wool for *śrī* (Geldner—zum Prunk; Griffith—for adornment).

श्रियो वसानश्चरति स्वरोचिः । (3, 38, 4)

Self-luminous Indra proceeds clothing in glory and splendour.

श्रिय·········दधे हस्तयोर्वज्रमायसं । (1, 81, 4)

Indra takes up the thunderbolt in both his hands for showing his supremacy

श्रिये न गाव उप सोममस्थुः । (4, 41, 8)

The hymns of praise glorify Indra and Varuna. As the milk of cattle adds *śrī* to the Soma juice, the hymns of praise glorify Indra and Varuna.

Three kinds of ingredients—milk, sour milk and barley were added to the Soma juice. This admixture is figuratively called a garment or shining robe of Soma. Hence it is spoken of as richly adorned. Thus it is said—

शिशुं न यज्ञैः परि भूषत श्रिये । (9, 104, 1)

Like parents decorating a child, decorate Soma for beautifying it. Here beautifying Soma really means—"enriching and invigorating" the Soma drink by the addition of milk, curd etc.

इंदवः············सुश्रियः । (9, 7, 1)

The drops of Soma have flowed forth the drops of Soma are *suśriyah*—endowed with all types of glory.

विश्वा अर्षन्नभि श्रियः । (9, 16, 6)

Soma purified in a sieve attains all sorts of beauty or splendour.

विश्वा अधि श्रियोऽधित । (10, 127, 1)

The goddess Night has put on all her glory and splendour.

अधि श्रियं शुक्रपिशं दधाने । (10, 110, 6)

Let holy Night and Morning be seated at their station assuming all their fair and radiant beauty. Complaining of the coldness and neglect of her husband Lopāmudrā says—

मिनाति श्रियं जरिमा तनूनां । (1, 179, 1)

Old age impairs the beauty of my limbs,

श्रिये गावो न धेनवोऽनवंत । (10, 95, 6)

Like milch cows the companions of Urvaśi lowed in competing with one another. Though with reference to the context this is the meaning, according to Pischel[5] and Geldner[6], yet the derivative meaning according to Geldner is 'um den Vorrang'.

In ṚgVeda there are some instances where *śrī* is connected with particles like *abhi*, *anu* and *adhi*.

भुवनानामभिश्रीः । (1, 98, 1)

Agni who leads all beings to *śrī* (gloriousness)[7] prosperity. Pischel (p. 55) "ein uber die Welten herrschender konig" Geldner (p. 127)... 'Oberherr der Geschopfe.'

घृतवती भुवनानामभिश्रियोर्वी । (6, 70, 1)

Lovely are the heaven and the earth, the asylum of created beings.

नियुतामभिश्रीः । (7, 91, 3)

5. Pischel, *Vedic Studian*, Erster Band, p. 273.

6. Geldner, *DER RIG Veda*, Dritter Teil, H.O.S. 35. Vide F. Note 6d, p. 301

7. Oldenberg, *S.B.E.*, 42, A, p. 127.

Vāyu adorns the team of his horses. He is the supreme lord of the team of his horses.

अग्निं·········अध्वराणामभिश्रियं । (8, 44, 7)

Agni is the supreme lord of sacrifice[8].

अध्वराणामभिश्रियः (10, 66,8)

Gods are supreme lords of sacrifices.

वर्धस इन्द्र विश्वा अभि श्रियः । (3, 44, 2)

Oh Indra, do thou increase upon as all sorts of prosperity (*śriyaḥ*)

अयं विश्वा अभि श्रियोऽग्निर्देवेषु पत्यते । (8, 102, 9)

Of all the gods this Agni alone possesses all glory and splendour.

विराण्मित्रावरुणयोरभिश्रीः । (10, 130, 5)

Virāj added to the power and might of Mitra and Varuna

विश्वा अर्षन्नभि श्रियः । (9, 16, 6)

Soma purified in a sieve attains all sorts of beauty and splendour.

बृहती अभिश्रिया । (9, 144, 6)

The mighty heaven and earth are endowed with *śrī.*

युवोरुषा अनु श्रियं । (1, 46, 14)

8. Geldner puts the meaning—"den oberherrn der opfer" Pischel in *Vedische Studian* (p. 53-55) supports Geldner. In justifying the meaning of 'power', 'lordship' Pischel comments that—Agni and Soma form the essential ingredients of sacrifice. Without Agni and Soma sacrifice cannot be performed and it remains incomplete. In this sense—Agni and Soma are said to have control over sacrifice.

In addressing Aśvins invited to the morning libation of Soma it is said—Dawn follows the beauty and splendour of your path.

अनु श्रिया तन्वमुक्षमाणाः । (6, 66, 4)

The Maruts manifesting their bodies with beauty and splendour are watering the earth.

अधि श्रिया विराजतः । (1, 188, 6)

Day and Night shine forth in their beauty.[9]

विश्वा अधि श्रियो धिषे । (10, 21, 3)

With black and white colours in its flames Agni is said to be in possession of all glory and splendour.

युवोर्विश्वा अधि श्रियः पृक्षश्च । (1, 139, 3)

The Aśvins are in possession of all *śriyaḥ*—benefit, prosperity, refreshment or nourishment.

यस्मिन्विश्वा अधि श्रियो रणन्ति । (8, 92, 20)

We are inviting that Indra to Soma drink in whom are embedded all benefits and prosperity.

विश्वा अधि श्रियोऽधित । (10, 127, 1)

The goddess Night has put on all her glory and splendour.

विश्वा अधि श्रियो दधे । (2, 8, 5)

Agni is possessed of all glory.

अधि श्रियं शुक्रपिशं दधाने । (10, 110. 6)

9. Geldner in translating this mantra comments upon *śrī* eigentlich das Bessersein, druckt vorrang, Ansehen und Schonheit aus.

Let holy Night and Morning be seated at their stations assuming all their fair and radiant beauty.

अधि श्रियो दधिरे पृश्निमातरः । (1, 85, 2)

Maruts, the sons of Pṛśnī have put on splendour. Then we come to a discussion of compounds like *Kṣatraṣrī, Ya jñaśrī, Janaśṛī etc.*

Varuna is *kṣatraśrī*—lord of material power, welfare, prosperity, (1,25,5). The son of Pratardana is *kṣatraśrī* (6,26,8).—endowed with the *śrī* of ruling power. Pūṣan is called *Janaśrī* (6, 55, 6), that is through Pūṣan people are endowed with *śrī* which may mean dignity, pre-eminence. The Maıuts are *ganaśriyaḥ* (1, 64, 9 ; 8, 23, 4 ; cf. 5, 60, 8), that is they form the choicest group. The intoxicating Soma drink is *Yajñaśrī* (1, 4, 7,)—which makes the sacrifice rich and prosperous. Agni is designated as *maryaśrī* (2, 10, 5)...beautiful like a youth Agni is *ghṛīaśrī* (1, 128, 4)—enriched with ghee. *Adhvaraśrī* is another epithet of Agni (144, 3.), it means Agni makes the sacrifice beautiful or more appropriately perfect and full-fledged. The horses who bring the Aśvins to the libations are called *adhvaraśriyaḥ* (1,47,8.) Here it is not so much important as to beautify the sacrifice rather as to make the sacrifice complete and perfect in every respect. Because unless horses bring the Aśvins to the sacrifice, they will not be able to enjoy the libations. So the sacrifice will be incomplete. Soma is called *adhvaraśrī* (10. 36, 8) that is, that Soma drink which enriches the sacrifice or which makes the sacrifice perfect. cf. R.V. 10, 78, 7 ; 8, 4, 14)

Usages like *aśrīrą* found in Ṛg Veda help us to get the meaning of the word *śrī*.

अश्रीरा तनूर्भवति रुशती पापयामुया । (10, 85, 30)

When the bridegroom wraps his own body with the

garment of his wife after defloration, the bridegroom's body becomes *aśrīra*...inauspicious.[10]

अश्रीर इव जामाता। (8, 2, 20)

The invoker prays Indra not to delay in coming to him like ugly (*aśrīra*) son-in-law.

यूयं गावो मेदयथा कृशं चिदश्रीरं चित्कृणुथा सुप्रतीकं। (6, 28, 6)

You cows, fatten the lean and emanciated, and make the ugly (*aśrīra*)[11] beautiful.

Now let us discuss the cognate words of *śrī* like *śreyas* and *śreṣṭha.* The use of the term *śreyas* is very rare in the ṚgVeda occurring only once in 10,31,2....

श्रेयांसं दक्षं मनसा जगृभ्यात्।

—let the sacrificer meditate in his mind the god who is better and the most mighty.

The few instances of the use of *śreṣṭha* show that this term is used as an adjective of *rūpa* and *peśa* (appearance), *rayi* and *draviṇa* (wealth), *bhāga* (portion), *kratvādā* (sacrificer), *sumati* (benevolence), *savīman* (protection, guidance), *jyoti* (luminary), of *Rudra*, *Bhānu* (rays), *sava* (libation), *bhojana* (food) etc.

10. Gonda prefers the meaning 'inauspicious' to the other meaning 'unlovely'. On the basis of the usages like *aślīka* , *aśrīka* found in post-vedic texts, Gonda takes the meaning to be inauspicious or unlucky (vide p. 182).

11. Oldenberg's interpretation of a son-in-law's ugly appearance is not accepted by Geldner, who takes it in the sense of 'Unfeiner Tochtermann'. Pischel connects *aśrīra jāmātā* with *vijāmātā* of R.V. 1,109,2. and takes the meaning 'ein unnobler Schwiegersohn'—a son-in-law bereft of nobility (*Ved. stu.* Vol. II, p. 79) Gonda interprets *aśrīra jāmātā* as one whose *śrī* has gone, in otherwards as an inauspicious son-in-law.

सूर्यस्य श्रेष्ठै रूपैस्तन्वं स्पर्शयस्व। (10, 112, 3)

श्रेष्ठं······पेशो। (4, 36, 7)

श्रेष्ठं वपुषं। (5, 62, 1)

Wealth, possessions etc. are called *śreṣṭha.*

श्रेष्ठं···द्युमन्तं······रयिं। (2, 7, 1)

इंद्र श्रेष्ठानि द्रविणानि धेहि। (2, 21, 6)

श्रेष्ठं नो······द्रविणं। (4, 54, 1)

श्रेष्ठं·········वरेण्यं भागं। (10, 35, 7)

श्रेष्ठं नो धेहि वार्यं। (10, 24, 2; cf. 3, 21, 2)

The Indra is invoked for *śreṣṭham vāryam* (*praśastatamam paśvādidhannm-Sāyaṇa*)

The sacrificer is *śreṣṭha*

क्रत्वा दा अस्तु श्रेष्ठ:। (6, 16, 26)

Agni is implored to bestow wealth on those praying with most prospering benevolence (*śreṣṭhayā sumatyā*)--(5,25,3.)

सवितु: सवीमनि श्रेष्ठे (6, 71, 2)

"May we live under the most beneficial of the god Savitṛ in order to receive wealth, who art concerned with giving a resting place to and the furtherance of all existing things" (cf.10,36,12).

The light of Uṣas is *śreṣṭha* among all lights.

इदं श्रेष्ठं ज्योतिषां ज्योतिरुत्तमं (10, 170, 3) cf. (1, 113, 1)

Rudra who shines in splendour like the sun, refulgent as gold is *śreṣṭh*a among the gods.

श्रेष्ठो देवानां वसु:। (1, 43, 5)

श्रेष्ठो जातस्य रुद्र श्रियासि (2, 33, 3)

Uṣas is addressed to shine upon the person praying and his relation---

अस्मे श्रेष्ठेभिः भानुभिः (7, 77, 5)

श्रेष्ठं सवं सविता साविषन् (1, 164, 26)

May Savitṛ accept the excellent libation.

श्रेष्ठं सवनं सुनोतनात्यो न (10, 76, 2)

Press the most excellent libations.

भोजनं श्रेष्ठं (5, 82, 1)

Svitṛ is expected to procure best type of food to man. Mitra and Varuna are *śreṣṭha varcasa*

श्रेष्ठवर्चसस्त उ नः (6, 51, 10)

Svasti well being fortune is *śreṣṭha*

स्वस्तिः·········श्रेष्ठं (10, 63, 16)

Yajurveda

In the Samhitas of the Yajurveda we come across the use of *śrī* in different contexts. When a man departs from this mundane world and attains heaven, he is said to have attained *śrī*.

श्रीर्हि मनुष्यस्य सुवर्गो लोको (T. S. 7, 4, 4, 2)

For a man the world of heaven is *śrī* (prosperity), In other places we find injunction to the effect that only those who have attained *śrī* (*gataśrī*) can perform a particular sacrifice.

नागतश्रीर्महेन्द्रं यजेत (T. S. 2, 5, 4, 4)

One who has attained *śrī* should offer a cake baked on eleven potsherd to *arkavat*, *aśvamedhavat* Indra (Maitrayani Samhita 2,2,9 ; T.S, 2,2,8,6.)

Similarly one who has attained *śrī* (*gataśrī*) should draw first the *sukragraha* (name of the pot for Aditya)--- *śukrāgrān gṛhnīta gataśrīyḥ* (Kathaka Samh 30, 3). There are three classes of people who are *gataśriyaḥ*—have attained *śrī* :

शुश्रुवान् ग्रामणी राजन्यः (T. S. 2, 5, 4, 4)

a learned (Brahmin), a village headman and a warrior.

A new concept which we find in these Samhitas, is that there are instructions for performing sacrifices to obtain *śrī*. In order to attain *śrī* and win over one's enemies one has to perform the *pañcadaśarātra* (fifteen days) sacrifice :

तेनासुरान पराभाव्य विजित्य श्रियमगच्छत् (T. S. 7, 3, 7, 1)

--With it he overcame and conquered the Asuras and attained *śrī* (prosperity). Similarly those who perform the twentyfour night (*Caturviṁaśtirātram*) sacrifice attain *śrī* (prosperity) - *śriyam gacchanti* (T.S. 7,4,2,1.) : The sacrificer who wants to excel persons of his equal status in *śrī* (prosperity) should perform the Kaukili Sautrāmaṇi sacrifice with his formula—

तेषां श्री मयि कल्पतां

(Kathak S. 38,2; Maitrayani S. 3,11,10)

Let their *śrī* be bestowed upon me. Offerings are offered to Indra for those who are worthy of *śrī*—

योऽलं श्रियै (T. S. 2, 2, 8, 6) :

Savitṛ is the promoter of *śrī*, a bull is sacrificed to Savitṛ for attaining *śrī*—

स एनं पुन: श्रिये प्रसूवति

(Kathaka S.13,6; Maitrāyaṇi S.2,5,5)—

he again promotes *śrī* for him. On another occasion a white goat is prescribed to be sacrificed to Vāyu for attaining *śrī*—

स एनं आशिष्टं श्रियं अभिप्रणयति
(Kathaka S.12,13,)—

he (Vāyu) brings him the desired *śrī*

Another feature noticed in these Saṃhitās is the close relation between *śrī* and *yaśas*. These two terms are found to be used together. In the Kaukili Sautramani sacrifice the Adhvaryu sprinkles water or milk on the sacrificer with the arms of Aśvins and hands of Pūṣan for gaining strength, wealth, *śrī* and *yaśas*—

श्रियै यशसे अभिसिंचामि (K a t h a k a S. 38. 4)

While sprinkling, the sacrificer touches his own limbs with the forumla—my head is *śrī*, and fame is my mouth—

शिरो मे श्री यशो मुखं (Kathaka S.38,4; Maitrāyaṇi S.3,11,8).

In the coronation ceremony for endowing the king with *bala yaśas* and *śrī* he is sprinkled with water with the following *Mantra*—

बलाय श्रियै यशसे अभिसिंचामि (V. S. 20, 3.)

—Oh king, I enthrone thee with strength and valour, *śrī* and *yaśas*. In the Pūrṇāhuti Mantra of a certain sacrifice the sacrificer prays for the attainment of *śrī* alongwith food, fame, wealth, etc.—

पशुनां रूपं अन्नस्य रसो यशः श्रीः श्रयतां मयि स्वाहा

(Kathaka S.39,2,2; V.S.39,4)—

May the ornament of cattle, the savour of aliment, fame, and *śrī* continue in my abode. Let this oblation be effectual.

The identification of *śrī* with different items or objects of sacrifice which is dealt with in wealth of details in Brahmana literature can be traced here. The intoxicating Soma drink has a very important role to play in the sacrifices. The Soma drink is identified with *śrī*—

श्रीः वै सोमः (Kathaka S.14,6;26,2,27,10; Maitr S.1,11,6; Kapiṣtha katha S.40,5)—

Soma is *śrī*. Again *śrī* is identified with the year—

एष व अस्थित श्रीः यत् सम्वत्सरो (Kathaka S.22,1; Maitr S.3,4,6).

Thus from a perusal of Samhitas of the Yajurveda we notice that the term *śrī* connotes prosperity, well-being, auspiciousness etc.

Śrī in Atharva Veda

In the Atharvaveda we come across the use of the term *śrī* in certain different contexts. The proclamation of victory in war through the beating of drums distributes *śrī*—

श्रेयो वन्वानो (5,20,9).

Śrī is connected with *bhūti* meaning 'growth, thriving and material prosperity.' Mother earth is invoked to make the sacrificer well established in *śrī* and *bhūti*

श्रियां मा धेहि भूत्याम् (12, 1, 6, 3) ;

It expresses the state of prosperity.

The amulet which Bṛhaspati bound on the gods for the destruction of Asuras is accompanied with *ūrja*—invigorating food, *payas*—milk, *draviṇa*—wealth and *śrī*—fortune, well-being (10, 6, 26). The amulet which helped Moon to conquer Dānavas yields to him *śrī* alongwith other power substance like *ājya* 'sacrificial butter', *bala* 'strength' *varcas* 'lustre', *bhūti* 'growth', *vājin* 'vigour', *kṛṣi* 'ploughing', *mahas* 'greatness', *sunṛta* 'youthful vitality', *amṛtam* 'immortality', *satya* 'truth', *jiti* 'victory', etc. (10, 6, 6-17)

The householder who takes his food without first entertaining his guest is said to lose his *śrī* alongwith such other power substances like *payas* 'milk', *rasa* 'sap', *ūrja* and *sphāti*—fatness, increase, prosperity, *prajā* 'progeny *paśu*, 'cattle', *kīrti* 'fame', *yaśas* 'glory', etc. (9,6,36.) In Pancodana sacrifice, to destroy the *śrī* of one's rival a goat is sacrificed—

भ्रातृव्यस्य श्रियं दहति 9, 5, 31

But if a Kṣatriya takes away an Agnihotra cow of a Brahmin, he loses his *śrī, dharma*, etc.—

श्रीश्च धर्मश्च 12, 5, 7

Śrī applies to concrete and visible welfare or prosperity.[12]

The night pictured as a woman and maiden of God Savitṛ, is said to have assembled all *śrī* in her—

संभृतश्री: 19, 49, 1

Śrī in Brāhmaṇas

When we come to the Brāhmaṇa literature we find that the concept of *śrī* has become more wide. We find that *śrī*

12. Gonda *Op. cit.* p. 182.

has been identified with different concepts like *prajā* (off-spring), *anna* (food), *kṣatra* (ruling power, dominion, chief-taincy, *rāṣṭra* etc.)

Śrī and Yaśas

Śrī is put on a par with *yaśas*. In order to be equal to Indra in *śrī* and *yaśas*—

श्रिया यशसा स्याम । (S. B. 2, 3, 4, 11)

One should make offerings to the three domestic fires when they are in full blaze. For attainment of *śrī* and *yaśas*—

श्रियं गच्छेयम् यशसा स्याम । (S. B. 2, 4, 4, 1)

Prajāpati performed the Dākṣāyaṇa sacrifice. Because of drinking all the Soma juice of Tvaṣṭṛ - Indra had to lose all his *śrī* and *yaśas*—

श्री यशसान्यू छ्वन्युदक्रामं । (S. B. 12, 8, 3, 1)

Svetaketu attains *śrī* and *yaśas*—

अजस्र एव श्रिया यशसा भवति । (S. B. 11, 6, 2, 2)

by performing the Agnihotra sacrifice in a particular manner *i.e.* because in the Agnihotra sacrifice he makes offering to both Agni and Sūrya. That *kṣatra* which is endowed with *śrī* and *yaśas* appears to be more covetable—

क्षत्रं श्रिया यशसा स्याम । [S. B. 2, 1, 3, 7]

The sacrificer is anxious to have *śrī* endowed with *tejas* 'fiery energy', *yaśas* 'renown' and *brahmavarcas* 'holy lustre' (S.B. 11,4,4,11).

Śrī and *Anna*

Anna (food) is equated with *śrī*—

अन्नं वै श्रीः। [J.B. 1, 11, 7]

and those who are rich in food are *śreṣṭha* among their people,—

अन्नादः······श्रेष्ठ। [J. B. 1, 108]

In the Newmoon and Fullmoon sacrifice by mixing powdered rice with water (*piṣṭabhiḥ*), the Adhyaryu is said to increase food and *śrī*—

श्रिये अन्नाद्याय।

of the sacrificer (S.B.1,2,2,3).

Śrī and Prajā

Śrī and *prajā* 'offspring' are often used in the same context (S.B.2,3,1,3), The benedictory formula in Iḍā offering (libation and offering of milk) runs thus—

प्रजा मे स्यात् श्रियं गच्छेयम्।

may I have off-spring, may I obtain *śrī* (S.B.1,8,1,36), The sole puropse of Prajāpati for performing Dākṣāyana sacrifice was the attainment of off-spring, cattle and *śrī*—

प्रजया पशुभिः स्याम् श्रियं गच्छेयम्।
[S. B. 2, 4, 4, 1 ; 2, 4, 4, 2 ; 2, 3, 4, 4]

Śrī and Cattle

Because of desecrating the sacrifice and drinking off Tvaṣṭṛ's Soma juice, *śrī* and *yaśas* passed off from Indra (S.B.

12,8,3,1). The cattle is *śrī* ; so a person who possesses enough of it is designated as *śrīmān*—

श्रीमान् पशुमान् [P. B. 13, 2, 2]

Payas (milk) is put on a par with *śrī*—

श्रीर्हि पयः । [S. B. 12. 8, 1, 21 ; 12, 7, 3, 13]

Like *payas vasā* (gravy) of the cattle is *śrī*—

श्रीः वै पशूनां वसा । [S. B. 12, 8, 3, 12]

In a Sautrāmaṇi sacrifice, the sacrificer is sprinkled with the gravy of the animal sacrificed for his *śrī*. The *rasa* (life-sap) of human beings is *śrī*

पुरुषाणां श्रीः यो रस S.B.6,1,1,4

Śrī and Other Worldly Possessions

In the description of the Fullmoon and Newmoon sacrifice, the S. B. (11, 1, 6, 23) defies. the different quarters. In that connection the western quarter is represented as hope—

तां आशां अकुर्वत्

then that 'hope' is represented as *śrī*, and lastly this *śrī* is again represented as earth ; because he who attains most from the earth becomes *śreṣṭha*. The earth of the *Karīṣa* (molehill) is conducive to the attainment of *śrī*. The man who has attained *śrī* is called *purīṣya* 'rich in manure or loose earth (S.B.2,1,1,7). *Pilippilā* 'the beautiful, shining and slippery earth after rains' is identified with *śrī*—

श्रीर्वै पिलिप्पिला [S. B. 13, 2, 6, 16]

The rain which fertilises the earth and aids to the growth of food crops is equated with *śrī*—

श्रियो वै पर्जन्यो वर्षति [S. B. 12, 4, 1, 11 ; J. B. 1, 117]

Loss of *śrī* is hunger (S.B.11.4,2,10). The topmost point of the tree where the power of vegetation and fertility rests is identified with *śrī*—

श्रीर्वै वृक्षस्याग्रं [T. B. 3, 9, 7, 4]

In Soma sacrifice the pitcher which is left out after others are put in pairs is called '*sadhana*'- common property. The pitcher designated as '*sadhana* is conducive of *śrī*—

सधनं......शियं अभ्यतिरिच्यते [S. B. 3, 9, 3, 34]

Various other objects or entities which are either *śrī* or add to the *śrī* of the sacrificer can be denoted by the same term. The Chandasya bricks used to construct the fifth layer of the fire altar are identified with *śrī* (S. B. 8, 6, 2, 1,). So Chandasya bricks are given to a king or a headman desirous of *śrī* (S. B. 8, 6, 2, 1). The great hymn of praise *mahad* (*uktham*) which is recited in the construction of the fire altar is *śrī* (S.B. 8, 6,2, 4; 8, 6,2,2,) The metre Bṛhati to which cattle are related is identified with *śrī* (S. B. 2, 7, 2, 15; 12, 8, 3, 24 ; T. B · 3, 11, 1; 20). Pṛṣṭha a particular arrangement of *Sāman* which is recited in the pressing of Soma is *śrī—śrīrvai pṛṣṭhāni* (A. B. 6, 5, 2, ; G. B. 2, 5, 11). Because a great number of *sāmans* is used on the ninth day of the ten-day sacrifice, the ninthday is identified with *śrī—śrīr navamam ahaḥ* (P. B. 15, 4, 5). In Asvamedha sacrifice the queen had to play a major role and anoint the horse ; because the wife is a form of *śrī*

पत्नयः·········श्रिय वा एतत् रूपं । [T.B. 3,9,4,7 ; S.B. 13,2,6,7·]

The lute, the sound of which is auspicious is a form of *śri* ; *śri* is conferred upon a person by playing on a lute—

वीणा श्रियमेवास्मिन् तत् धत्त । [T.B. 3,9,14,1 ; S.B. 13,1,5.1]

Śrī is frequently identified with the metre Virāj which expresses the ideas like— 'exellent, splendid ruling far and wide, preeminence, high rank, majesty'. The Virāj is regarded as food—

श्री: वै विराट् यशोहन्नाद्यं। [G. B. 1, 5, 20 ; A. B. 4, 11, 8 ; 6, 36, 6 ; S. B. 8, 3, 2, 13 ; 9, 2, 3, 40]

When the sacrificer prays for food Virāj metre is used (S. B. 11, 4, 3, 18). Virāj is also identified with *śrī* and food (G. B. 2, 1, 19 ; T. B. 3, 9, 8, 2). To obtain *śri*, off-spring and Virāj Sautrāmaṇi sacrifice is prescribed (T. B. 2, 6, 18, 2).

The householder who generally enjoys special honour and dignity among the other members of the household is identified with *śrī— śrīr vai gārhapatam*— (S.B. 5, 3, 3, 3 ; 5,4,3,15). That person is designated as *gataśrī*[13]—(of established prosperity) who would not wish to become economically better (*śreyān*) or worse (*pāpīyna*)

य: इच्छेत् न श्रेयान् स्याम न पापीयान्। [S. B. 1, 2, 5, 12]

As it is wrong to speak ill of man who is well-to-do (*śreyas*). One should not speak ill of *śrī*.

Śrī and Kṣatra

There is relation between *śrī* and *kṣatra* "ruling power, dominion, chieftaincy." Agniṣtoma sacrifice is recommended for a person desirous of *śrī* and *kaṣtra*. In the same context *śrī* is identified with *kṣatra*—

क्षेत्रं वै श्री:। (J.B.1, 272).

kṣatra and *śrī* are used together. In the construction of sacred fire altar, by laying down a single brick in the fifth layer of the fire altar, *Śrī* and *kṣatra* are attached to a single person.

13. *S.B.E.*, Vol.XII, Part I, p. 98

एकस्यं तत् क्षत्रं एकस्थं श्रियं करोति । [S. B. 8, 7, 2, 3,]

By offering oblation to Agni one endows a person with *śrī* and *kṣatra* (S.B.9,3,1,14). By constructing a single fire altar *Śrī* and *kṣatra* are endowed upon a single person (S.B. 9,4,32). By offering a single oblation of Vaisvānara cake one concentrates on a single person *kṣatra* and *śrī* (S.B.6,6,1,8). The close relation of *śrī* and *kṣatra* are better illustrated in the (A. B. 1,30 30)

क्षत्रं स श्रीः तत् आधिपत्यं ।

"this is *kṣatra*, this *śrī*, this over-lordship. One desirous of *kṣatra, śrī* and *yaśas* offers oblations to Agni in the summer.

क्षत्रं श्रिया यशसा स्याम इति । [S. B. 2, 1, 3, 7]

Śrī and Rāṣṭra

There is identification of *śrī* with *rāṣtra* (rule)—*śrī vai rāṣṭram* (T.B. 3, 9, 7, 1 ; S.B.6,7, 3,7). Through some sacrifice Varuṇa bestowed upon gods like Rudra, Aditya and Maruts royal power whereby they got *śri* and *rājya*

अश्नुते श्रियं गच्छति राज्यं य एवं वेद । [J. B. 3, 152]

The centre of the kingdom is identified with *śrī* (T.B. 3, 9, 7, 2, S.B. 13, 2, 9, 4). Śrī is identified with *rāṣṭra* and Aśvamedha (horse sacrifice)

श्रीः···राष्ट्रं···अश्वमेधं । [S. B. 13, 2, 9, 2]

In a horse sacrifice the priest endows the performer with *śrī* and *rāṣṭra*

श्रियं एवास्मिन् राष्ट्रं अधिनिदधति । [S. B. 13, 2, 9, 3]

Besides *śrī* being equated with *kṣatra* and *rāṣṭra* in Brahmana literature we get some examples where *śrī* is connected with a royal position. In Rājasuya sacrifice which is performed at the time of coronation as a mark of undisputed sovereignty, for attainment of *śrī yāṣas* and *annādya* the king is anointed (A.B. 8,6; 8,7,8,9). The anointment gives the king *śrī, aiśvarya* and *ādhipatya*- (A.B. 7, 20, 3). The king performing the Rājasūya sacrifice obtains tributes from all, and is established in *Śrī* (A. B. 7, 34, 9)

आदित्य इव···श्रियं प्रतिष्ठित ।

In such a ceremony the royal person's being is wedded to *śrī* who is presented here as a female being: ;

राज्यं इ वैप्राप्नोति···एतेनो हास्या सपत्नामुबाधा श्रीः भवति ।
[S. B. 2, 4, 4, 6]

The priest coming to the king while consecrating the water meant for washing his feet, says—In this kingdom I am depositing *śrī* :

अस्मिन् राष्ट्रे श्रियं आवेशयामि । [A. B. 8, 27, 2]

In a coronation ceremony the king ascends the royal throne. The Brahmana texts speak of this throne in glorifying term. Vadic metres and *sāmans*, ṛks, *vajus* etc. are identified with different parts of the throne. Important divinities like Prajāpati, Bṛhaspati, Soma and Varuṇa appear as the legs of the throne ; and the *upabarhaṇam* (cushion) on which the king takes his seat is identified with *śrī—śrīr* upa *barhaṇam* (A.B. 1, 12 , J.B. 2, 25). This identification of the cushion and *śrī* is significant in so far as the cushion adds to the *śrī* of the king. It is this cushion which actually endows the king with all sorts of power and prosperity like the tiger skin used in the Rājasūya sacrifice.

The possession of *śrī* expresses the state of prosperity and well-being in life, which leads to distinction or social preeminence. When it rains upon a person's Agnihotra milk, the sacrificer should know that *śukra* (sap) has come to him from above, that the gods have rendered assistance to him that he shall become Sreyān- *sreyān bhaviṣyāmi*-(S.B,12,4,2,10) that is his *śrī* will increase. When one peforms the sacrifice for one's own sake, he becomes *śreyān*- prosperous in cattle and off-spring; but when one performs the sacrifice for some body else, the personconcernedflourishes, but the priest remains like a withered trunk-

शुष्क एव स्थाणुः परिशिष्यत । [S. B. 9,5, 2, 13]

If it rains during Agnihotra sacrifice, the herbs and trees are produced on earth, seed flows from man and animals, and therefrom is everything generated; when abundant production has accrued to the Agnihotrin he becomes *śreyān*-

बहुः प्रजया पशुभिः भविष्यामि श्रेयान् भविष्यामि । [S. B. 12, 5, 1, 7

When the sepulchral mound is made on a ground which inclines towards the north the deceased man's off-spring becomes *śreyas* (more prosperous) (S.B. 13,8,1,6). In the Trirātra sacrifice the sacrificer has to donate three hundred thirty three cows on each of the three days of the sacrifice; the thousandth (*sahaśrī*) cow is to be released on the last day; and if this cow goes southward the sacrificer will shortly die; but if the cow goes northward the sacrificer will be more prosperous (*śreyan*) (S.B. 4,5,8,11).

Food is identified with *śrī*; one who has enough of it becomes *śreṣṭha* among other - *annāda śreṣṭha* (J.B. 1,108). One who knows and reveres *śrt* in a particular way becomes *śreṣṭha* of his region; even the princes reveres him (J.B. 1,271). The expression like *śreṣṭha svānām* means for who occupies social distinction or pre-eminent position among his fellow beings (S. B. 1, 6, 3, 22; 10. 3,5, 10). Indra is regarded as *śreṣṭha* among gods (T.B 2, 3, 1,3 : S. B. 1, 6, 3, 22 : 9, 2,2,3), so his equals yield to his supremacy (*śreṣṭhyāya*)—(P.B, 16,4 1,2;6,3, 9 ; 7, 52, 2). By virtue of early birth or superiority in knowledge one enjoy some social position which is called *jyeṣṭha* and *śreṣṭha* among others (P. B. 21, 2, 4 ; A. B. 4, 25:)

J. B. 2, 67: S. B. 10, 3, 5,10). *Śreṣṭha* and *baliṣṭha* run parallel, which mean superior in force strength and power among others. Indra and Agni are *balistha* (most powerful deities) so they are adored as *śreṣṭha* (S. B. 11, 5, 4, 2). One who performs Sarvamedha sacrifice attains *śreṣṭhya, svarājyam* and *ādhipatyam* (S. B. 13. 7, 1, 1).

In the Brahmanas we find that *śrī* is not used in the sense of beauty or brilliance ; but the scope of use has become wider. It has often, been used in connection with welfare, prosperity, advantage, food, material comfort, etc ; the possession of *śrī* and a state of thriving and prosperity, of enjoying economic, social and political pre-eminence is often expressed by the use of the terms *śreyas* and *śreṣṭha*. The significance of *śrī* becomes clear through numerous examples where *śrī* and *pāpmān*—evil, misfortune, unhappiness misery, wickedness and the state of being affected by sin are contrasted. Soma which is the drink of immortality and favoured libation of the sacrificer, is identified with *śri*, but a physical evil or disease called *yakṣma* is identified with *pāpmān*—

श्री: वै सोम: पाप्मा यक्ष्म: । [S.B. 4,1,3,9]

When Soma and Surā are contrasted Soma stands for ṣrī but Surā for *pāpmā*—

सोम: श्री:·········पाप्मा सुरा ।
[S.B. 5,1,2,10;5.1,5,28;2,3,3,13;5,3,2,13;14,1,1,31]

As thirst is removed through drink, darkness through light, *pāpmā* is removed by *śrī* (S.B. 10,2,6,19). *Śrī* can be attained by warding off *pāpmā*—

अपहत पाप्माऽनन्त्य श्रियं अश्नुते । [G.B. 1,1,38; A.B. 7,15]

Through some sacrifice one can repel evil and attain *sri*

अपशुचं हते·····श्रियं उपैति । [P.B. 12,6,10]

In the Rājasūya sacrifice by making a particular offering to Soma, Rudra the king is freed from *pāpmā* (evil), and becomes the very light by *śrī* and *yaśas* (S.B. 5,3,2,3,). Agni is the repeller of evil; the sacrificer by passing through the Āhavanīya and Gārhapatya fire repels *pāpma* (evil) and becomes the very light of *śrī* and *yaśas.*

अपहत पाप्मा ज्योतिरेव श्रिया यशसा भवति । [S. B. 2 ; 3, 3, 13]

One who speaks the truth becomes *śreyān* ; but one who speaks the untruth (*anṛta*) becomes *pāpīyān* (S.B. 2,2,2,19) Indra was *śreṣṭha* (pre-eminent) among gods ; this pre-eminence of Indra consisted of *vīryam somapīṭham* and *annādyam* : but when he lost all of these through Namuci he was overtaken by *pāpmā* (evil) (S.B. 12, 7, 1, 10). With regard to the exclamation *Vaṣaṭ* it is said—by pronouncing the formula *Vaṣaṭ* in a depressed tone one makes one's rival worse ; but by pronouncing it in a raised voice one places one's friend in prosperity—

शनैःतरं वषट् कुर्यात् पापीयांसं एव तत् करोति,

उच्चैतरं वषट् कुर्यात् श्रिये एव (A. B. 3, 7)

Thus we have seen above that various objects or entities which bring material prosperity, economic welfare and social well-being have been identified with *śrī*. Oldenberg[14] after long deliberation chiefly finds out the term *śrī* used in the sense of beauty. In addition to that we come across such usages of *śrī* where it is used in the context of material wealth, well-being, fortune and social pre-eminence for which one commands position of honour and respect among one's people. Ultimately we reach a point in Satapatha Brāhmaṇa where *śrī* is personified and is represented as being born from Prajāpati when he was practising fervid penance—

तस्मात् श्रान्ताद् तपनात् श्रीः उदक्रामत् । [11, 4, 3, 1[

14. H. Oldenburg, 'Die Vedischen Worte fur "Schon" und "Schonhut' und das Vedische Schonhutsgefuhl", *Kleine Schriften*, p. 830 ff.

She stands resplendent, shining and trembling. The gods were envious of her possessions and wanted to kill her and take away all her possessions. Prajāpati dissuaded them from killing Śrī because she happens to be a woman; he rather advised the gods to take all her possessions and to leave her unhurt. Agni took her *annādya* (food), Soma her *rājya* (royal power), Varuṇa her *sāmrājya* (universal sovereignty), Mitra her *kṣatra* (noble rank), Indra her *bala* (strength, power,) Bṛhaspati her *brahmavarcas* (holy lustre), Savitṛ her *rāṣṭra* (dominion), Pūṣan her *bhaga* (wealth), Sarasvatī her *puṣṭi* (prosperity), Tvaṣṭṛ her beautiful *rūpa* (form) (S.B. 11, 4, 3,1—3). On the advice of Prajāpati she recovers her possession by performing Mitravinda sacrifice. It appears from the above account that Śrī personified represented food, royal power, universal sovereignty, lustre, power, beauty and other qualities through which her personality manifests. If we take a critical view of the account we notice that the different divinities who robbed off the specific qualities from Śrī were actually in possession of these qualities long before Śri attained pre-eminence. Once Śri's personality developed, and she came to represent all these different aspects of glory and honour the different deities were pictured as having borrowed those specific qualities from Śrī. In the very text (S.B. 14, 9, 3, 8) alongwith other deities like Soma, Lakṣmī, Sāvitrī, Sarasvatī, etc. oblations are offered to Śrī for achieving something great—

महद् प्राप्नुयाम् इति श्रियै स्वाहा······लक्ष्म्यै स्वाहा।

From separate mention of Lakṣmī it becomes clear that Śrī has not yet been fused with Lakṣmī but moves side by side as an independent deity accepting offerings or oblations from the sacrificer. In T.A. (3,13,2) the resplendent shining deity Śrī born from Prajāpati appears as his wife, her co-wife being Lakṣmī.

श्रीश्चते लक्ष्मीश्च पत्न्यौ।

In the period of the *Saṁhitas*, *śrī* referred to beauty, brilliance, splendour, etc. Different deities, their grace and their chariot were endowed with *śrī*. In the Brāhmaṇa period particularly in the Śatapatha Brāhmaṇa we find that the personality of Śrī becomes more and more clear. Her birth from the primal creator, Prajāpati, the greed and avarice of different gods to rob of her royal power, lustre, beauty, etc., the offering of oblations to her for attaining something great, and lastly her position as the consort of Prajāpati—all these indicate that Śrī is gradually rising to the position of a divinity capable of bestowing wealth and splendour.

Śrī in the Upaniṣads

When we come to the Upaniṣads we find that this literature does not throw any new light on the development of the concept of *Śrī*. As in the Brāhmaṇas here *Śrī* is identified with woolly animlas.—

श्रियं······लोमशं । [Taitt. UP. 1, 4, 2]

The Bṛhad Āraṇyaka Upaniṣad (2.3,6,) speaks of *śrī* of lightning ; the Maitrī Upaniṣad (1,4) speaks of *mahatī Śrī* (opulence or well-being) of great kings like Nahuṣa and Yayāti ; the only case of personification of *śrī* appears in Bṛhad Āraṇyaka Upaniṣad (6,4,6) where the woman after defloration is represented as an embodiment of *Śrī* (definitely referring to the divinity personified)—

श्रीः वा एषा स्त्रीणां यत् मलोद्वासः ।

It is but natural to identify a female ready to produce and procreate after menstruation with *Śrī*—personification of growth and prosperity.

Śrī in the Kalpasūtras

The Śrauta Sūtras are concerned with giving a clear and systematic account of all Vedic sacrifices described in the Brāhmaṇa literature. Naturally one notices little in the development of the concept of *Śrī* in such texts. As in older literature—the Saṁhitās and Brāhmaṇas *śrī* denotes wealth, prosperity, etc. Different offerings and sacrifices are prescribed for attaining *śrī*.[15] The Kātyāyana Śr. S. 4, 15, 4 recommends offering of oblation very early in the morning in the Agnihotra sacrifice for attaining *Śrī*—

शयान श्रीकामस्य प्रातः ।

The chanting of some mantra in the Newmoon and Fullmoon sacrifice is said to bring *śrī* (Āpastamba Śr. S. 4, 2, 1 ; Bhāradvāja Śr, S. 4, 2, 5 ; Hiraṇykeśī Śr. S. 1, 2). At the time of Agnihotra sacrifice by taking the fire from Āhavanīya to Gārhapatya one carries the divinity along with *Śrī* (Āśvalāyana Śr. S. 2,2,2). In Soma sacrifice by reciting a particular mantra the priest is said to endow himself with *śrī*, *bhadra*, *yaśas* and *vibhūti* (Śāṅkhāyana Śr. S. 5, 1, 10). The new garments are a form of *śrī* and those who put it on become *śrīmān* (Jaiminīya Śr. S. 2, 11).

In the Gṛhya Sūtras which deal with the rites and customs concerned with the domestic rites of the Aryans, *Śrī* appears as a divinity personified. In the description of marriage which is the pivot of all household ceremonies *Śrī* appears as one of the presiding deities along with Brahmā, Viṣṇu, Rudra and Hutāśana (Agni, Gr.

15. (*Baud. Sr. S.* 13, 14, 8 ; *Mānava. Sr. S.* 5, 19, 37 ; *Hiranyakeśī Sr. S.* 18, 2, 6 ; *Kātyāyana Sr. S* 4, 15, 14 ; *Āpastamba Sr. S.* 4, 2. 1 ; *Bhāradvāja Sr. S.* 4, 2. 5 ; *Hiranyakeśī Sr. S.* 1, I, 2 ; *Āpastamba Sr. S.* 23, 4, 11 23, 6, 9, 22, 13, 4 , *Hirayankeśī. Sr. T.* 18, 3, 2 , *Āpastamba Sr. S.* 23,7,5 , 22, 10, 6 , *Śāṅkhāyana Sr. S.* 16, 30, 13).

S. 2, 6. 7). The Baudhāyana Gr. S. (1, 3, 37) recommends that in the marriage ceremony one should perform sacrifices in honour of Śrī, Puṣṭi, Virupākṣa and others. In a pre-wedding rite described in Kāṭhaka Gr. Sūtra, the bride is made to put on new garments and is seated on a soft chair when the family priest sacrifices the oblations of cooked food to Śrī and Lakṣmī alongwith other gods and goddesses like Indra, Indrāṇī etc.—

श्रियै स्वाहा लक्ष्म्यै स्वाहा (17, 1)

In describing the offering of Madhuparka to the bridegroom the Agni. Gr. S.[16] (2,6,7) speaks of making a Maṇdala on a place besmeared with cowdung ; and alongwith Brahmā, Viṣṇu, and Rudra Śrī is represented as one of the presiding deities of the Maṇḍala.

The Gṛhya Sūtras contain ceremonies connected with cattle welfare, house building and agricultural operation. The ceremony relating to agriculture consists in making an offering to the agricultural deity Sītā (which literally means a furrow.) In this Sītāyajña Śrī is invoked alongwith Bhūti, Bhūmi etc. for protecting the creatures.—

श्री: प्रजां इह आवतु स्वाहा। (Pāraskara Gṛ. S. 2,17,9)

The Navānnabhakṣaṇa is one of the prominent rites in an agricultural community. The Vaikhānasa Gr. S. recommends sacrifice of newly cooked rice together with clarified butter (first fruits or crop) to *Śrī* together with Agni, Śrīpati and Oṣadhīśa (4,8). The Gṛhya Sūtras give elaborate descriptions for building a house, and describe the rites to be performed during its construction and when the owner enters the house after it is ready.

16. The Agni Gr. S. is later in age in comparison with other Grhya Sutras, Prof. Ram Gopal in his '*India of Vedic Kalpasutras*' (p. 30) testifies to its composition to a much later date on the basis of its style or subject matter.

When a house is built *Śrī* alongwith Yaśas is invoked to protect the eastern point. (Pāraskara Gṛ. S. 3,4,10,) Dharma is identified with the pillar of the newly built house, and *Śrī* is the roof which covers the structure (Pār. Gṛ. S. 3,4,18). The Gṛ. Sūtras recommend Vaiśvadeva sacrifice in which oblation of the Vaiśvadeva food are offered into the fire to various deities. After this *devayajña* where offerings are made in the fire, follows the *baliharaṇa* or *bhūta-yajña* in which the householder offers *bali* (the offerings of food) to different deities and beings in various places outside the fire. The Sankhayana Gṛhya Sūtra in its treatment of the *baliharaṇa* rite recommends that the householder should offer *bali* to Śrī at the head of the bed and to Bhadrakālī at the foot of the bed—

नमः श्रियै सज्यायाः शिरसि पादतः भद्रकाल्यै ।

[Śaṅkhāyana Gṛ. S. II, 14, 14]

The Kauśika Sūtra on the other hand recommends offering of *bali* to Śrī around the domestic fire.

In prescribing the performance of ṣaṣṭhī Kalpa *i. e.* a ritual sacred to goddess Saṣṭhī to be performed on the sixth day of the lunar fortnight for getting sons and cattle, treasures and corn etc. the Mānava Gṛ. S. and the Kāṭhaka Gṛ. Ś. identify the goddess ṣaṣṭhī with a female divinity called Padmacāriṇī. In the subsequent stanzas one can notice the fusion of individuality of Saṣṭhī with that of other female goddesses like Śrī, Hrī, Lakṣmī, Upalakṣmī etc—

श्रियै स्वाहा, ह्रियै स्वाहा, लक्ष्म्यै स्वाहा, उपलक्ष्म्यै स्वाहा । [Mānava. Gṛ. S. 2, 13, 6 ; Kāṭhaka. Gṛ. S. 19, 7]

In the Agni Gṛ. S. (2,5,3) one can notice Śrī and Lakṣmī originating from Brahmā and each having its individual existence.

From what has been narrated above we can safely draw

the conclusion that in the period of the Gṛ. Sūtras Śrī And Lakṣmī were two separate individual divinities. And Śrī. though coming up as a distinct goddess and getting the offerings of *bali* in the *bhūtayajña*, is debarred from getting any place in the *devayajña*, whereas for gods like Agni and Prajāpati oblations are offered in the fire itself ; *balis* are offered to Śrī at the head of the bed (Śāṅkhāyana Gr. S. II, 14, 14), or around the household fire (Kauśika Sūtra 74, 8-10).

Lakṣmī in Saṁhitās and Brāhmaṇas

After dealing with the occurrence of Śrī in the different Saṁhitās and Brāhmaṇas we turn our attention to the other concept Lakṣmī which has become later on the most common epithet of the goddess of wealth. In this connection we have to take note of two terms *lakṣman* and *lakṣmī* used in the Saṁhitās and Brāhmaṇas. When Yamī wants to cohabit with Yama the latter rejects her plea on the ground—

सलक्ष्मा यद् विषुरूपा भवति । [RV. 10, 10, 2 ; 10, 12, 6]—

a blood relation (*salakṣma*—literally a peron having the same mark) is behaving like a stranger. In *vasā-yajña* offering of omentum in fire for god Tvaṣṭṛ, thou who art different be of one form—

विषुरूपा यद् सलक्ष्माणो भवथ [TS 1, 3, 10, 1; 6, 3, 11, 2]

literally *salakṣma* means having the same mark or sign). Vājasaneyī Saṁhitā uses the same expression with variant reading in the same context—

सलक्ष्म यद विषुरूपं भवति [6, 20]

The injunction is to the effect that the Hotṛ priest is to put on the sacred thread over the right shoulder during the *Pitṛyajña* and over the left shoulder during *devayajña*. By putting on the sacred thread over the left shoulder the Hotṛ priest is said to carry the distinctive mark of the gods—

देवलक्ष्मं एव तत् कुरुते । [T.S.·2, 5, 11, 1]

The *dūrvā* grass offered in sacrifice is called *devalakṣma* (symbol or sign of the gods) (T.S. 5, 2, 8, 2). The gods placed the *dūrvā* grass with the uppermost mark (*uttara-lakṣmāṇam*), the demons placed it with the mark lower most (*adhara-lakṣmāṇam*) (T.S. 5, 2, 8, 3). In the T.S. 7, 4, 19, 2—*kṛṣṇa lakṣma* is used in connection with the female organ—

य श्रासां कृष्णे लक्ष्मणि सदिगृंदि परावधित् ।

In the Atharva Veda *puṣṭika*-mantras speak of the mark to be made with knives of copper in the ears of cows—

श्रकृतं श्रश्विना लक्ष्म ।

"The Aśvins have made the mark (6, 141, 2). In the same context the Aśvins are implored to make the mark thousand-fold—

सहस्त्र पोषाय कृणुत लक्ष्म श्रश्विना । [A.V. 6, 141 ,1—3]

The white mark of the leper is called *śveta lakṣma* (A.V. 1, 23, 4).

We can notice the development of the concept of *Lakṣmī* in the sense of prosperity, well-being etc. from the term *lakṣma*. The Vedic usages of *lakṣma* was in the sense of sign or mark ; any sign, mark or symbol (*lakṣma*) which was conducive to the attainment of good luck and fortune was taken as *puṇyā lakṣmī*. and any other sign indicating misery or misfortune was called *pāpī lakṣmī*. The development of *Lakṣmī* from *lakṣma* becomes clear in the following cases. Laying a brick on the right side of the fire-altar is like placing *puṇyā lakṣmī*. Eulogizing the placing of a brick on the right side of the fire altar tne Brāhamaṇa text continues—

यस्य दक्षिणतो लक्ष्म भवति तं

पुण्यालक्ष्मीक इति आचक्षत। [S.B. 8, 4, 4, 11]

"he who has *lakṣma* on the right side is said to be *puṇyālakṣmīka* but it is just the opposite in case of female *i.e.* in case of a female who has *lakṣma* on her left side is *puṇyālakṣmīka*. The bricks used in the construction of the fifth layer of the fire altar are called *puṇyālakṣmyah*. In that connection the text says—he who has *lakṣmas* on all sides is *puṇyālakṣmīka*—

यस्य सर्वतो लक्ष्म भवति तं पुण्यालक्ष्मीक इति आचक्षते।

[S. B. 8, 5, 4, 3];

so the close relation between *lakṣman* and *lakṣmī* cannot be ignored. The Ājyā verse chanted at the time of offering oblations is *puṇyālakṣmī*—

पुण्या इव लक्ष्मीः पुण्यं एव तत् लक्ष्मी संभावयति (A. B. 2, 40)

The cattle wealth which is identified with metre is *puṇyā-lakṣmī*—

ये ते पशवः पुण्याः त लक्ष्म्यः। [S.B. 8, 4, 4, 8]

While extolling the speech of the Vedic seers it is stated, "The blessed sign is retained in the sacred speech of the Vedic poets—

भद्रा एषां लक्ष्मीः निहिताधिवाचि। [R. V. 10, 71, 2][17]

17. For a detail discussion of the verse refer to Prof. Palsule's article

The bull which is humpbacked is *lakṣmī* (prosperity) thousandfold—

भवति साहस्री वा एषा लक्ष्मी य एव पशून्

अवरुंधे । [T. S. 2, 1, 5, 2 ; M. S. 2, 5, 3]

Thus the development of the concept of *lakṣmī* in the sense of prosperity, well-being can be connected with *lakṣma* meaning - sign or symbol. Kalidasa's use— लक्ष्म लक्ष्मीं तनोति । (Abhijñāna śākuntalam. I, 17) is not accidental. That *lakṣma* which was found to bring good luck, prosperity could very easily be turned as *Lakṣmī*. In practising witchcraft the T.S. recommends offering of a hornless goat to Brahmaṇaspati ; and this hornless goat is designated as *Lakṣmī* ; because the particular *lakṣma* of having no horns leads to prosperity and well-being—

क्षुरपविः वा एषा लक्ष्मी यत् तूपरः समृद्ध्यैः । [T. S. 2, 1, 5, 7]

Those particular signs or symbols which are indicative of prosperity, well-being, opulence are called *lakṣmī* and gradually the term *lakṣmī* itself came to denote prosperity, well-being, opulence etc. The hump-backed bull which is taken as a sign of prosperity, and which is to bring prosperity to the person, became identified with *lakṣmī*. Similarly the hornless goat which is a sign of prosperity, when sacrificed to Brahmaṇaspati destroys one's enemies, and brings about the prosperity of the sacrificer ; the object which served as a symbol or sign (*lakṣmī*) of prosperity subsequently was identified with prosperity. On the other hand, if that sign or symbol of prosperity is taken away from others, it causes the loss

on Patanjali's interpretation of Rgveda 10, 71, 2 in *Indian Antiquary* Vol *3* (1969) pp. 1—3

of *puṇyā lakṣmī* to the person doing such work. When a Kṣatriya carries away a Brāhmin's cow which is a sign of *lakṣmī* (prosperity, opulence, good-luck), the Kṣatriya loses his *puṇyā lakṣmī* due to stealing.

In a particular Sūkta (7, 115, 1-4) of A.V. used in a propitiatory rite against Nirṛti the goddess of death and destruction, we notice the frequent use of the term *lakṣmī*. For a clear understanding, we quote the Sūkta in full :

प्र पतेत: पापि लक्ष्मि नश्येत: प्रामुत: पत ।
अयस्मयेनांकेन द्विषते त्वा सजामसि ।। [7, 115 ,1]

"Fly forth from here, oh evil sign (*pāpī lakṣmī*), disappear from here ; fly forth from there, with a hook of metal we attach thee to him that hates us"[18]

या मा लक्ष्मी: पतयालुरजुष्टाभिचस्कंद वंदनेव वृक्षम् ।
अन्यत्रास्मात् सवितस्तामितो धा
हिरण्यहस्तो वसुनो रराण: ।। [7, 115, 2]

"The unenjoyable flying sign (*lakṣmī*) that hath mounted me, as a creeper a tree-that, O Savitar, mayest thou put hence else-where than on us, being golden-handed, granting good to us."

एकशतं लक्ष्म्यो मर्त्यस्य साकं
तन्वा जनुषोऽधि जाता ।
तासां पापिष्ठा निरित: प्र हिण्म:
शिवा अस्मभ्यं जातवेदो नि यच्छ ।। [7, 115, 3]

"A hundred and one (are) the signs (*lakṣmyaḥ*) of a mortal born from his birth together with his body ; the worst

18. Translation is taken from Whitney.

of these we send forth out from here ; to us, O Jātavedas, grant propitious (*śivā*) ones".

एता एना व्याकरं खिले गा विष्ठित इव

रमन्तां पुण्या लक्ष्मीया: पापीस्ता अनीनशम् ।। [7, 115, 4]

"These signs (*lakṣmī*) I have separated like kine separated in a barren (*khila*) pasture ; let the good signs (*puṇyā lakṣmī*) stay, those that are evil (*pāpī lakṣmī*) I have made to disappear."

In a charm used for driving away *Pāpī Lakṣmī* called *arāti*, an evil spirit, which frustrates good intentions and disturbs happiness, and for establishing *Puṇyā bhadrā Lakṣmī* the text runs :

निर्लक्ष्म्यं ललाम्यं निररातिं सुवामसि ।

अथ या भद्रा तानि नः प्रजाय अरातिं नयामसि ।।

[A. V. 1, 18, 1]

The object or entity which leads one to prosperity, well being, opulence etc. came to expresss prosperity, opulence and well-being. In the above Sūktas we mark the development of the concept in two ways viz-the *pāpī lakṣmī* and *puṇyā*, *śivā*, *bhadrā* laksmi. The signs or symbols which bring fortune good-luck are designated as *puṇyā lakṣmī*; but the signs which bring bad-luck misfortune and misery are designated as *pāpī lakṣmī*. In the mantra quoted above (7,!15,2)- there is reference to *pāpī lakṣmī* which sticks to the tree like a creeper. This *pāpī lakṣmī* ultimately became Alakṣmī of the later age, and carried all the evil traits which bring misfortune, misery, badluck in one's life. A separate section is devoted to such a deity. The concept of *puṇyā*, *bhadrā* or *śivā lakṣmī* can be traced in the above mantras (A.V. 7, 15, 3 ; 4 : 1, 18, 1). that *lakṣmī* which leads one to the state of prosperity, thriving well-being or opulence is taken as *bhadrā*, *śivā* or *puṇyā lakṣmī*. So one is anxious to have such *lakṣmī* in one's life which would lead one to a prosperous state. Different rites were devised to get rid of *pāpī lakṣmī* so that one can enjoy the *puṇyā lakṣmī*. But after citing the above examples Gerda Hartmann[19] came to the conclusion that originally *lakṣmī* represented a sign which was evil and unholy without any trace of auspiciousness in it. That *lakṣmī* was sticking to a person like a creeper to a tree. But really Hartmann's view point seems to be one-sided. In the hymn of the A.V. cited above it is clearly said that out of hundred and one signs (*lakṣmī*) of an individual the evil ones (*lakṣmī*) are sent forth, and the propitious *lakṣmīs* are invoked to remain with the individual. In the last mantra of the said hymn the idea of *Lakṣmī* (both *pāpī* and *puṇyā*) is put side by side. The Vedic seer emphatically gives expression to his feelings—Let the *puṇyā lakṣmī* stay and the *pāpī lakṣmī* disappear. So one hundred and one *Lakṣmīs* referred to in mantra (7, 115,3) cannot be said to be all evil or inauspicious. Meyer[20] rightly points out this lacuna ; his conjecture is that *Lakṣmī* is possibly derived from the root *lag* ; and originally *Lakṣmī* a disease of the crops stuck to the plants like a scar or a mark, and *Lakṣmī* 'der romischen Robigo, der Genie des Getreiderostes'—'the spirit of dry corn' were originally related to each other. Later the attributes of *Lakṣmī* sticking to the plant as disease were transferred to a new divinity Alakṣmī which developed later on. The auspicious corn-spirit, 'der romischen Robigo' merged with Śrī and developed into *Lakṣmī*, the goddess of wealth and fortune of the later period. Latest of all we come across Prof. Gonda[21] who seems to have given a balanced opinion on the problem. According to him

19. Gerda Hartmann, *Beitrage Zur Geschichte der Gottin Laksmi*, p. 13 ff.

20. J.J. Meyer, *Trilogie*

21. J. Gonda, *op. cit.*, p. 215

"*Lakṣmī* is an object or a being, the very existence or presence of which means something (auspicious-*puṇyā lakṣmī* or evil *pāpī lakṣmī*) ; a *lakṣma* is more vaguely a token or mark, a fact connected with the external form of beings or objects as perceived by the senses, which may induce man to infer that there is something auspicious, favourable. "Because the feminine polysyllabic (ī) stem in vedic denote as a rule beings or objects like *tandrī*—weariness ; *nandī* refreshment, bliss, Gonda concludes *lakṣmī* to be an object signifying sometimes auspicious sometimes evil. This *lakṣmī* (sign) which indicated something auspicious (*puṇyā*), which was instrumental in bringing prosperity, good fortune, well-being to the person possessing it, turned into the divinity representing the signs or prognostications of luck and prosperity.

— o —

CHAPEER II

Sri-Laksmi in Sri-Sukta

Introduction

Though Śrī and Lakṣmī appear as two distinct deities right from Vājasaneyī Saṁhitā (31, 22) onwards, the earliest text eulogizing Śrī and Lakṣmī as two different divinities is the Śrī-Sūkta[1] which forms the Chapter 2, Varga 6 of the Khilas appended to the Rg. Veda. Like other Khilas it is handed down in a large number of manuscripts. As Śrī-Sūkta is *puṣṭivardhana* 'promoter of prosperity' (Viṣṇudharmottara Purāṇa 2, 128, 2) and is used in different rituals, it attracted the attention of the composers of the different Vedas. Though certain mantras of the Sūkta were used in part or as a whole in different Vedic texts, the compilers of other Vedas also were anxious to have Śrī-Sūkta of their own. So we find the Śrī-Sūkta of each Veda[2] to be different. The Śri-Sūkta of the Yajur Veda occurs in the Taittirīya Brāhmaṇa 2, 7, 7, 2 :

रथे अक्षेषु वृषभस्य वाजे, वाते पर्जन्ये वरुणस्य सुष्मे ।
इंद्रं या देवि सुभगा जजाना सा न आगन् वर्चसा संविदाना ॥

The third mantra of Rg. Veda (8,99) which is repeated

1. *RgVeda Samhitā*, Vol. IV, pp. 927 ff.

2. Sri-Sukta of each Veda is mentioned in brief in the *Viṣṇudharmottara Purāna*, 2, 128, 2fi and *Agni Purāna*, 263, 1-4 See P.V. Kane, *History of Dharmasatra*, Vol. III, p. 77, F.N.110.

in the Sāma Veda (3, 26⁷, 5) is called the Śri-Sūkta of the Sāma Veda :

श्रायन्त इव सूर्यं, विश्वेदिन्द्रस्य भक्षत ।

वसुनि जातो जनमान्योजसा प्रति भागं न दिधिमः ।

The particular mantra of Āpastamba Śrauta Sūtra (4,7,4) is identified as the Śri-Sūkta of the Atharva Veda. The mantra is :

श्रियं धातर् मयि धेहि ।

श्रियो माऽधिपतिं कुरु ।

विशमिशानो मघवेन्द्रो मा यशसा नयत् ।

Even the composers of the Purāṇas[3] for propitiating Śrī Lakṣmī did not lag behind in composing Śrī-Stotra after their own fashion.

Number of Mantras

Anyway the Śri-Sūkta appearing in the Khilas appended to the Ṛg. Veda was an old composition but the number of mantras constituting the Śri-Sūkta differs from one recension to the other. In Aufrecht's[4] edition of Rg. Veda the Śri-Sūkta consists of twenty-three mantras and in the Ṛg. Veda edited by Max Müller,[5] the Śrī-Sūkta contains twentynine mantras. In the last thirteen mantras of Śrī-Sūkta in the Max Müller's edition, Śrī is brought into relation with Viṣṇu, her relation with Viṣṇu is definitely later. Besides, the mantra sixteen in the Max Müller's edition is a *phalaśrati* :

3. *Agni Purāna*, Ch. 237 and *Brahmavaivarta Purāṇa*, 2, 39 deal with Sri Stotra.

4. Aufrecht, Die *Hymnen Des, Rig Veda*, Vol. II, pp. 674-676.

5. Max Muller *Rg. Veda.* Vol. IV, pp. 523-28.

य: शुचि: प्रयतो भूत्वा
जुहुयात् आज्यं अन्वहं ।
सूक्तं पंचदशर्चं च
श्रीकाम: सततं जपेत् ।।

'Whoever desires that the goddess Śrī should always reside in his family, being pure and well-prepared must daily offer clarified butter and mutter the fifteen mantras dedicated to Śrī.'

This mantra is also referred to in the ṚgVidhāna[6] [2, 18, 1] which limits the Śrī-Sūkta only to the fifteen verses—*sūktam pañcadaśarcam.* The Kashmir version of the Ṛg Veda also drops the last thirteen mantras. The Baudhāyana Gṛhya Śeṣa Sūtra (3, 5), the Viṣṇudharmottara **P**urāṇa (2, 128, 3) and the Agni Purāṇa (263, 2) refer to only the first fifteen mantras. The great Vedic commentator, Sāyaṇācārya comments only on these fifteen mantras. This clearly establishes the spuriousness of the last thirteen mantras of Max Muller's edition. So we shall discuss the first fifteen mantras which constitute the genuine Śrī-Sūkta. In order to have a clear idea of the concept of the goddess, Śrī-Lakṣmī we quote the Sūkta below :

Śrī Sūkta text

हिरण्यवर्णां हरिणीं सुवर्णरजतस्रजाम् ।
चंद्रां हिरण्मयीं लक्ष्मीं जातवेदो ममा वह ।।1।।

तां म आवह जातवेदो लक्ष्मीमनपगामिनीम् ।
यस्यां हिरण्यं विन्देयं गां अश्वान् पुरुषान् अहं ।।2।।

अश्वपूर्णां रथमध्यां हस्तिनादप्रमोदिनीम् ।
श्रियं देवीमुपह्वये श्रीर्मा देवीजुषताम् ।।3।।

6. J. Gonda, *The Rg. Vidhāna*, 2, 18, 1.

कांसोस्मितां हिरण्यप्राकारामार्द्रां ज्वलन्तीं तृप्तां तर्पयन्तीम् ।
पद्मे स्थितां पद्मवर्णां तामिहोपह्वये श्रियम् ।।4।।

चन्द्रां प्रभासां यशसा ज्वलन्तीं श्रियं लोके देवजुष्टामुदाराम् ।
तां पद्मनेमिं शरणं प्रपद्ये अलक्ष्मीर्मे नश्यतां त्वां वृणोमि ।।5।।

आदित्यवर्णे तपसोऽधिजातो वनस्पतिस्तव वृक्षोऽथ बिल्वः ।
तस्य फलानि तपसा नुदन्तु या अन्तरा याश्च बाह्या अलक्ष्मीः ।।6।।

उपैतु मां देवसखः कीर्तिश्च मणिना सह ।
प्रादुर्भूतोऽस्मि राष्ट्रेऽस्मिन् कीर्तिं वृद्धिं ददातु मे ।।7।।

क्षुत्पिपासामला ज्येष्ठा अलक्ष्मीर् नाशयाम्यहम् ।
अभूतिमसमृद्धिं च सर्वां निर् नुद मे गृहात् ।।8।।

गन्धद्वारां दुराधर्षां नित्यपुष्टां करीषिणीम् ।
ईश्वरीं सर्वभूतानां तां इहोपह्वये श्रियम् ।।9।।

मनसः काममाकूतिं वाचः सत्यमसीमहि ।
पशूनां रूपमन्नस्य मयि श्रीः श्रयतां यशः ।।१०।।

कर्दमेन प्रजा भूता मयि संभ्रम कर्दम ।
श्रियं वासय मे गृहे मातरं पद्ममालिनीम् ।।11।।

आपः सृजन्तु स्निग्धानि चिक्लित वसमे गृहे ।
नि च देवीं मातरं श्रियं वासय मे कुले ।।12।।

आर्द्रां पुष्करिणीं यष्टीं सुवर्णां हेममालिनीम् ।
सूर्यां हिरण्मयीं लक्ष्मीं जातवेदो ममा वह ।।13।।

आर्द्रां पुष्करिणीं पुष्टिं पिङ्गलां पद्ममालिनीम् ।
चन्द्रां हिरण्मयीं लक्ष्मीं जातवेदो ममा वह ।।14।।

तां म आ वह जातवेदो लक्ष्मीं अनपगामिनीम् ।

यस्यां हिरण्यं प्रभूतं (गाव दास्योऽश्वान्)
त्विन्देयं पुरुषान् अहम् ॥15॥

Translation

Invocation to Goddess Lakṣmī

mantra 1. Jātavedas is implored on behalf of the sacrificer to invoke Lakṣmī, who is *hiraṇyavarṇā, hiraṇmayī*, 'radiant as gold', *hariṇī*, 'reddish yellow', who is bedecked with a necklace of gold and silver, *suvarṇarajatasrajā, candrā*, 'radiant as the moon.'

mantra 2. The presence of Lakṣmī, who is firm and steady, '*anapagāminī*', bestows gold, milch cattle, horses and human-beings.

Invocation to Goddess Śrī

mantra 3. *Śrī* is the lord of all creatures '*īśvarī*' and has the best of horses, *aśvapūrṇā* ; she is seated on the middle of the chariot, *rathamadhyā* ; she is delighted by the roaring of the elephant, *hastinādapramodinī*.

mantra 4. She is dressed in gold, *hiraṇyaprākārā*; she is moist *ārdrā*; she is seated on a lotus *padmesthitā* and she has the colour of lotus *padmavarṇā*; she is lustrous like fire *jvalantī*.

mantra 5. Goddess *Śrī* is bountiful *udārā*; she is honoured by all the divinities; she appears like a lovely lotus *padmanemī*; she is radiant as the moon *candrā*. Goddess *Śrī* is resorted to so that Alakṣmī may be removed.

mantra 6. Goddess *Śrī* is resplendent as the sun *ādityavarṇā* ;

through the austerities of *Śrī* the Bilva tree was born; the goddess is prayed so that through her favour the Bilva fruits may dispel Alakṣmī.

mantra 7. *Śrī* is implored to bestow fame and prosperity.

mantra 8. *Śrī* is prayed for banishing *abhūti*—want, *asamṛddhi* —poverty and Alakṣmī, who is characterised by dirty qualities of hunger and thirst *Kṣutpipāsāmalā*.

mantra 9. Goddess *Śrī* is perceptible through odour, *gandhadvārā* ; ever abundant in harvest *nityapuṣṭā*; she lives in cowdung *kariṣiṇī*.

mantra 10. Śrī is prayed for conferring food and cattle.

mantra 11. Kardama 'mud, mire, slime' is referred to as the illustrious progeny of Śrī. Kardama is invoked to abide along with his mother Śrī, who is described as *padmamālinī*.

mantra 12. Ciklita 'mire, ooze', another son of Śrī is prayed to dwell in the abode of the invoker in company with his mother Śrī.

Invocation to Goddess Lakṣmī

mantra 13. Goddess Lakṣmī is described as *ārdrā* 'moist', she is bedecked with lotus flowers *puṣkariṇī* ; she is slim and slender *yaṣṭī*; she is like the sun in splendour *sūryā*. She is radiant as gold *hiraṇmayī, hemamālinī, suvarṇā*.

mantra 14. She is *ārdrā*—moist ; she is bedecked with lotus flowers *puṣkariṇī* ; she wears a garland of lotus flowers *padmamāliṇī*. She has the brilliance and splendour of the moon *candrā* and abundance personified *puṣṭi*. She is of golden colour *hiraṇmayī, piṅgalā*.

mantra 15. Lakṣmī is firm and steady *anapagāminī*, through her grace the invoker attains gold and cattle etc.

Date of Composition

Scholars are not unanimous as regards the date of composition of the Sūkta. The Bṛhaddevatā[7] whose date of composition is taken to be the 4th century B.C. refers to Śrī-Sūkta. According to Oldenberg[8] the Sūkta is older in age than the Buddhistic cannonical poetry. Prof. Kashikar[9] is of opinion that the Sūkta was composed during the period of Yajur Veda and the Brāhmaṇas. Scheftelowitz made a thorough analysis of Śrī-Sūkta. After critically examining all the mantras he has found out that the mantras 1 and 2 refer exclusively to Lakṣmī and in mantras 3 to 12 there is reference only to Śrī; in the mantras 13 and 14 there is fusion of the two divinities Śrī and Lakṣmī. On this basis he comes to the conclusion that the mantras 1 and 2 and the group of mantras 3 to 12 must have been composed very early when *Śrī* and Lakṣmī were treated as two separate deities, because a very old text like Vājasaneyī Saṁhitā (31, 22) refers to *Śrī* and Lakṣmī as two separate divinities—

श्रीः च ते लक्ष्मीः च पत्न्यौ

Out of the last three mantras, the mantra 15 is repetition of the mantra 2, and the other two mantras (13-14) are of later date. Scheftelowitz[10] takes these two mantras to have been composed in the Upaniṣad period, as here there is fusion of the two divinities—*Śrī* and Lakṣmī. Besides, he has taken into consideration the metres used, the words and expressions of the

7. *Bṛhaddevatā*, Vol. 1, Introduction, P. XXII ; Vol. II, pp. 188-189.

8. Oldenberg, *Op. Cit.*, p. 942.

9. *Rig. Veda*, IV, pp. 901-902.

10. Scheftelowitz, 1. '*Śrīsukta*', *ZDMG*, 75, p. 43.

Śrī-Sūkta appearing in other Vedic texts and the individual mantras of *Śrī*-Sūkta quoted in ancient Vedic texts and has come to the conclusion that the mantras 3 to 12 must have been composed in the Brāhmaṇa period, because individual mantras of this group (3-12) are found quoted in the Taittirīya Āraṇyaka, Mahānārāyaṇa Upaniṣad etc. The other reason for assigning great antiquity to the *Śrī*-Sūkta is that by the time of the composition of this hymn, *Śrī* and Lakṣmi were treated as separate divinities. So he is of opinion that the whole of *Śrī*-Sūkta excluding the last three mantras must have been composed during Brāhmaṇa period at the latest, and the last two mantras must have been composed during the period of Upaniṣads when the personality of *Śrī* and Lakṣmī was mingled together.

Sāyaṇācārya's Commentary

Sāyaṇa has commented on these fifteen mantras of *Śrī*-Sūkta and in a different context he has commented on mantras 8 and 9 as they appear in Taittirīya Āraṇyaka (10,66; 10,1) and Mahānārāyaṇa Upaniṣad (66, 9; 1,47) ; and on mantra 10 as it appears in Kāṇva Saṁhitā (39,2,2,) Taittirīya Saṁhitā (3,1,4,3) and Taittirīya Brāhmaṇa (2,4,6,6).

His commentary on Śrī Sūkta

As is usual with Sāyaṇa he has first mentioned the names of the seers of *Śrī*-Sūkta. According to him they are—Ānanda 'the state of contentment', Kardama 'mud, mire' and Ciklita 'mire, ooze', who are taken as sons of Indirā. The divinities invoked in these verses are *Śrī* and Agni.

In mantra 1, Sāyaṇa besides interpreting *hariṇī* as *haritavarṇā* gives an alternative explanation of *hariṇī* and he justifies the meaning of *hariṇī* by alluding to a pauranic story that *Śrī* is called *hariṇī*, because she roamed in the forest assuming the form of a female deer. In place of *aśvapūrṇā* Sāyaṇa takes *aśvapūrvā* and gives the meaning as 'that *Śrī* in front of whom horses are marching forward' and *rathamadhyā* is explained by him as oue 'who is in the midst of chariots'. Sāyaṇa takes the word *prabodhinī* in place of *pramodinī* and gives the meaning—'*Śrī* who makes her presence known through the roaring of elephants'. Because the mantra refers to horses, elephants and chariots, for Sāyaṇa *Śrī* is *senārūpā* or has the form of an army (mantra 3). In the first pāda of mantra 4, there is an expression—*kāṅsosmitām.* Sāyaṇa breaks up this as *kāṅ* and *sosmitām* and his interpretation is—*Śrī* is of the nature of Brahman and she is of smiling appearance. The appellation of *ārdrā* given to *Śrī* is explained in two different ways by Sāyaṇa : She is *ārdrā*, because she was born from the milky ocean ; it may be, she was born in *ārdrā* constellation.

The first half of mantra 7 is interpreted as—Kubera '*devasakha*' and Renown '*kīrti*' may come to me along with Maṇibhadra—'the name of a Yakṣa. Taking into consideration the expressions—*gandhadvārā*, *nityapuṣṭā* and *karīṣiṇī* in mantra 9, Sāyaṇa takes this mantra as referring to *Śrī* in the form of Earth '*Bhūrūpā*'.

Mantras 13 and 14 are nearly identical. There are two expressions used with reference to Lakṣmī—*puṣkariṇī* and *yaṣṭī*. By connecting the word *puṣkariṇī* with *puṣkara* meaning—*gajaśuṇḍāgra* 'the tip of the trunk of an elephant', Sāyaṇa interprets *puṣkariṇī*—Goddess Lakṣmī touched by the tips of the trunks of elephants ready for her *abhiṣeka*—consecrating her by sprinkling water. The other term *yaṣṭī* is interpreted as—*daṇḍarūpā* 'a mace personified to wrong-doers.

Ritualistic application

Unlike other Khila Sūktas *Śrī*-Sūkta came to be very popular ; since very old age, different texts on rituals prescribed the recitation of *Śrī*-Sūkta or its individual mantras on different occasions like coronation of the king, for happiness and prosperity, in marriage, for getting abundant rain etc.

Śaunaka in his Ṛg.Vidhāna gives the traditional use of some mantras of *Śrī*-Sūkta on different religious rites. The mantra 7 of *Śrī*-Sūkta—

उपैतु मां······

—is prescribed to be recited for consecrating the king after he has taken the ceremonious bath with water infused with all sorts of herbs (Ṛg.Vidhāna 2, 18, 4). A person desirous of cattle is to be consecrated with the recitation of the mantra 10—

मनसः कामम्······

whereas the mantra 11—

कर्दमेन प्रजाभूता······

should be muttered by a person desiring off-spring (Ṛg. Vidhāna 2, 18, 5,). A man desiring kingdom should mutter mantra 3—

अश्वपूर्णां रथमध्यां······

at the time of bath. After this ritual bath the Brahmin is directed to offer oblations of clarified butter along with lotus flowers by muttering the mantra 5—

चन्द्रां प्रभासां······

of *Śrī*-Sūkta, and oblation of Bilva fruits is to be performed with the mantra 6—

आदित्यवर्णे तपसो······

[Ṛg.Vidhāna 2,19,3]

For one desirous of *Śrī*, sacrifices should be performed where the fuel of the fire should consist of Bilva, and the number of oblations differ according to the desire of the sacrificer. The possession of *Śrī* for eternity (*śāśvatī śrī*) which can be possible only by offering oblation for hundred thousand times, can be very easily accomplished just by the *japa* (muttering) of *Śrī*-Sūkta for ten thousand times.

The Mānava Gṛhya Sūtra (2, 13,6) prescribes the performance of Ṣaṣṭhī-kalpa—a ritual sacred to the goddess Ṣaṣṭhī, and according to this Gṛhya Sūtra the Ṣaṣṭhīkalpa should be celebrated in the night of the sixth lunar day of bright fortnight ; the goddess Ṣaṣṭhī is here invoked to grant abundant crops, cattle wealth and treasure to the worshipper. *Śrī*, Lakṣmī and Padmacāriṇī are spoken of as different names of goddess Ṣaṣṭhī. In this ritual of Ṣaṣṭhī, along with other mantras, three mantras of *Śrī*-Sūkta—

mantra 3—अश्वपूर्वां रथमध्यां······

mantra 7—उपैतु मां देवसखः······

mantra 9—गन्धद्वारां दुराधर्षां······

are recommended for recitation.

The Baudhāyana Gṛhya Śeṣa Sūtra (1, 28) discusses the procedure of the coronation of the king. In that connection the text recommends that the cleaning and washing of the crown, a symbol of power and prestige is to be taken up only after goddess *Śrī* is worshipped with the recitation of *Śrī*-Sūkta. The same text (3,5) refers to the worship of *Śrī* in a ceremony called Śrīkalpa. In describing the method of worshipping this divinity, *Śrī*, the text makes full use of *Śrī*-Sukta. At the time of inviting (*āvāhana*) goddess *Śrī*, mantras 1 and 2 of *Śrī*-Sūkta—

हिरण्यवर्णां हरिणीं······(1)

तां म आवह जातवेदो······(2) ;

and the mantras 11 and 12—

कर्दमेन प्रजाभूता ······(11)

आप: सृजन्तु स्निग्धानि ·····(12)

are to be recited at the time of sprinkling the divinity with water ; the ceremonious bath of the divinity is to be performed by the recitation of mantra 3—

अश्वपूर्वां रथमध्यां

The different offerings such as fragrant substances like sandal and camphor *gandha,* flowers, incense *dhūpa,* lamp *dīpa* and food *naivedya*— each of these offerings is to be made to the goddess *śrī* with the accompaniment of the mantras 9, 4, 7, 14, and 5.

गन्धद्वारां······ (9)

कांसोस्मितां······ (4)

उपैतु मां······ (7)

आर्द्रां पुष्करिणीं······ (14)

चन्द्रां प्रभासां······ (5)

respectively. At the time of offering oblations, the worshipper has to recite all the fifteen mantras of *Śrī*-Sūkta, and lastly while rubbing lotus flower all over his body, the worshipper has to recite the mantra—*Kṣutpipāsāmalā jyeṣṭhā*...and thus he repels Alakṣmī from him.

Reference to Śrī-Sūkta in the Purāṇas

By the time of the Purāṇas *Śrī*-Lakṣmī was firmly established as a goddess of crops, cattle-wealth and prosperity. Any type of prosperity was attributed to the grace of Lakṣmī. With the growing popularity of the goddess Lakṣmī, though many popular stotras were composed by the Paurāṇikas.

in honour of Lakṣmī, yet the *Śrī*-Sūkta so popular in the Vedic age continued to be equally popular with the composers of the Purāṇas.

When the milky ocean was churned and goddess Lakṣmī came out with all her splendour, the sages and seers glorified her by chanting the *Śrī*-Sūkta in her honour (Viṣṇu Purāṇa 1, 9, 101 ; Padma Purāṇa 5, 4, 59). The Agni Purāṇa prescribes the recitation of *Śrī*-Sūkta on different occasions. While laying the foundation stone of a temple, the Agni Purāṇa (41, 8) recommends the muttering of *Śrī*-Sūkta three times apparently to endow the temple with glory and prosperity. In any ritual or sacrifice, consecration of sacrificial pitcher (*kumbhādhivāsa*) is an indispensable rite ; and this is to be performed with the muttering of *Śrī*-Sūkta (57, 20). This text (62, 1.ff) also recommends that the different mantras of *Śrī*-Sūkta should be recited at the time of the installation of goddess Lakṣmī. While offering water for washing the feet (*pādya*) to different deities, the recitation of *Śrī*-Sūkta is recommended (Agni Purāṇa, 264, 2). Because *Śrī*-Sūkta glorifies the goddess Lakṣmī, the symbol of glory and fortune, the Agni Purāṇa (263, 1.ff) in its chapter on *utpātaśānti* prescribes its recitation whenever any misfortune or calamity befalls.

Analysis of Śrī-Sūkta

The first two mantras (1-2) are exclusively devoted to Lakṣmī, she is invoked and her personal traits are described. She is *hiraṇyavarṇā, hiraṇmayī, hariṇī*—all these expressions referring to her golden colour. Because she is the goddess of plenty and prosperity, it is but natural to describe her outward appearance as of gold. In the Ṛg.Veda Agni is brought into close relation with wealth and prosperity. In Rg.Veda 4,5,15—Agni is an abode of wealth, in Ṛg. Veda 10, 45, 5—Agni is stated to be very liberal in offering various kinds of prosperity and to be a keeper of riches—

श्रीणां उदारो धरुणो रयीणां

Therefore, it is in the fitness of things that of all the gods Agni (Jātavedas) has been requested to lead Lakṣmī, the goddess of wealth towards the invoker—

तां म आ वह जातवेदो लक्ष्मीमनपगामिनीम्

In these two mantras, the description of Laksmī is very sketchy and it does not help us in getting any knowledge about her except her colour, adornment, and things she can bestow upon the invoker. But in the mantras 3—12, which are exclusively devoted to goddess *Śri*, we are in a position to get a detailed picture. Like Lakṣmi *Śrī* gets the epithets—*hiraṇyaprākārām*, *jvalantī*, *padmavarnā*. *candrā*, *prabhāsā*, *padmanemī*, *ādiṭyavarṇā*. Besides these refrences, which bring out her glory and splendour she is brought into relation with *kīrti* and *yaśaṣ*, both the words implying fame. In the mantra, 5, *Śrī* is *yaśasā jvalantī* and in the mantra 7, she is prayed to bestow *kīrti* 'esteem, renown,' along with *vṛddhi* 'success. welfare, prosperity—

कीर्तिं वृद्धिं ददातु मे

(mantra 7.). Whereas Lakṣmī is prayed only for material prosperity (vide mantra 2), *Śrī* is invoked for mental happiness as well as material prosperity. In mantra 10, the invoker besides praying for cattle, food and fame prays for getting the knowledge and purpose of mind—

मनसः काममाकूतिं

and the truth of speech—

वाचः सत्यं

The significant expressions which present before us a clear picture of the goddess *Śrī* are—*ārdrā* 'moist' *gandha-*

dvārā 'perceptible through odour', *karīṣiṇī* abounding in cowdung'. Because she is goddess of vegetation and fertility she is called *ārdrā* 'moist', also implying fresh green as a plant living.[11] The prosperity of agriculture depends upon water. In many ancient cultures there was a belief that life originated in the waters. The gr wth and abundance of vegetative life is always dependent upon water either of clouds or of rivers. In the Atharva Veda (4,5,6 and 9) rain water is identified with milk of the rain-god Parjanya. 'From rain originates virility, sap, well-being (S.B.1,8.3,15). Like the Yakṣas, divinities connected with wealth and fertility, and intimately associated with waters,[12] *Śrī*, goddess of vegetation has been brought into relation with water through expression —*ārdrā 'moist'*. She is *gandhadvārā* 'perceptible through odour'. Probably it refers to the smell coming out of the earth after the first shower of rain. She is *Karīṣiṇī* 'abounds in cowdung'. *Karīṣa* 'cowdung', *kardama* 'mud, mire, slime' and *ciklita* 'mire, ooze'—all these epithets bring home to us the concept of *Śrī* who is definitely a goddess of fertility and vegetation. That is why mud, water and cowdung are brought into relation with her.

Like water cowdung or manure is important for a good harvest. Dubois[13] has referred to a custom of South India—during the Deepāvalī festival every householder prostrates himself before the dunghill collected for manuring and offers flowers, lighted tapers, boiled rice and fruits and begs it to fertilize his lands and to produce him abundant harvest. The present writer is aware of the fact that in many parts of Orissa on the day of the Deepāvalī Amāvasyā, the agriculturist worships the dunghill with lamps and incense. The importance of cowdung for getting good harvest is too well-

11. Gonda, *Op. Cit.*, p. 213

12. For intimate connection of water with Yaksas, see A.K. Coomaraswamy, *Yaksas*, Part II, p. 13 ff

13. Dubois and Beauchamp, *Hindu Manners Customs and Ceremonies, p. 571.*

known to be described. Goddess *Śrī* has been made to reside in cowdung *karīṣiṇī* as she represents the spirit of vegetation. Because of her relation with crops she is *ārdrā* 'moist' and for the same reason she has been brought to relation with cowdung. Cowdung is always brought into relation with the cult of fertllity. The Gobhila Gṛhya Sūtra (4, 8, 18) recommends that those who want plenty and prosperity should make an offering of cowdung. The same text (4, 9, 13 cf. Khādira Gṛhya Sūtra 4,13,16) recommends the offering of cowdung for a man desirous of cattle wealth. During the festival of Navarātra,[14] one of the most important item of the worship of the goddess Durgā is *mahāsnāna* 'the great bathing', in which cowdung forms an important part. In laying down the procedure of selecting a bride, Bhāradvāja Gṛhya Sūtra (1,11, cf. Āpastamba Gṛhya Sūtra 1,3,14-17) states that different lumps of earth either from the field or the burial ground or the cowdung are to be put covered up before the bride. In case the bride touches the lump of cowdung, that is taken up as a sign of prosperity for the bride.

The goddess's relation with lotus is very significant. In the Sūkta she is described as *padmesthitā* 'seated on lotus', *padmavarṇā* 'of the colour of lotus'; she is garlanded with lotus—*padmamālinī, puṣkariṇī.* From ancient days she maintains her close relation with lotus. Lotus was primarily understood to represent water (S.B. 7, 4, 1, 8). In the early Art, the plants whose virility and healing power are stressed so much are generally represented by lotus[15] because of its direct origin in the waters. The flower signifies 'preservation and procreation of life' (E.R.E., Vol. VIII. p. 144). Due to its direct relation with water and as a symbol of fertility, the lotus is associated with the goddess, who is a divinity of fertility and vegetation.

14. Chintaharana Chakravarty, *The Tantra, Studies on their Religion and Literature*, p. 98.

15. A.K. Coomaraswamy, *Op. Cit.*, p. 57 ; D.R. Patil has collected enough materials on lotus and its relation with Lakṣmī in his thesis to prove its significance, *Cultural History from the Vāyu Purāna*, pp. 234-235.

CHAPTER III

Laksmi in the Puranapancalaksna Texts[1]

The Basis of Purāṇapañcalakṣaṇa

In course of investigation of historical tradition of ancient India from the Purāṇas, Pargiter points out that the Purāṇas like Vāyu and Brahmāṇḍa have one text kernel and contain the oldest version of the Pañcalakṣaṇa text; Matsya, Brahma and Harivaṁśa have the next best versions.[2] However he did not prepare any concordance to prove his thesis. Kirfel following Pargiter made an intensive investigation of the Purāṇas. In order to find out the urkern of the Purāṇas he depended on the five chief characteristics which have been clearly mentioned in different Purāṇa texts as pañcalakṣaṇa. These five characteristics are *sarga* 'creation', *pratisarga* dissolution and recreation', *vaṁśa* 'divine genealogies', *manvantara* 'ages of the Manus' and *vaṁśānucarita* 'genealogies of kings.' All the Paurāṇikas agree that these are the chief characteristics of Purāṇa literature in general.[3] These characteristics formed the kernel of the Purāṇas and different topics like festivals, rituals, Vratas and the glorification of different holy places were added to this text kernel later. On this basis

1. W. Kirfel, *Das Purāṇa Pancalakṣaṇa*; In order to find out the urkern of the Purāṇas, Prof. Kirfel has to toil hard, *Das Purāṇa Pancalakṣana* is the result of his long research where the original texts of the Purānas have been arranged in a chronological order.

2. F. E. Pargier, *Ancient Indian Historical Tradition*, pp. 23-24.

3. The following traditional verse which can practically be traced in all the purāṇas—

through the deductive method of a comparative study of different Purāṇas, Kirfel prepared a concordance which consists of four chapters i.e. *sarga* and *pratisarga* (abschnitt I), *vaṁśa* (Abschnitt 2), *manvantara* (Abschnitt 3) and *vaṁśānucarita* (Abschnitt 4).

After collecting different Purana texts Kirfel came to the conclusion that in the Purāṇas one can notice different versions of the Pañcalakṣaṇa texts. According to him the Pañcalakṣaṇa texts in the Brahma Purāna and Harivaṁśa are by far the oldest ; next to these two Purānas come Brahmānḍa Purāṇa and Vāyu Purāṇa where the Pañcalakṣaṇa texts have undergone some changes and the pañcalakṣaṇa texts of Matsya Purāṇa can be called a revised form of the two text-groups-Brahma- Harivaṁśa and Brahāmṇḍa- Vāyu.[4]

The version of the Pañcalakṣaṇa texts occurring in the Brahma and Harivaṁśa have been put by Kirfel in text-group I. In order to show the gradual change in the basic Purāṇa texts through addition, elaboration and mutilation, Kirfel has made further division of the texts like text-group II A, II B and III. In text-group I of Ist Abschnitt (*sarga* and *pratisarga* constituting the texts from Brahma and Harivaṁśa. p.4) the number of mind-born sons created by Brahma to help him in the creation of the universe is limited to seven only; they are Marici, Atri, Aṅgiras, Pulastya, Pulaha, Kratu, and Vaśiṣtha. In the versions of Mārkaṇḍeya Purāṇa. 50,5 ; Padma Purāṇa 1.

सर्गश्च प्रतिसर्गश्च वंशमण्वन्तराणि च ।

वंशानुचरितं चैव पुराणं पंचलक्षणम् ।।

Quoted in *Brahmāṇḍa Purāṇa*, 1, 1, 37-38 ; *Vāyu Purāṇa*, 4, 10-11 ; *Matsya Purāṇa*. 53,65 ; *Kurma Purāṇa* 1, 1, 12 ; *Varāha Purāṇa*, 2. 4, *Garuḍa Purāṇa*, 1, 215, 14 ; *Bhaviṣya Purāṇa*, 1, 2, 4-5 ; *Brāhmavaivarta Purāṇa*, 4, 133, 6 ; *Devī Bhāgavata* 1, 2, 18 ; differently expressed in *Viṣṇu Purāṇa* 3, 6, 25 ; *Agni Purāṇa* ; 1, 14; wrongly in *Bhāgvata Purāṇa* 12, 78. 10 ; Pargiter is of opinion that the five characteristics are ancient and characterise the earlier Puranas and express their primary contents. *Ibid p.* 36.

4. Vide Kirfel. Intro. p. XLV.

1, 3, 167 ; 168 ; Padma Purāṇa 2, 5, 3, 159b ; 160a ; Viṣṇu Purāṇa. 1, 7, 5 forming the text-group II A (p. 35) the number of mind-born sons increases to nine with the addition of Bhṛgu and Dakṣa ; and in the Purāṇa texts of Brahmāṇḍa. 1, 5, 70, Liṅga 70, 181b ; 182a constituting the text-group II B (p. 67), though the number of mind-born sons remains the same, the order of narration changes ; but in the text-group III (p. 137) comprising the Matsya 3,8, the number of mind-born sons increases to ten with the addition of Nārada. The above reference to the number of ṛṣis and their gradual development very nicely justifies Kirfel's analysis of the Purāṇa text and their division into different text groups.

In the Pañcalakṣaṇa texts we come across different myths formed around Lakṣmī. In one group of texts Lakṣmī is described as the daughter of Dakṣa-Prajāpati and in another as the daughter of Bhṛgu and in some other text-groups she is pictured as an emanation from Satī, the consort of Śiva. When a group of Purāṇas describes her as the wife of Dharma, another set of texts mentions her as the consort of Viṣṇu. In view of such heterogenous traditions they are taken up in chronological order.

Lakṣmī attends upon Soma (the Moon)

Taking into consideration the different Pañcalakṣaṇa texts in Kirfel, we notice in Brahma-Harivaṁśa as well as in Brahmāṇḍa-Vāyu, forming text-group I A, of Abschnitt 4, Kapitel 3 dealing with *vaṁśānucarita,* a passage on Lakṣmī which seems to be the oldest reference to her—

तं सिनी च कुहूश्चैव द्युतिः पुष्टिः प्रभा वसु : ।
कीर्तिर्धृतिश्च लक्ष्मीश्च नव देव्यः सिषेविरे ॥

PPL. p. 351 ; Brahmāṇḍa Purāṇa. 2, 65, 26 ; Brahma Purāṇa. 9, 16 ; Harivaṁśa. 1337 ; Vāyu Purāṇa. 90, 25.

The nine divinities like Sinī, Kuhū, Dyuti, Puṣṭi, Prabhā, Vasu, Kīrti, Dhṛti and Lakṣmī attended upon him (Soma).

The myths narrated in the Purāṇas derive all the dynasties reigning in India sometimes from the sun, sometimes from the moon and sometimes from the mythical seers. In narrating the *vaṁśānucarita* of the lunar race the Purāṇa version of Brahmāṇḍa. 2, 65, 1f (p. 349f) constituting the text-group I A, 3 Kapitel, appearing in the Abschnitt 4, *vaṁśānucarita* refer to a mythical seer—Atri, who is represented as the father of Soma, the moon. After the birth of Soma, Brahmā makes him the lord of waters and plants and gives him a divine chariot on which he travels the whole universe. Then Soma performs a Rājasūya sacrifice on a grand scale. Hiraṇyagarbha acts as the Udgātṛ priest, Hari-Nārāyaṇa becomes the assistant at the sacrifice. Soma gives the three worlds as *dakṣiṇā* to his priests. Then nine divinities including Lakṣmī come forward to attend upon him; they are Sinī, Kuhū, Dyuti, Puṣṭi, Prabhā, Vasu, Kīrti, Dhṛti and Lakṣmī : [5]

स तत् प्राप्य महद्राज्यं सोमः सोमवतां वरः ।
समाजह्रे राजसूयं सहस्रशतदक्षिणाम् ॥ (22)

5. In this apparently earliest reference to Laksmī, she is described as attending upon Soma along with other eight divinities. But this version of Laksmī attending upon Soma is found in a revised and elaborate form in the Matsya *Purāṇa* and Padma *Purāṇa* (PPL. p. 400), where Laksmī is represented as coming to attend upon Soma after forsaking her husband Nārāyaṇa :

लक्ष्मीर्नारायणं त्यक्त्वा सिनीवाली च कर्दमम् ।
द्युतिर्विभावसुं त्यक्त्वा पुष्टिर्धातारमव्ययम् ॥ (24)

प्रभा प्रभाकरं त्यक्त्वा हविष्मन्तं कुहुः स्वयम् ।
कीर्तिर्जयन्तं भर्तारं वसुर्मारीचकश्यपम् ॥ (25)

धृतिस्त्यक्त्वा पतिं नन्दिं सोममेवाभजंस्तदा ।
स्वकीया इव सोमोऽपि कामयामास तास्तदा ॥ (26)

हिरण्यगर्भश्चोद्गाता ब्रह्मा ब्रह्मत्वमीयवान् । (23)

सदस्यस्तत्र भगवान् हरिर्नारायणः प्रभुः ।
सनत्कुमारप्रमुखैराद्यैर्ब्रह्मर्षिभिर्वृतः ॥ (24)

दक्षिणामददत् सोमस्त्रींल्लोकान् इति नः श्रुतम् ।
तेभ्यो ब्रह्मर्षिमुख्येभ्यः सदस्येभ्यश्च वै द्विजाः ॥ (25)

तं सिनी च कुहूश्चैव द्युतिः[6] पुष्टिः प्रभा वसुः ।
कीर्तिर्धृतिश्च लक्ष्मीश्च नव देव्यः सिषेविरे ॥ (26)

PPL: p. 351 ; Brahmāṇḍa Purāṇa. 2, 65, 22f ; Brahma Purāṇa. 9, 13f ; Harivaṁśa. 1333f ; Vāyu Purāṇa. 90, 22f.

In this reference to Lakṣmī 'Wealth and Splendour', we find the mention of different deities like Kīrti 'Fame' Dyuti, Prabhā 'Radiance, Splendour', Dhṛti 'Patience', Puṣṭi 'Nourishment', Vasu 'Beneficence'. Except the two divinities like Kuhū and Sinī (which are personifications of the day of the new-moon and the day preceding new-moon day) all other divinities are only personifications of abstract qualities. After the performance of Rājasūya sacrifice, the king Soma was endowed with fame and glory, wealth and splendour etc. This can be the only interpretation of the nine divinities attending upon Soma. So here Lakṣmī is represented as a pure and simple female divinity ; there is reference neither to her birth and parentage nor to her marital relation.

ppl. p. 400 ; Matsya Purana. 23, 24-26 Padma Purāṇa. 2, 5, 12, 24-26 : put by Kirfel in 3 kapitel text-group IIA, Abschnitt 4, *vaṁś-ānucarita.*

It is clear that the redactor must have put this revised and elaborate version only after Laksmī became a constant companion of Viṣṇu. In order to bring into harmony the two accounts—the earliest reference to Laksmī attending upon Soma and the later account of Laksmī represented as the consort of Viṣṇu (Vide p. 40) the redactor had to make this revision — *Lakṣmī Nārāyaṇam tyaktvā*).

6. *Brahmāṇḍa Purāṇa.* 2, 65, 26 ; *Vāyu Purāṇa.* 90, 25—वपुः

This passage referring to Lakṣmī and other divinities put in the *vaṁśānucarita* section (Abschnitt. 4) occurs in Brahma Purāṇa. 9, 16 ; Harivaṁśa. 1337, and the same passage is repeated in Brahmāṇḍa. Purāṇa. 2, 65, 26 and Vāyu Purāṇa. 90, 25 without any change. In this connection Kirfel's statement on the chronology of the different Pañcalakṣaṇa texts is proved to be valid. According to him Brahma-Harivaṁśa, Brahmāṇḍa-Vāyu and Matsya contain the complete forms of the Pañcalakṣaṇa texts ; the texts of Brahma-Harivaṁśa and Brahmāṇḍa-Vāyu are parallel, whereas the third Matsya presents a disorganised or revised version of the above two texts--Brahma-Harivaṁśa and Brahmāṇḍa-Vāyu.[7]

Lakṣmī daughter of Dakṣa *and wife of Dharma*

The birth of Lakṣmī from different parentage and her marriage with different persons are found only in the Pañca lakṣaṇa texts coming under 1st Abschnitt, *sarga* and *pratisarga*. The same text kernel underlying text group IIA has been further elaborated and expanded in text group IIB. The texts common to these two groups have been very prominently put by Kirfel in spaced print.[8]

Brahmāsvayambhū[9] with the desire of creation created nine Prajāpatis (*nava-brahmāṇa*) ; they are — Bhṛgu, Pulastya, Pulaha, Kratu, Aṅgiras, Marīci, Dakṣa, Atri, and Vaśiṣṭha and along with the Prajāpatis three others were mentioned—Rudra, Saṁkalpa and Dharma. Then Brahmā-Svayambhū created Manu Svāyambhūva and a female Śatarūpā by name. Manusvāyambhuva had Śatarūpā as his wife and through her brought forth two sons—Priyavrata and Uttānapāda, and two

7. Kirfel, *Op. Cit.*, Intro., p. XXIX.
The Matsya Purāṇa account of the divinities like Lakṣmī and others attending upon Soma is a revised and elaborate one and is discsused before.

8. *Idid.*

9. *Ibid*, p. 35f.

daughters—Ṛddhi and Prasūti. Prasūti was married to Dakṣa, one of the Prajāpatis created by Brahmā. Dakṣa begot twentyfour daughters through Prasūti ; they are Śraddhā, Lakṣmī, Dhṛti, Tuṣṭi, Puṣṭ', Medhā. Kriyā, Buddhi, Lajjā, Vapu, Śānti, Ṛddhi, Kīrti, Khyāti, Satī, Sambhūti, Smṛti, Prīti, Kṣamā, Sannati, Anasūyā, Ūrjā, Svāhā and Svadhā. Out of these twentyfour daughters Dharma married thirteen daughters, like Śraddhā, 'Faith', Dhṛti 'Steadiness', Tuṣṭi, 'Resignation, Puṣṭi, 'Thriving', Medhā 'Intelligence', Kriyā 'Action', Buddhi 'Intellect, Lajjā 'Modesty', Vapu 'Body', Śānti 'Expiation,' Siddhi 'Perfection', Kīrti 'Fame', and Lakṣmī 'Prosperity'. Each of the rest eleven daughters was married to a particular seer or divinity. Khyāti was united with Bhṛgu. Satī to Bhava. Sambhūti to Marīci, Smṛti to Aṅgiras and so on. Each of the thirteen daughters of Dakṣa in consequence of their marriage with Dharma produced offsprings. Lakṣmī gave birth to Darpa 'Pride', Śraddhā to Kāma 'Desire', Dhṛti to Niyama 'Precept', Tuṣṭi to Santoṣa 'Content', Puṣṭi to Lobha 'Cupidity' etc. :

प्रसूत्यां च तथा दक्षः चतस्रो विंशतिं तथा ।

ससर्ज कन्याः तासां तु सम्यङ् नामानि मे शृणु ॥ (20)

श्रद्धा लक्ष्मीर् धृतिस्तुष्टिः पुष्टिर् मेधा क्रिया तथा ।

बुद्धिर्लज्जा वपुः शान्तिर् ऋद्धिः[10] कीर्तिः त्रयोदशी ॥ (21)

पत्न्यर्थं प्रतिजग्राह धर्मो दाक्षायणीः प्रभुः ।

ताभ्यः शिष्टा यवीयस्य एकादशः सुलोचनाः ॥ (22)

ख्यातिः सत्यथ सम्भूतिः स्मृतिः प्रीतिः क्षमा तथा ।

संनतिश्चानसूया च ऊर्जा स्वाहा स्वधा तथा ॥ (23)

10. *Mārkaṇḍeya Purāṇa.* 50, 21 *a* ; *Padma Purāṇa.* 2, 5, 3, 175b; *Viṣṇu Purāṇa* 1, 7, 21—सिद्धिः

मृगुर्भवो मरीचिश्च तथा चैवाङ्गिरा मुनिः ।
पुलस्त्यः पुलहश्चैव क्रतुश्चर्षिवरस्तथा ।। (24)
अत्रिर्वशिष्ठो वह्निश्च पितरश्च यथाक्रमम् ।
ख्यात्याद्या जगृहुः कन्या मुनयो मुनिसत्तमाः ।।[11] (25)
श्रद्धा कामं चला[12] दर्पं[13] नियमं धृतिरात्मजम् ।[14]
सन्तोषं च तथा तुष्टिर्लोभं पुष्टिरसूयत ।। (26)
मेधा श्रुतं[15] क्रिया दण्डं नयं विनयमेव च ।
बोधं बुद्धिस्तथा लज्जा विनयं वपुरात्मजम् ।। (27)
व्यवसायं प्रजज्ञे वै क्षेमं शान्तिरसूयत ।
सुखं ऋद्धिर्यशः कीर्तिरित्येते धर्मसूनवः ।। (28)

PPL. p. 37f. Garuḍa Purāṇa. 1, 5, 24ff ; Mārkaṇḍeya Purāṇa. 50, 19bff ; Padma Purāṇa 1. 1, 3, 182ff; Padma Purāṇa 2. 5, 3, 174ff; Viṣṇu Purāṇa. 1, 7, 20ff arranged in the 7th kapitel, text-group IIA, Abschnitt I, *sarga* and *pratisarga* by Kirfel.

The above account of Dakṣa and his creation is repeated with revision and elaboration in the Purāṇa texts of Brahmāṇḍa, Vāyu, Kūrma and Liṅga, which forms the text group IIB in spaced prints, which indicates that this common text kernel was known to the redactors of the Purāṇas of Garuḍa, Mārkaṇḍeya, Padma and Viṣṇu forming text group

11. *Padma Purāṇa* 1. 1.3, 187b, *Padma Purāṇa* 2, 5, 3, 179b—रजसत्तम *Visnu Purana* 1, 7, 25b— मुनिसत्तम

12. *Mārkaṇḍeya Purāṇa*. 50, 25b—श्रीश्च

13. *Padma Purāṇa* 1.1.3,18--बलं लक्ष्मीः

14. *Padma Purāṇa* 2, 5, 3, 180—
तथा लक्ष्मीर्दर्पं च नियमं धृतिः

15. *Padma Purāṇa* 2, 5, 3, 181—श्रियं

IIA, 7 Kapitel as well as to the redactors of Brahmāṇḍa, Vāyu, Kūrma and Liṅga of text group IIB. 7 kapitel :

प्रसूत्यां च तथा दक्षश्चतस्रो विंशतिं तथा ।
ससर्ज कन्या नामानि तासां सम्यक् निबोधत[16] ॥ (23)
श्रद्धा लक्ष्मीधृतिस्तुष्टिः पुष्टिर्मेधा क्रिया तथा ।
बुद्धिर्लज्जा वपुः शान्तिः सिद्धिः कीर्तिस्त्रयोदशी ॥ (24)
पत्न्यर्थं प्रतिजग्राह धर्मो दाक्षायणीः प्रभुः ॥ (25a)

× × ×

ताभ्यः शिष्टा यवीयस्य एकादश सुलोचनाः ।
ख्यातिः सत्यथ सम्भूतिः स्मृतिः प्रीतिः क्षमा तथा ॥ (26)
संनतिश्चानसूया च ऊर्जा स्वाहा स्वधा तथा ।
भृगुर्भवो मरीचिश्च तथा चैवाङ्गिरा मुनिः ॥ (27)
पुलस्त्यः पुलहश्चैव क्रतुः परमधर्मवित् ।
अत्रिर्वशिष्ठो वह्निश्च पितरश्च यथाक्रमम् ॥ (28)

16. Brahm*āṇ*da — V*ā*yu ond Liṅga retain an elaborate and revised version of the same text thus—

तस्यां कन्याश्चतुर्विंशत् दक्षस्त्वजनयत् प्रभुः ।
सर्वास्ताश्च महाभागाः सर्वाः कमललोचनाः ॥ (23)
योगपत्नयश्च ताः सर्वाः सर्वास्ताः योगमातरः ।
सर्वाश्च ब्रह्मवादिन्यः सर्वा विश्वस्यमातरः ॥ (231)

PFL. P. 116. *Brahmāṇda Purāṇa*. 1, 49, 47b—9a : *Vāyu Purāṇa*, 10, 23-24, *Linga Purāṇa*. 70, 282b-284a, by the time of the composition of this text-piece, these twentyfour divinities must have attained supremacy among other deities : so they are differently glorified as *Brahmavādinyaḥ Yogamātaraḥ Viśvasyamātaraḥ* etc.

ख्यात्याद्या जगृहुः कन्या मुनयो ज्ञानसत्तमाः ।। (29)

× × ×

श्रद्धा कामं व्रिजज्ञे वै, दर्पो लक्ष्मीसुतः स्मृतः ।

धृत्यास्तु नियमः पुत्रस्तुष्टयाः संतोप उच्यते ।। (33)

पुष्ट्या लोभ सुतश्चापि मेधापुत्रः श्रुतस्तथा ।

क्रियायां अभवत् पुत्रो दण्डः समय एव च ।। (34)

बुद्धेर्बोधः सुतश्चापि अप्रमादश्च तावुभौ ।

लज्जया विनयः पुत्रो व्यवसायो वपोः सुतः ।। (35)

क्षेमः शान्ति सुतश्चापि सुखं सिद्धेर्व्यजायत ।

यशः कीर्तेः सुतश्चापि इत्येते धर्मसूनवः ।। (36)

PPL. p. 116-117 ; Brahmāṇḍa Purāṇa. 1, 9, 49bff ; Kūrma Purāṇa. 8, 15ff ; Vāyu Purāṇa. 10, 25ff and Linga Purāṇa. 70, 284ff put under text-group IIB, 7 kapitel of Abschnitt I, *sarga* and *pratisarga*.

As is evident in both the versions Lakṣmī is born from the union of Dakṣa and Prasūti, she is married to Dharma and her son is Darpa.

In enumerating the Prajāpatis created by Brahmā, the *sarga* and *pratisarga* section of Brahma and Harivaṁśa speaks of only seven Prajāpatis (*sapta brahmāṇa*).[17] This earliest account of *sarga* and *pratisarga* does not even mention the name of Dakṣa, what to speak of Dakṣa's marriage and his progeny. But in the elaborate version of *sarga* and *pratisarga* preserved in the Mārkaṇḍeya Purāṇa, Padma Purāṇa and Viṣṇu Purāṇa coming in text-group IIA, (p. 35) the number of

17. PPL. p.4.

Prajāpatis rises to nine including Bhṛgu and Dakṣa,[18] Through Dakṣa-Prajāpati Prasūti gives birth to twentyfour daughters. Of the nine divinities who waited upon Soma (नव देव्यः सिषेविरे —p. 351) after he performed the Rājasūya sacrifice, the four divinities—Puṣṭi, Kīrti, Dhṛti and Lakṣmī are included here in the list of twentyfour daughters of Dakṣa and Prasūti. And these four divinities including Lakṣmī are given in marriage to Dharma and produced offsprings.

Lakṣmī daughter of Bhṛgu and wife of Viṣṇu

In the last account Dakṣa-Prajāpati and Prasūti have twentyfour daughters. Out of these Dharma marries thirteen daughters, one of whom is Lakṣmī. And among the rest eleven is mentioned the name of Khyāti who marries Bhṛgu. The Pañcalakṣaṇa texts as quoted before concluded with just this account of the marriage of Khyāti with Bhṛgu. But there was further elaboration of this marriage of Bhṛgu with Khyāti in the Pañcalakṣaṇa texts of other Purāṇas :

देवौ धातृविधातारौ भृगोः ख्यातिरसूयत ।

श्रियं च देवदेवस्य पत्नी नारायणस्य या[19] ।। (14)

PPL. p. 40 ; Mārkaṇḍeya Purāṇa 50, 14b-15a ; Padma

18. भृगुं पुलस्त्यं पुलहं क्रतुं अंगिरसं तथा ।
मरीचिं दक्षं अत्रिं च वशिष्ठं चैव मानसम् ।। (5)
नव ब्रह्माण इत्येते पुराणे निश्चयं गताः ।। (6A PPL. p. 35.)

19. *Padma Purāṇa* 2·5, 23, 201— वासुदेवपरिग्रहम् The same text-piece which is repeated in the *Kurma Purāṇa*. 13, 1 and *Viṣṇu Purāṇa*. 11, 10, 2 under Kapitel 9, I st Abschnitt, *sarga* and *pratisarga* is shown by Kirfel to be interpolated—

भृगोः ख्यात्यां समुत्पन्ना लक्ष्मीर्विष्णुपरिग्रहः ।

तथा धातृविधातारौ ख्यात्यां जातौ सुतौ भृगोः ।। (1, 2 ; PPL. p. 41.)

Purāṇa 1. 1, 3, 205b-206a ; Padma Purāṇa 2. 5, 3, 201 ; Viṣṇu Purāṇa 1, 8, 13 grouped by Kirfel under Kapitel 8 of text-group IIA, Abschnitt I, *sarga* and *pratisarga*.

Besides giving birth to two sons—Dhātā and Vidhātā, Khyāti gave birth to Lakṣmī [20] who was united with Viṣṇu. This account making Lakṣmī a daughter of Bhṛgu and getting her married to Viṣṇu is definitely a later tradition. [21] This tradition has been elaborated in text-group IIB. The Purāṇa texts of Brahmāṇḍa and Vāyu do not stop just with the marriage of Bhṛgu and Khyāti, the birth of Lakṣmī from their union and her marriage with Viṣṇu, but they proceed further in giving an account of the offsprings of Lakṣmī after she is united with Viṣṇu:

सातुनारायणं देवं पतिं आसाद्य शोभना ।
नारायणात्मजौ तस्यां बलोन्मादौ व्यजायताम् ।
बलस्य तेजः पुत्रस्तु उन्मादस्य तु संशयः ।। (3)
तस्यान्ये मानसाः पुत्रा आसन् व्योमविचारिणः ।
ये वहन्ति विमानानि देवानां पुण्यकर्मणां ।। (4)

PPL. p. 128; Brahmāṇḍa Purāṇa 1,12,3-5a ; Vāyu Purāṇa 28,2-3; classed under 9 kapitel of text-group IIB, Abschnitt I, *sarga* and *pratisarga*.

20. The above text in the Kapitel 8 (p. 40.) and 9 (p. 41) distinctly preserves the tradition of *Śrī* and Lak*ṣ*m*ī* as two separate divinities.

21. In the primary stage of development, La*k*smī rose as an independent deity. Then she became the consort of Dharma. But later with the development of Vai*ṣṇ*avism Lak*ṣ*mī was adopted to the Vai*ṣ*ṇava pantheon and she became the consort and costant companion of Vi*ṣṇ*u. After thorough examination of different images of Lak*ṣ*mī and Vi*ṣṇ*u, Jaiswal came to the conclusion that Lak*ṣ*mī was admitted into the Vai*ṣ*ṇnva pantheon during the Gupta age (3rd-4th centuries A.D.), during which she was united with Viṣṇu. Cf. Suvira Jaiswal, *The Origin and development of Vaiṣṇavism*, Delhi, 1967, p. 102f.

Lakṣmī married Nārāyṇa and from her were born two sons —Bala and Unmāda and those who were born from the mind of Lakṣmī were engaged in carrying the chariots of gods in heaven. Teja became the son of Bala and Saṁśaya that of Unmāda.

Bala and Unmāda represented as sons of Lakṣmī are nothing but personifications of abstract qualities, which are again brought to relation with personified attributes like Teja and Saṁśaya.

Lakṣmī a form of Satī

In the first tradition[22] of text-group IIA Satī was one of the twentyfour daughters of Dakṣa; out of these, thirteen daughters were given in marriage to Dharma, the other eleven daughters were married to other gods. Among them tradition contained in the Pañcalakṣaṇa texts [23] of Vāyu and Liṅga a different version of the birth of Satī is mentioned. Out of Brahmā's wrath was created Rudra whose body was half man and half woman. Out of the male half eleven Rudras were created and the female half of Rudra became Satī, the great goddess :

प्रागुक्ता तु महादेवि स्त्री सैवेह सती ह्यभूत् ।

22. For an elaborate discussion on this creation, refer to P. 69f of this chapter.

23. prof. Kirfel is right when he states in his introduction to *Das Purāṇa Pancalakṣaṇa* (p. XXXf) on the Ist Abschnitt, *sarga* and *pratisarga*, that the texts of Linga Purāna which preserves the preliminary version of the Brahmāṇḍa-Vāyu runs parallel witn them and the texts of Brahmāṇḍa and Vāyu developed out of one text kernel. But the text dealing with Lakṣmī appears only in the Vāyu Purāṇa and Liṅga Purāṇa. Though the redactor of Liṅga Purāna (Ch. 70) knew the Urkern of Brahmāṇḍa-Vāyu and preserved it faithfully, the redactor of of Vāyu could retain the preliminary version of this account whereas the redactor of Brahmāṇḍa Purāṇa might have skipped it over. So the preliminary version of the account of Lakṣmī as a form of Satī is traced out in the Liṅga Purāṇa and only in Vāyu Purāṇa but not in Brahmāṇḍa Purāṇa.

हिताय जगताँ देवी दक्षेणाराधिता पुरा ।।[24] (69)

PPL., p. 108 ; Liṅga Purāṇa. 70, 327.

Satī again divided herself into two parts - the bright half and the dark half. Out of the bright half were created different female divinities like Svāhā, Svadhā, Mahāvidyā, Medhā, Sarasvatī, Lakṣmī etc. and out of the dark half were produced Mahākālī, Raudrī, Durgā, Kālakarṇī etc. All these different divinities are but different manifestations of the great goddess Satī who is of the nature of the universe—

विश्वरूप श्रथार्यायाः पृथग् देहविभावनात् ।

In glorifying Satī, the female counterpart of Rudra, the Pañcalakṣaṇa text represents Lakṣmī and Sarasvatī as only different forms of the one supreme goddess, that is Satī. Later on the same account depicts Prajñā and Śrī as the most important goddesses born from Satī, the great goddess and out of these two — Śrī and Prajñā, thousands of female divinities have originated :

कायार्धं दक्षिणं तस्याः शुक्लं वामं तथासितम् ।

श्रात्मानं विभजस्वेति प्रोक्ता देवी स्वयंभुवा ।। (70)

सा तु प्रोक्ता द्विधा भूता शुक्ला कृष्णा च वै द्विजाः ।

तस्या नामानि वक्ष्यामि शृणुध्वम् सुसमाहिताः ।। (71)

24. The redactor of Vāyu Purāṇa. 9.83*a* gives a different account of the origin of Satī—

प्रागुक्ता तु मया तुभ्यं

स्त्री स्वयंभोर्मुखोद्गता ।। (69)

PPL., p. 108.

स्वाहा स्वधां महाविद्या मेधा लक्ष्मीः सरस्वती । (72a)

× × ×

महादेवी कुले द्वे तु प्रज्ञा श्रीश्च प्रकीर्तिते ।
आभ्यां देविसहस्राणि यैर्व्याप्तं अखिलं जगत् ।। (82)

PPL., p. 109-10 ; Liṅga Purāṇa. 70, 328. ff ; Vāyu Purāṇa. 9, 83bff arranged under 6 Kapitel of text-group IIB Abschnitt I. *sarga* and *partisarga.*

Innumerable female divinities both benevolent and malignant had their independent existence in the Hindu pantheon and they were popular among the common folk. With the development of Śakti cult all these female divinities lost their independent existence and their origin was attributed to the great goddess Satī. Like Sarasvatī, Lakṣmī also came to be represented as a manifestation of the great goddess.

CHAPTER IV

Lakṣmi in the Epics and Purāṇas

In the earlier texts different legends regarding the origin of Lakṣmī has been traced out. In some text groups she is mentioned as the daughter of Dakṣa and in the other she is procreated through Bhṛgu and Khyāti etc. But in later literature there is a very popular myth of the churning of the ocean where Lakṣmī is described to have emerged out of the ocean. This tradition has been recorded in the Epics and Purāṇas. So in order to have a complete picture of her character the myth of the churning of the ocean[1] is taken up with reference to her origin from the ocean.

Lakṣmī and the churning of the Ocean

Purāṇa Pañcalakṣaṇa Texts

The earliest version of this myth[2] is referred to in connection with the genealogy of Yaduvaṁśa. Kārtavīryārjuna, is said to be so valiant that he could agitate the turbulent ocean by his thousands of hands. This agitation of the ocean by

1. For different interpretations of the myth, see S.A. Dange, *Legends in the Mahābhārta*, p. 242 ff, T.K. Taimni, *An Introdnction to Hindu Symbolism*, p, 73ff ; Klaus Ruping, *Amrtamcnthana und Kùrma Avatāra* ; J. Gonda, Change *and continuity in Indian Religion:* V.M. Bedekar, *The Legend of the Churning of the Ocean in the Epics and the purāṇas : A comparative Study*," *Purāṇa*. Vol. 1X, No. 1. Jan. 1967, p. 7ff.

Kirfel, *Op. Cit.*, p. 416

Kārtavīrya is compared with the churning of the ocean by the mountain Mandara thrown into it by the gods and the demons :

> प्रवर्तयत् तदा राजा सहस्रेण च वाहुना ।
> देवासुर समाक्षिप्तः क्षिरोदं इव मन्दरः ॥

Brahma Purāṇa 13,181; Harivaṁśa 1873; Brahmāṇḍa Purāṇa 2,69,33; Vāyu Purāṇa 94,33 ; Matsya Purāṇa 43,356.

Besides this casual reference to the churning of the ocean, this myth also is referred to in connection with the birth of Dhanvantarī[3]

> धन्वन्तरे संभवोऽयं श्रूयतां इह वै द्विजाः ।
> सः संभूतः समुद्रात् तु मथ्यमानेऽमृते पुरा ॥

Brahmāṇḍa Purāṇa 2,69,10 : Harivaṁśa 1524 ; Vāyu Purāṇā 92.9.

Apart from this occasional reference to Dhanvantarī,s birth from the churning of the ocean, we are told that Prahlāda was defeated in the war which took place during the time of Amṛtamanthana:[4]

> प्रह्लाद निर्जितो युद्ध इन्द्रेणामृतमन्थने ।

Brahmāṇḍa Purāṇa 2, 72, 79 a: Matsya Purāṇa 47, 48ab; Padma Purāṇa 1.1.13, 185b, Padma Purāṇa 2.5,13, 189a: Vāyu Purāṇa 97, 79b.

It appears from the above citations that the basic story element of the myth forms a part of the Purāṇa Pañcalakṣaṇa texts. Here the only motif of the Samudramanthana is to get back amṛta. The gods and the demons churned the ocean

3. Kirfel, *Op. Cit.*, p. 370
4. *Ibid*, p. 490

whereas the mountain Mandara serves the purpose of the churning rod.

This myth though casually referred to in different contexts in the Purāṇa Pañcalakṣaṇa texts, appears before us in a definite form in the Rāmāyaṇa. In the later literature[5] there are frequent references to Lakṣmī's origin from the ocean for which she is called—*Kṣirodatanayā*, *Kṣirasāgarakanyā*, *Dogdhābdhītanayā*, *Sindhukanyā* etc. So it is better to take up the study of the myth of the churning of the ocean for getting an insight to her birth from the ocean.

Out of the two versions of the myth in the Rāmāyaṇa and the Mahābhārāta, the Rāmāyaṇa version appears to be older than the version in the Mahābhārata. In the Rāmāyaṇa the narration is straight and simple without much elaboration.

Rāmāyaṇa 1.44.

In the Kṛtayuga the sons of Diti and Aditi wanted to be ageless, immortal and free from disease. So they decided to churn the ocean to get the elixir of life—

क्षिरोद मन्थनं कृत्वा रसं प्राप्स्याम तत्र वे ।। 17b,

The gods and the demons use Mandara mountain as the churning rod and the snake Vāsuki as the rope, and churn the ocean. As a result of churning six gems appear ; they are - 1. Dhanvantarī, 2. Apsarasas 'heavenly nymphs', 3. Vāruṇī, the daughter of Varuṇa, 4. Uccaiḥśravas, 'the heavenly horse, 5. Jewel Kaustubha and 6. Amṛta. In the above enumeration of

5. *Amarakoṣa*, 1, 27

in different Purāṇas she is designated in the above manner.

objects there is no mention of the goddess Lakṣmī.[6]

Mahābhārata 1, 15-17.

The same myth is narrated in an elaborate manner in the Mahābhārata. On the advice of Nārāyaṇa the gods and the demons churn the ocean for getting amṛta, the jewels and the herbs:

देवैरसुरसंघैश्च मथ्यतां कलसोदधिः ।
भविष्यत्यमृतं तत्र मथ्यमाने महोदधौ ।

[Mahābhārata 1, 15, 12]

6. The description of the goddess Lakṣmī rising out of the ocean occurs in the three south Indian manuscripts (M1, M2, M3) of Rāmāyaṇa : and in view of its later addition to these texts, the editor of the Rāmāyaṇa (Critical edition) has put it to the foot note No. 966, p. 257 :

ततो दीर्घेन कालेन चोत्पन्ना कमलालया ।
अतीव रूपसम्पन्ना प्रथमे वयसि स्थिता ।
सर्वाभरणपूर्णाङ्गी सर्वलक्षण लक्षिता ।
मुकुटाङ्कितचित्राङ्गी नीलकुंचित मूर्धजा ।।
तप्तहाटक संकाशा मुक्ताभरण भूषिता ।
कन्या यस्याः प्रभावेन इन्द्र ऐश्वर्यं माप्नुयात् ।।
चतुर्भुजा महादेवी पद्महस्ता वरानना ।
सा च देवी तथोत्पन्ना पद्मा श्रीर्लोकविश्रुता ।।
सा पद्मा पद्मनाभस्य ययौ वक्षस्थलं हरेः ।।

The above description of the goddess *Śrī*, her beauty and brilliance seems to be much later ; and this might have been possible only when *Śrī* could attain the state of supremacy as the divinity per excellence and was finally united with Viṣṇu, but it is evident that she could not reach this state during the composition of the earlier version of the text. The later redactors have tried to insert it to make it a complete whole. Similarly, the editor of the critical edition of Harivaṁśa did not accept the chapter on the churning of the ocean, which appeared in the Bhaviṣya parva (3) Ch. 30 of the old edition and has placed it under the Appendix 1 (No. 41) in the Vol. II in view of its posterity.

With the Mandara mountain as the churning rod and Vāsuki as the rope churning continues, in consequence of which seven different entities emerge from the ocean viz.1. Soma 'the moon', 2. *Śrī*. 3. Surā, 4. the white steeds, 5. Kaustubha, 6. Dhanvantarī ; and 7. amṛta. Out of these goddess Śrī rises as only the second object clad in white raiment—

श्रीरनन्तरमुत्पन्ना घृतात् पाण्डुरवासिनी

[Mahābhārata 1, 16, 34a. [

Thereafter accompanied by Soma, Surā and Uccaiḥśravā *Śrī* goes to the gods. When the gods take possession of *Śrī*, Soma, Surā etc. the demons are greatly offended, in consequence of which there is a great scramble among them for the possession of amṛta.[7]

As it appears from the Mahābhārata version, goddess *Śrī* does not attain so much prominence ; and the attainment of Śrī is never the motif of samudramanthana.

Purāṇa versions of the myth

(*a*) *Brahmāṇḍa* Purāṇa 1, 25—*Vāyupurāṇa*, 54.

In the Brahmāṇḍa Purāṇa—Vāyu Purāṇa version, the story takes a different turn and on the request of the gods and sages, Vāyu relates the story in order to justify as to how Śiva's throat

7 The Mahābhārta (Critical Edition) does not include the possession of Laksmī by the gods as the cause of discontent among the demons, but the manuscripts like VI, DN, DI, 3,4 of Mahābhārata state that the bone of contention between the demons and the gods was not only amṛta but also the graceful divinity Lakṣmī, which is taken to be a later addittion. So it is put in the footnote 277, p. 125 to the Mahābhārata (Cr. Edn.)

अमृतार्थे च लक्ष्म्यर्थे महान्तं वैरमाश्रितः

But as the goddess Lakṣmī did not attain so much prominence by that time, the text has been put in the footnote only.

becomes black. In order to show the super power of Śiva, who is the only powerful god to drink poison, the ferocious nature of the poison has been described in detail and Viṣṇu himself has been described to be black by the heat of the poison—

निर्दग्धो रक्त गौरांगो कृत कृष्णो जनार्दन ।

Brahmāṇḍa Purāṇa 1, 25, 57a ; Vāyu Purāṇa 1. 54, 58 and the story ends just with the drinking of the Kālakūṭa poison by Śiva. This is definitely a Śaivaite redaction of the myth which does not refer to the cause of the churning of the ocean or any other entity born from the ocean.

(b) *Matsya Purāṇa* 248—250.

The myth in the Matsya Purāṇa shows definite improvement over the Brahmāṇḍa Purāṇa—Vāyu Purāṇa version and it seems clear that though the redactors of Matsya Purāṇa knew the text tradition of the Mahābhārata and have preserved and elaborated it, still like the Brahmāṇḍa Purāṇa—Vāyu Purāṇa version, they have tried to insert the glory and greatness of Śiva into it.

In course of narration of the myth, the redactor has tried to picture the terrible form of Kālakūṭa poison which appears in a corporeal form with devastating effect. It is about to devour the world unless it is devoured by anybody ; at last at the behest of Brahmā, Viṣṇu and other gods, Śiva devours that world-devastating poison and thereby saves the three worlds from a perilous situation.

In addition to the seven entities in the Mahābhārata version the Matsya Purāṇa adds seven objects and as a result the number of gems arising out of the ocean rises to fourteen. In the Mahābhārata version for the first time Śrī rose out of the ocean and goes to the gods, but the Matsya version is more definite. Here goddess *Śrī* and the gem Kaustubha are taken possession of by Viṣṇu. So by the time of the formation of this version *Śrī* must have been united with Viṣṇu as his consort.

In the epics the purpose of the churning of the ocean is to get amṛta for the gods and the Brahmāṇḍa—Vāyu account speaks of the rise of the poison Kālakūṭa only out of the churning ; but the Matsya Purāṇa version brings about a compromise between the two versions and states that in course of churning of the ocean by the gods and the demons for amṛta, while the terrible poison Kālakūṭa rises up Śiva has to drink it up to save the gods from such a dangerous situation. Now let us examine the myth as depicted in some other Purāṇic texts where it seems to have taken a Vaiṣṇavite trend.

In the previous account of the myth, the motif is to get amṛta, but in these versions that becomes secondary. Goddess Lakṣmī, who in the earlier accounts is like any other entity to rise out of the ocean, occupies the most important position, and the myth centres round her and her loss and recovery becomes the main motif of the myth. In order to bring out the glory and greatness of the goddess, the curse of Durvāsā has been introduced into this myth to make it a complete whole. So the myth of her birth from the ocean takes a new turn because of inserting the Durvāsā episode.

Viṣṇu Purāṇa 1, *9ff—Padma Purāṇā* (*Sṛṣṭikhaṇḍa*) 5, *4ff*

The Viṣṇu Purāṇa 1,9ff and Padma Purāṇa (Sṛṣṭikhaṇḍa) 5,4ff state the story thus : In course of his journey the sage Durvāsā gets a garland of Santānaka flowers from a Vidyādharī and presents it to Indra whom he meets on the way. Indra due to the infatuation of power fails to realise the importance of the garland which is the dwelling of *Śrī* (*Śriyo dhāma*) and places it on his heavenly mount Airāvata; but the elephant throws it on the ground. So the sage becomes furious at his behaviour and curses him that *Śrī* would disappear from the three worlds (whose lord is Indra). Indra apologizes to the sage but to no effect. The goddess *Śrī* disappears from the three worlds. As a result of her absence, no sacrifice is performed, the ascetics do not observe penance. Gifts are not given away. People are overpowered by cupidity. The sun and the moon lose their brilliance and vigour. The sacrificial fire loses its heat. The gods lose their strength, energy and merit and become so weak that they are vanquished by the demons. So they all approach Brahmā for help and on the advice of Viṣṇu they churn the milk-ocean to recover the goddess Śrī.

When the churning of the ocean continues, different objects and entities emerge from the ocean ; and the goddess Lakṣmī comes out as the last entity. She comes out seated on a full-blown lotus with a lotus in her hand. She appears radiant with beauty and brilliance. The sages enraptured by her presence pray her by chanting the mantras of Śrī-Sūkta. Viśvāvasu and other Gandharvas sing her praise. Ghṛtācī and other celestial nymphs dance before her. The elephants of the quarters take up the waters in the vases of gold and bathe her. The milk-ocean in person presents her with a garland of unfading lotus flowers. Viśvakarmā, the architect of the gods decorates her body with heavenly ornaments. Thus bathed, adorned and decorated she casts herself upon the breast of Hari.[8] When the goddess in the lap of Viṣṇu adds to his glory and splendour and turns her eyes towards the gods, they attain the state of highest bliss ; but Vipracitti and other demons are terribly shocked because of this union of the goddess with Viṣṇu.

In addition to the above account Viṣṇu Purāṇa (1, 9, 117-133) adds a long hymn of praise which Indra addresses her after she is united with Viṣṇu. Śrī is moved by praises and prayers of Indra, she assures him to grant his wishes. So Indra prays for two boons—the first boon asked for is that Lakṣmī would not deprive the three worlds of her presence ; and the second prayer is that she should not turn away from those who would praise her with the hymns of praise uttered by

8. The Padma Purāṇa (Sṛṣṭikhaṇḍa 5,4, 66-69) states that when she originates from the milk-ocean, all the gods, demons etc. are interested to have her, but Brahmā interferes and aks Viṣṇu to accept the goddess Lakṣmī as his bride and the goddess also is advised to accept Viṣṇu as her companion. As a result she goes over to Viṣṇu and remains as his consort.

Indra. Both of these prayers asked for by Indra and granted by Lakṣmī are in fact a recognition of her superiority over other divinities ; and Indra may be considered to have inaugurated her cult.[9] In addition to this Indra is assured by Lakṣmī that she would remain a constant companion of Viṣṇu in all his different incarnations.

The Bhāgavata Purāṇa—8, 5, 15—8, 12, 47.

Though the Bhāgavata Purāṇa account conforms to the Padma Purāṇa (Sṛ.)—Viṣṇu Purāṇa versions to a certain extent still it differs from it on certain points. Like the versions of Padma-Viṣṇu and Brahmāṇḍa also in the Bhāgavata Purāṇa the churning of the ocean is taken up for getting back Lakṣmī who vanishes because of the curse of Durvāsā.

As in other versions, here also the emergence of Lakṣmī from the ocean is depicted in a very beautiful manner.

When the goddess rises out of the ocean, all the celestials, demons and human-beings enamoured by her grace, complexion and beauty cherish her company. Mahendra offers a wonderful seat for her pedestal. The sacred rivers bring water in golden jars for her bath. The Earth 'Bhūmi' brings for her all medicines and the cows present their five auspicious Products '*pañcapavitrāṇi*'. The elephants of the quarters perform her bath accompanied by the music and dance of heavenly beings. After her bath the Spring in person presents her with fruits. The Ocean presents her with two pieces of yellow silken raiments for her dress. When Varuṇa brings her the garland of Vaijayantī and the goddess Sarasvatī a beautiful garland, Brahmā decorates her with a lotus in full bloom. The serpents bring ear-rings. Viśvakarmā presents her a beautiful dress. Thus beautifully dressed and decorated she looks for a suitable partner. But finding no other god equal to Viṣṇu she chooses him as her partner.

9- J. Gonda, 'A Note on Indra in Purāṇic Literature' *Purāna*, Vol. IX, No. 2, July, 1947, p. 256.

Viṣṇudharmottara Purāṇa 1, 40-42

There is little difference between the versions of Bhāgavata and Viṣṇudharmottara Purāṇa. Lakṣmī comes out as the seventh and the last entity out of the ocean. She is very beautifully dressed. With Kuṇḍalas shining in her ears, and a garland of Santānaka flowers round her neck, the goddess holds a lotus and a garland of Vaiḍūrya in her hands. She casts her favourable glances at the different divinities and at last she goes over to Viṣṇu.

Brahmavaivarta Purāṇa. 2, 35-39—*Devī Bhāgavata.* 9, 39-41

The version in the Brahmavaivarta Purāṇa and Devī Bhāgavata is somewhat different. Due to the curse of Durvāsā goddess Lakṣmī is furious and relinquishes heaven out of pain and sorrow and merges herself with Mahālakṣmī in Vaikuṇṭha (Brahmavaivarta Purāṇa 2,8,5,-DevīBhāgavata 9, 40, 4) ; then on the advice of Nārāyaṇa in the Kaliyuga she incarnates herself as the daughter of the ocean '*Sindhukanyā*'. The gods under the leadership of Brahmā approach Viṣṇu and Viṣṇu advises Brahmā for churning the ocean and placing Lakṣmī with the gods:

मथित्वा सागरं लक्ष्मीं देवेभ्यो देहि पद्मज ।

Brahmavaivarta Purāṇa 2, 38, 56b—DevīBhāgavata 9, 41, 52b.

Out of this churning Lakṣmī appears from the ocean. She presents a chaplet of wood-flowers to Viṣṇu and accepts him as partner. Adored by Brahmā, Śankara and others she releases the gods from the curse of Durvāsā.

Padma Purāṇa (Brahmakhaṇḍa) 3, -8-10*Padma Purāṇa (Uttara khāṇḍa)* 6, 259-260.

In the Padma Purāṇa (Brahmakhaṇḍa and Uttarakhaṇḍa)

because of the curse of Durvāsā Lakṣmī disappears from the three worlds. In consequence, the residents of the three worlds are afflicted with hunger, poverty and thirst. Because of want of rain all the reservoirs of water are dried up. All the trees and the plants wither and dry up. Having faced such distress and suffering due to the disfavour of Lakṣmī the different divinities approach Viṣṇu who advises them to churn the ocean for the recovery of Lakṣmī.

On the auspicious Ekādaśī day when the gods and the demons begin to churn the ocean, Alakṣmī and the Kālakūṭa poison come out. And on the subsequent day comes out Lakṣmī.

Agni Purāṇa 3.

The Agni Purāṇa version of the myth is very short and sketchy. While narrating the Kūrmāvatāra of Viṣṇu it states that the churning of the ocean is taken not only for amṛta but also for Lakṣmī :

अमृतार्थं श्रिये सुराः

It does not go into details of the myth.

Lakṣmī's relation with Indra

Before finally settling with Viṣṇu as his consort. Lakṣmī had relation with various gods, one of them is Indra. In the Mahābhārata we come across different accounts of her relationship with Indra. When Indra is sitting with Nārada, goddess Lakṣmī approaches him on the back of Garuḍa. The heavenly nymphs follow her and with the divinity come her seven inseparable companions who are Jayā, Āśā 'Hope, Śraddhā 'Faith',Dhṛti 'Firmness', 'Content', Kṣānti 'Forbearance', Vijiti 'Triumph', Saṁnati, 'Humility', Kṣamā 'Patience'. When Lakṣmī sits beside Indra, he begins to pour down rain upon the crops, which grow in the proper season; the cows give plenty of milk ; gods and men enjoy a prosperous state and the earth flourishes in all directions (Mahābhārata 12, 221, 14 ff).

In the same book when Indra in disguise begs the noble nature '*śila* from Prahlāda. on which his power rests, Lakṣmī looking like a flame, comes out of Prahlāda to Indra (Mahābhārata 12, 124, 54). On different occassion when the goddess leaves Bali to remain with Indra, he is surprised at her sudden appearance. As she is very fickle by nature and does not live with anybody for ever, Indra is not hopeful to enjoy her company for a longer period. But when the god Indra, requests her to live with him for ever, the divinity out of her own accord advises Indra to divide her into four parts and to put one quarter of her essence in the earth, another in the water, the third in the fire and the fourth part in the good men, who are devoted to Brāhmaṇas and are truthful. Thus she expresses her desire to remain with Indra for ever (Mahābhārata 12, 218, 11ff).

The Rāmāyaṇa (6,50,25) refers only to the loss and recovery of Lakṣmī by Indra ; the Purāṇas on the other hand try to elaborate the story of her disappearance fron Indra and her subsequent recovery through the churning of the ocean,[10] for which Indra is designated as *Śrīmān*. The Brahmavaivarta Purāṇa (3,21, 3ff) states that Indra has to lose the company of Lakṣmī because of running after bad women. Indra is advised to perform sacrifice and to chant her mantras to get her back. So he praises her in different hymns and practises penance, in consequence of which Hari finally presents Lakṣmī to Indra as a boon.

Another story from the Mahābhārata (1, 189, 1ff) helps us to establish her close association with Indra : Indra with four earlier Indras is sent by Śiva to a cave to practise penance and at last these five Indras are reborn as Pāṇḍavas and his

10. For the loss of Lakṣmī through the curse of Durvāsā and her recovery through the churning of the ocean, see pp. 84-85.

consort Lakṣmī is reborn as the wife of those five Pāṇḍavas. This legend points to her prior association with Indra.[11] Later on when Viṣṇu rises to eminence and appropriates the characteristic features of Indra, Lakṣmī is given to Viṣṇu as his wife; thus he drives away Indra from his former position; then only it becomes imperative on the part of the redactor of Mārkaṇḍeya Purāṇa (5, 24ff) to remodel the above legend of the Mahābhārata. He puts some justification for the prior birth of Draupadī. So he has to describe Draupadī not as an incarnation of Lakṣmī but of Indrāṇī, the consort of Indra. Lakṣmī does not relinquish her former association with Indra. In Kaumudī Mahotsava or Kojāgara Pūrṇimā (Āṣvina pūrṇimā) Lakṣmī is duly adored with Indra on the back of Airāvata (Nirṇaya Sindhu, Vol. II, p. 60) and on the Śrīpañcamī day (Māgha śuklapañcamī) also she is worshipped with the same god (Kālikā Purāṇa 82, 21).

According to Pāraskara Gṛhya Sūtra (2, 17, 9) Indra's wife is Sītā, that is the personified Furrow. In a sacrifice to Sītā, offerings are made to Indra, Bhūti etc. which consist of rice and barley. Indra, in various ways is connected with the fertility of the field and crops.[13] He is the lord of ploughs (R.V. 2, 21, 1 ; 6, 20, 1). Though in later mythology Indra is deprived of his former greatness still he rides on an elephant and carries a thunder-bolt in his hand. This clearly indicates his original nature as god of rain, In addition to that one of his epithets is *pākaśāsana* 'crop-controller'.[14] Thus Indra who is related to vegetation and fertility, is associated with Lakṣmī, the goddess of prosperity and vegetation.

Lakṣmī's relation with Kubera

Lakṣmī the goddess of wealth is assorted with Kubera, the

11. H. Jaeobi, *The Rāmāyaṇa*, p. 104 Note 82.
12. J. Gonda, *Op. Cit.*, p. 252.
13. E.W. Hopkins, 'Indra as god of fertility', *JAOS*, Vol. 36, 1917, p. 242 ff.
14. E. W. Hopkins, *Epic Mythology*, p. 122.

lord over treasures and the giver of wealth. In the Mahābhārata (2, 10, 18) Lakṣmi is said to have lived in the Kubera's palace and is united with him (Mahābhārata; 3, 164, 13).

The Rāmāyaṇa 5, 6, 14, mentions the pictorial representation of the goddess with lotus in her hand on the chariot of Kubera and is stated to have remained with him (Rāmāyaṇa 5, 7, 8). But the later Nārada Purāṇa 84, 12, explicitly mentions this divinity as the wife of Kubera. This relation of Kubera with Lakṣmī is well-illustrated in the Mahābhārata (2, 16, 14), which states that Laksmī belongs to Kubera as Tejas belongs to the sun, Kṣamā 'patience, indulgence' to the Earth and anger to Yama. This shows their mutual and close relation.

Kubera is the king of Yakṣas-*Yakṣarāṭ*—(Mahābhārata 3, 41,14; 5,16,33) and is surrounded by other Yakṣas like Maṇibhadra, Śvetabhadra etc (Mahābhārata 2, 10, 14-16). In the representation of Yakṣa and Yakṣīs in the Bharhut relief (2nd century B.C.) the names of Lakṣmī and Kubera are mentioned[15] In Sirikālakannī Jātaka 392 she is the daughter of Dhataraṭṭa who is enumerated as a Yakṣa at Bharhut. In the ancient Indian Art [16] Laksmī is often represented as a Yakṣī ; Kubera and Lakṣmī are put together[17]. The Yakṣa—male and female are earth genii and are patrons of wealth and fertility.

In the Purāṇas, the relation of Lakṣmī with Kubera is

15. A.K. Coomaraswamy. *Yakṣas*, Part 1, p. 5.

16. J.N. Banerjea. 'Padminī Vidyā, *Jaurnal of the Indian Society of Oriental Art*. Vol. IX, 1941, p. 142 ff.

17. In course of his examination of Brahmanical images in the Mathurā museum V.S. Agrawala definitely states that Lakṣmī is often represented with Kubera, because at certain period she is regarded as his wife. V.S. Agrawala, *A Catalogue of Brahmanical Images in Mathurā Art*, U.P. Historical Society, Lucknow, 1951, p. 151. On the other hand Coomaraswamy opines that in the Buddhist legends though Kubera as Pancikī is associated with Hāritā in later art Hāritī is closely assimilated with Lakṣmī. So Lakṣmī becomes his consort. A.K. Coomaraswamy, *Yakṣas*, Part II, p. 4.

mentioned in different manner. Kubera is the lord of treasures[18] *nidhināmadhipa* — (Harivaṁśa 34, 16) *Nidhīśa* Rāmāyaṇa 7, 3, 22), which are eight in number ; they are Padma, Mahāpadma, Makara, Kacchapa, Mukunda, Nanda, Nīla and Saṅkha. These treasures represent the different aspects of material wealth and prosperity, or are personified treasures. So wherever there is prosperity or opulence one or more of these treasures are found to be at the root of such good fortune and one attains such state only due to the divine favour and service to virtuous people. Each of these treasures is associated with one of the selected opulent professions and is presiding deity of that particular kind of wealth. The Padmanidhi stands for the wealth consisting of gold, silver, copper and other metals ; Mahāpadma for rubies, pearls and other gems etc. The treasures like Saṅkha and Padma are chief among those who are appointed as counsellors of Kubera (Mahābhārata 2, 10, 39).

Mārkaṇḍeya Purāṇa (Ch. 68) and Garuḍa Purāṇa (Ch. 53) which deal with these treasures and their functions extensively call it as Padminī Vidyā.[19] This Padminī Vidyā is defined as the knowledge which brings all types of pleasures or secures all sorts of enjoyments in life.

पद्‌मिनी नाम या विद्या सर्वभोगोपपादिका

(Mārkaṇḍeya Purāṇa 68, 7a)

and this knowledge brings the happy state by putting all the treasures under the disposal of the individual concerned. As the supreme divintiy of all treasures Lakṣmī

18. Coomaraswamy enumerates nine treasures adding Kharva as one, but the Purāṇas which deal with treasures speak of eight treasures (Mārkaṇḍeya Purāṇa 68, 8f; Garuḍa Purāṇa 53,1-2). These treasures are described as 'water symbols'—Coomaraswamy, *Op. Cit.*, Part II, p. 49, F.N. 4.

19. V.S. Agrawala, 'Padminī Vidyā of the Mārkaṇḍeya Purāṇa', Purāṇa Vol. I, No. 2, 1960, p. 181ff ; J.N. Banerjea, *Loc. Cit.*

presides over them all ;

पद्मिनी नाम या विद्या लक्ष्मीस्तस्याश्च देवता ।

तदाधारश्च निधय: ... .॥४॥

(Mārkaṇḍeya Purāṇa 68, 4)

These treasures are all under her control and work at her command. Whereas Kubera is the king of treasures '*nidhīśvara*' and is known as the treasurer of Lakṣmī ; Lakṣmī is the presiding deity of the treasurers, who are taken to be the supporter of the Padminī Vidyā. Thus Kubera, the god of riches and the goddess Lakṣmī are related together.

Various purāṇic legends are formed around Kubera as the possessor of wealth. He is conferred the power and privilege as the possessor of wealth—*dhanādhipatvam* (Mahābhārata 9, 46,22; 5,16,33; 3,258,12-16) immortality and the regent of the quarters—*lokapālatvam.* When the Yakṣas wanted to possess all wealth stored under the earth, Kubera served as the calf to milk it (Padma Purāṇa (Sṛ. khaṇḍa) 5,5,22). He is the lord and protector of especially that wealth which grows in the mountains and is stored under the earth[20] (Rāmāyaṇa 1, 76, 18 : Mahābhārata 6, 8, 25 ; 6, 7, 21) ; when Yudhiṣṭhira is in need of wealth stored under the earth, he has to make offerings of flowers, meat and other objects to Kubera and his followers before digging[21] (Mahābhārata 14, 64, 6ff). On the other hand Lakṣmī is the goddess of fertility and agriculture, which grows in the field. Like his Buddhist counterpart Jambhala, the god of wealth being united with Vasudhārā,[22]

20. V. Fausboll, *Indian Mythology According to the Mahābhārata*, p. 180ff; Hopkins, *Op. Cit*, p. 145

21. Hopkins, *Op. Cit.*, p. 146
22. B. Bhatchyarya, *The Indian Buddhist Iconography*, p. 89ff.

the goddess of wealth and agriculture, Kubera is rightly united with Lakṣmī.

Later on Kubera is also wedded with Bhadrā (Mahābhārata 1, 191, 6) and Ṛddhi (13, 146, 6) .Though the old order changes yielding place to the new, the old is allowed to continue side by side with the new. Kubera, still continues to have relation with Lakṣmī. On Dīpāvalī day (Nirṇaya Sindhu, Vol. II p. 714) Lakṣmī is worshipped with Kubera. The Mārkaṇḍeya Purāṇa 126, 10 ; 65, 2 prescribes her worship along with Kubera and the treasures.

Lakṣmī's relation with Bali

Though as a goddess of prosperity Lakṣmī maintains relation with other gods, her relation with a demon seems to be very unholy. However, it is striking to note how the demon king Bali possesses her. The epic and the Purāṇas bear the testimony of her relation with Bali.[23]

In the Vāmana Purāṇa (Saromāhātmya) 2, 13-20 it is stated that when Indra is defeated by Bali, the goddess Lakṣmī approaches him and speaks of the cause of her coming to Bali thus : "since you could prove your valour by defeating Indra, I am pleased with you and find in you the unparallel strength and high self-conscious respect for which I have been drawn towards you. "Having spoken thus the godess enters the body of Bali and is followed by such other sixteen divinities like Ṛddhi, Hrī, Kīrti, Dyuti, Kṣamā and all other qualities that appertain to sāttvika nature (Vāmana Purāṇa 49, 14-50).

23. For further discussion on Bali see J.J. Mayer, *Trilogie*, G. C. Tripathi, *Der Ursprung und die Entwickung der Vāmana Legend in der indischen Literature*, Wiesadon, 1968 ;G. S. Rai , 'Vāmana Legend in the Vedas, Epics and Purāṇas', *Purāṇa*, Vol. XII,, No. 1, January1970, pp. 102-140

After her close association with Bali, he rules the three worlds as the sovereign ruler. The three worlds prosper due to his benevolence and virtue. During his reign the earth produces grains and fruits in plenty without ploughing ; the cows give sufficient milk ; trees are full of flowers and fruits etc. (Padma Purāṇa 6, 4-5a ; Mahābhārata 12, 216, 16).

As a prosperous king he has to protect and nourish his subjects. Even though he used to donate profusely, he has to suffer no loss of wealth due to her presence (Mahābhārata 12, 216, 4ff). The kingdom flourishes in all respects. Even the people who approach Bali for wealth, enjoyment and liberation are never disappointed (Skanda Purāṇa 1, 1, 19, 61ff).

While Bali reigns so prosperously the gods who are exiled from heaven approach Viṣṇu for succour and at last Viṣṇu in the form of Vāmana appears before Bali while he performs Aśvamedha sacrifice. Vāmana asks for a gift of earth measuring three steps (Skanda Purāṇa 1, 1, 18, 115f). In his first step Vāmana covers the earth and in the second the heaven. When Bali is unable to provide space for the third step, he bends down his head to provide space for Vāmana; as a result Vāmana is pleased with Bali and asks him to enter Sutala with other demons for his habitation. When Bali expresses his unwillingness to leave Viṣṇu he assures him to remain as his gate-keeper in Sutala region. On the otherhand Vāmana is pleased to ask Bali for some boons. As Bali has to satisfy Vāmana with the gift of three steps *tripāda dāna*' he asks to enjoy his kingdom on the earth for three days every year, which has been forcefully taken away from him by Vāmana. Vāmana assents to it. So Bali visits his kingdom on the earth for three days every year (Skanda Purāṇa 2, 4, 9, 52ff).

The three days dedicated as the kingdom of Bali on the earth are—Kārttika Kṛṣṇa Caturdaśī, Amāvasyā and Śuklapratipadā days of the month Bali uses to visit the earth on these days with Bali comes Lakṣmī on the earth. So those who offer lamps on these days in their houses, Lakṣmī remains constant with them ; on the other hand those who keep their house dark during these days, Lakṣmī does not favour them and as a consequence they are debarred from having offspring ; and never enjoy prosperity and plenty throughout the year.

Thus goddess Lakṣmī has become the constant companion of Bali and lives in Sutala with him and follows Bali in his suite (DevīBhāgavata 8, 19, 15). When Bali visits the earth during Dīpāvalī festival, Lakṣmī follows him.

Lakṣmī : consort of Viṣṇu

In the earlier stages of development Lakṣmī appears to have been associated with different gods. The union of Lakṣmī with Viṣṇu is the latest development of her legend in the Mahābhārata. The Mahābhārata (12,59,133-134) narrates that the goddess is born from a golden lotus which originated from the forehead of Viṣṇu. She is then married to Dharma and bears a son named Artha, These three—Dharma 'duty, justice', Artha 'riches' and the goddess are established in sovereignty. When Viṣṇu has been elevated to the supreme position, the function of creation has been ascribed to him. During this period of glorification of Viṣṇu, he has been described as the progenitor of goddess Śrī which seems to be a later addition.[24]

In the Mahābhārata (1, 55, 34) Lakṣmī is tne consort of Kṛṣṇa and in the same text a part of her incarnates as Rukmiṇī (Mahābhārata 1, 61, 90, 95). The union of Viṣṇu with Lakṣmī forms an ideal couple, which has been referred to under different contexts (Mahābhārata 5, 115, 10 ; 1, 191, 6 ; 3, 186, 86). In the Rāmāyaṇa (2, 110, 19) her relation is recognised when it is said that Lakṣmī decorates Viṣṇu as his faithful wife. When Rukmiṇī sees Lakṣmī on Viṣṇu's lap, Lakṣmī describes her the places of her (Lakṣmī's) residence.

24. *The Age of Imperial Unity*, p. 471

The divinity dwells in rivers, lotuses, bulls, elephants, maidens, ruling sovereigns etc. in spirit only, but she lives with Nārāyaṇa in her embodied form—

नारायणेत्वेकमना वसामि सर्वेण भावेन शरीरभूता ।

(Mahābhārata 13, 11,19)

> The Amarakoṣa (1, 1, 27f) mentions Haripriyā 'the beloved of Hari' as an epithet of Lakṣmī and Viṣṇu is called Śrīpati, Lakṣmīpati (1, 1, 15 ; 1, 1, 28) 'husband of Lakṣmī'. While enumerating the thousand names of Viṣṇu, the Mahābhārata (13, 149) calls the god Śrīmān, Śrīvāsa, Śrīnivāsa 'abode of Śrī', Lakṣmī, Lakṣmīvān, Śrīpati, Śrīśa, Śrīmatāmvara, Śrīnidhi 'receptacle of Śrī,' Śrīdhara 'bearer of Śrī, Śrīda 'giver of Śrī, Śrīkara and Śrīvibhāvana. These names mentioned in the above enumeration very well prove the importance of the divinity and her association with Viṣṇu. The Viṣṇu Dharma Sūtra (1, 43, 99, 1) describes her as a constant companion of Viṣṇu who shampoos his feet while reclining.

The union of Lakṣmī with Viṣṇu reaches its final stage in the Purāṇas. The Viṣṇu Purāṇa states the legend of the churning of the ocean where she emerges from the ocean and goes to Viṣṇu as his consort (1, 9, 105). The worship of Lakṣmī with Viṣṇu is prescribed in the Viṣṇudharmottara Purāṇa (3, 216, 4 ; 6) and the divinity is said to have been dwelling in the breast of Viṣṇu.

The prominence of the goddess becomes so great that she is conceived to be the controller of the cosmic and human order. When she is united with Viṣṇu, the functions of Viṣṇu are transferred to her and she is given equal status with him. When Viṣṇu assumes different incarnations, Lakṣmī becomes his constant companion. When Viṣṇu is born as Āditya, she takes the form of Padmā, born of lotus. Lakṣmī appears as Dharaṇī while Viṣṇu descends as Paraśurāma. In the incarnation of Rāma she is Sītā[25] and when Viṣṇu is born as Kṛṣṇa, she is Rukmiṇī. Lakṣmī follows Viṣṇu as his constant associate in his different incarnations. When Viṣṇu appears in a celestial form, Lakṣmī is also born with a heavenly form, likewise when Viṣṇu is born as a mortal she takes human form. (Viṣṇu Purāṇa 1, 9, 142-145).

Lakṣmī is united to Dattātreya, who is an incarnation of Viṣṇu.[26] She takes her seat by the left side of Dattātreya when gods visit to appease him to win over the demons. When the demons rob him of Lakṣmī and carry her on their heads, they lose their strength and are defeated by gods (Mārkaṇḍeya Purāṇa 18, 38ff).

When Viṣṇu takes the incarnation of Nṛsiṁha[27], Lakṣmī follows him. She witnesses the fight between Nṛsiṁha and Hiraṇyakaśipu (Bhāgāvata 7, 9, 2) ; after the death of the demon, when Nṛsiṁha's wrath is not pacified, she appeases his anger at the request of gods and human beings (Padma Purāṇa 6, 265, 125). Rukmiṇī, the wife of Kṛṣṇa is described as an incarnation of Lakṣmī (Mahābhārata 1, 67, 156). Thus Lakṣmī takes different incarnations corresponding to Viṣṇu.

Before Lakṣmī is accepted as the consort of Viṣṇu, there is no reference to her incarnations. Only when she is accepted as the constant companion of Viṣṇu, the concept of incarnation is extended to her. Like the different incarnations of Viṣṇu, Lakṣmī has exclusive incarnations of her own. In different ages of creation Lakṣmī assumes different forms and originates from different sources. In the age of Svāyambhuva,

25. *Ramottaratāpinī Upaniṣad* 6, 120, 28 states—

सीता लक्ष्मीर्भवान् विष्णुः·········

26. Hopkins, *Epic Mythology*, p. 218 ; Mahābhārata 1, 63, 99 ; *Mārkaṇḍeya Purāṇa* 17, 6,

27. *Nṛsiṁhapurvatāpanīya Upaniṣad* 4, 15, 7.
J.N. Farquhar, *An Outline of the Religious Literature of India*, p. 188ff.

Lakṣmī is born as the daughter of Bhṛgu and rises from the fire in the age of Svāroci. She originates from the water in the age of creation of Uttama and in Tāmasa age she rises out of the abyss of the earth. In the ages of Raivata and Çākṣuṣa she appears from Bilva and full-blown lotus respectively. But in the age of Vaivaśvata she rises from the ocean, when the churning of the ocean is conducted. Thus she is born in different forms in different ages (Viṣṇudharmottara Purāṇa 1, 41, 33-36).

Prior to Lakṣmī's association with Viṣṇu, he is said to have certain powers and functions. He is thought to be the supreme lord of the universe and is the cause of creation, preservation and dissolution of the universe ; he pervades all beings. When Lakṣmī is united with Viṣṇu, she is said to have shared the powers and functions of Viṣṇu. Like Viṣṇu she also takes part in the function of creation, maintenance and destruction of the universe and both of them pervade all beings. She represents all that is female and he all that is male and both are ever-existent and complementary to each other (Viṣṇu Purāṇa 1, 8, 17ff.)

Goddess Lakṣmī appears as a popular deity unaligned with any other male god between the 3rd century B.C. and Ist century A.D.[28]. The Baudhāyana Dharama Sūtra (2, 5, 9, 10) mentions her as one of the independent divinities of the Vaiṣṇava pantheon. So there is no certainty as to the exact period in which she becomes Viṣṇu's wife. In the days of the Mahābhārata, Lakṣmī is also worshipped alone. In reply to Kṛṣṇa's querry about the divinities whom he worships, Nārada enumerates the names of a number of deities and Lakṣmī is mentioned as one of these deities (Mahābhārata 13, 31, 6).

Though in the Mahābhārata the relation between Viṣṇu and Lakṣmī is established as Kṛṣṇa's wife

28. *The Age of Imperial Unity*, p. 470; A. A. Macdonell, "The Development of Early Hindu Iconography", *JRAS.* of Great Britain & Ireland, 1916, p. 127.

(1, 55, 34), still in the same text her former relation with other deities are mentioned. She is the wife of Dharma (1, 60, 13) and belongs to five Indras (1, 169, 33) and others. From epigraphic and other evidences it is known that the divinity is coupled with Viṣṇu during the Gupta age[29], and then only her worship wlth Viṣṇu is prescribed.

Attributes and Emblems of Lakṣmī

In order to understand the character of the deity it is indispensable to enter into details of the goddess's emblems and attributes. Lakṣmī is represented as standing on a lotus pedestal wearing garland of lotus, holding a lotus and Bilva in her hands ; the elephants of the quarters sprinkle water in inverted jars and a bird serving as her vehicle. It is significant that the objects and animals attached with Lakṣmī have a close relation with her nature. So the study of these attributes is greatly helpful to understand the nature of the deity.

The relation of lotus with Lakṣmī is very significant. She is called Padminī ; she stands on a lotus *padmesthitā* ; she is *padmavarṇā*, she is of the colour of lotus and is born of lotus—*padmasambhavā*, *padmālayā*, *padmā*. She maintains her old association with lotus till now. In the Viṣṇu Purāṇa 1, 9, 100 she is said to have arisen from the ocean on a full-blown lotus *vikāsikamalesthitā* holding lotus in her hand *dhṛtapaṅkajā*. When the goddess is represented in sculpture either with four hands or two hands, she is stated to have

29. After thorough examination of different icons. Suvira Jaiswal comes to the conclusion that goddess is united with Viṣṇu during the Gupta age (3rd-4th centuries A.D.) and then only the god Viṣṇu appears with lotus as one of his emblems, which is closely connected with Lakṣmi. *The Origin and Development of Vaiṣṇavism*, pp. 102-103 ; *The Classical Age*, pp. 424-425; H.C. Roychoudhury, *Materials for the Study of Early Vaiṣṇavism*, p. 176 ff; D.A. Pai—*Monograph on the Religious Sects in India among the Hindus*, p.7.

held lotus in her hands (Viṣṇudharmottara Purāṇa 3, 82, 2-6 ; Matsya Purāṇa 257, 12). The lotus is attached to the divinity from the very early age ; but later on the same symbol is extended to other deities.

The Vāyu Purāṇa 37, 5ff and Vārāha Purāṇa 79, 1ff describe a lake named Śrīsara. In this Śrīsara, there is an unfading lotus named Mahāpadma, which is surrounded by other sweet-scented lotus flowers and is watched over by the gods. In this unfading lotus Mahāpadma resides the goddess Lakṣmī. The Śrīsara is surrounded by Śrīvana abounding in Bilva trees and the goddess is said to be worshipped by her followers there.

Brahmā, the creator of beings is also called *abjaja, abjayoni, padmasambhava* etc. 'lotus-born'. This lotus out of which springs Brahmā, grows from the navel of Viṣṇu or from a lotus which grows out of him (Mahābhārata 3, 12, 37 ; 203, 15). The navel of Viṣṇu is the place of origin of the lotus and it is stated that the universe is situated on it (Mahābhārata 12, 4, 7, 58). This navel is said to represent the sum total of the cosmic energy of the universe, whereas the lotus arising out of it represents the material aspect of evolution, the petals its consecutive forms (Agni Purāṇa 49).

The lotus which arises from the depth of water and expands its petals on the surface of it, gives the most beautiful evidence of the fertility of the bottom. It also proves the life-supporting power of the abyss. This may be a cause for which Kamalā is selected as an appropriate consort of Viṣṇu who represents cosmic water of the primordial ocean out of which all phenomena and elements of the universe arise and at the time of dissolution they all return to it. The dynamic force of creation which has been withdrawn at the time of dissolution reappears in the shape of the lotus to begin its circle of the perennial course anew.

The lotus out of which Brahmā, the creator of all arises, is the representative par excellence of the power of vegetation and fertility. It is the representative of the force or energy inherent in the water and in the moisture of the soil. As water is regarded as a female principle, lotus which is identified with such creative entity of female character, is the birth place of Brahmā, the creator and the goddess Lakṣmī. The relation of lotus and water indicates the character of fertility and procreation. The character of the goddess can very well be discernible from her relation with the lotus and Viṣṇu.

The Viṣṇu Purāṇa 1, 9, 103 states that when the goddess rises out of the ocean, she is sprinkled over by the elephants of the quarters[30] (*dīggajaiḥ*) with the water of the Ganges and other sacred rivers. From the earliest period such representation of the deity in Art is abundant, for which she is called Gaja Lakṣmī 'Lakṣmī of the elephants'. In a later text like Skanda Purāṇa 1, 1, 11, 67, we come across the description of the goddess arising out of the ocean, where she is said to have emerged riding a white elephant—

पाण्डुर गजमारूढा

The elephant like horse is an ancient symbol of water cosmogony.[31] We find the elephants of the quarters or cloud-elephants and water-elephants *jalahastin*, *jalebha*, who are associated with Yakṣas and Yakṣiṇīs as their vehicle. H. Zimmer[32] has tried to depict a very interesting story of their origin through Brahmā and how they have been entrusted to guard the quarters and are designated as *lokapālas*. These eight pairs of elephants—male and female, support the eight quarters of the earth with different gods. One of them is Airāvata and Abharamu who support the east and are attached to Indra.

Indra is the 'god of rains' (Mahābhārata 6,95,34; Rāmāyaṇa 7, 70, 10) and fosters the field with rain-water. The elephant Airāvata on which he sits, draws up water from the under

30. *Saubhāgya Lakṣmī Upaniṣad*, 1.

31. Coomaraswamy, *Op. Cit.*, Part II, p. 32ff.

32. H. Zimmer, *Myths and Symbols in Indian Art and Civilization* p. 103ff.

world for Indra (Mahābhārata 5, 97, 7). Thus the elephant who has been symbolised as the raining cloud is fittingly chosen as the vehicle of Indra.[33] The peculiar virtue of the elephant is to attract the heavenly counterpart and produce rain on earth. In popular myth and religion, it serves as the producer of rain. Abhramu 'producing clouds', who knits the clouds, the consort of Airāvata, exercises the special power. They specially attract the monsoon clouds which add to the fertility of the soil for vegetation. This also reminds us of its origin from the churning of the ocean and its relation with water.

As like Airāvata of Indra, the earthly king, who is the representative of gods on earth preserves elephants as a sign of royalty and strength. The elephant is the carrier of the king. It naturally claims worship as the symbol of strength and wisdom. The ideal king on earth is not only expected to administer justice and to protect his subjects from dangers and difficulties but also the fertility and prosperity of the country depend on king's virtue. In war and peace it is the symbolic mount of the king.

The elephant is an animal of adoration. If the officers of the kingdom do not pay due reverence to the elephant, a severe catastrophy is inevitable, as a result the king and the kingdom would perish. On the other hand if due honour is accorded to the elephant, the crop would flourish ; there would be plenty of rain for growth and vegetation.[34] If the royal elephant is given away, the country has to suffer from draught, failure of crops and famine.[35] It is a symbol of prosperity.

Thus we find that elephant is taken as an auspicious sign and is related with water. It is the insignia of rain-cloud which adds to fecundation ; moreover it is related to Indra, the Indian rain-god. The elephant in association with water

33. Asis Sen, *Animal Motifs in Ancient Indian Art*, p. 103ff.

34. *Hastyāyurveda*, 4, 22, 35-41 ; H. Zimmer, *Op. Cit.*, p. 52.

35. *Pali Jataka*, Vol. VI, *Jataka* No. 547; Vol. III, *Jataka* No. 276.

as the source of all life is very significant.

When Lakṣmī is installed as an independent deity she is represented with four hands,[36] out of which she holds a jar of amṛta in one hand and a Bilva fruit in the other. and the other two hands adorn lotus and conch respectively (Viṣṇudharmottara Purāṇa 3, 82, 5-7). Either represented with four hands or two hands, she holds Bilva in one of the hands. The Bilva 'wood apple' is called Śrīphala (Matsya Purāṇa 260, 43). Its unripe fruits are used for medical purposes. The fruit is applied to cure barrenness.[37] Persons desiring prosperity in offspring, cattle and food, pre-eminence in holiness or spiritual knowledge are advised to make a sacrificial post of Bilva (A.B. 2, 1 ; Ap. Ś. S. 7, 1, 15). The Ṛg-Vidhāna (2, 19, 3ff) designates it as *Vṛddhināmauṣadhi* the herb called after prosperity and those who desire endless fortune should offer oblation of Bilva wood to the deity. The Bilva leaf is favourite of Hari (Ṛg Vidhāna 3, 42,4).

As it grows on the very place where the sun is established on earth before he is lifted to the sky, it is regarded to be auspicious (T.A. 2, 1, 8, 1 ; Bṛhat Saṁhitā 85, 3). In the Śrī-Sūkta (V.6) the Bilva is related to the goddess. It is said to be born of her penance and is expected to remove illusion, distress and poverty. In order to drive away Alakṣmī, an amulet of Bilva is prescribed.

The Vārāha Purāṇa 79, 1ff and Vāyu Purāṇa 37, 8ff speak of a lake named Śrīṣara which is surrounded by a Bilva forest. This forest of Bilva is the favourite of Lakṣmī. Various purāṇic legends are formed to describe its origin and its relation with the divinity. The tree is born out of the hands of Lakṣmī (Vāmana Purāṇa 18, 8). After the churning of the ocean when the gods and the demons quarrel among them-

36. The *Padma Purāṇa* 6, 260, 41-45 presents an iconographical description of Lakṣmī with four hands. While rising from the ocean Laksmī stands on a golden lotus besmeared with sandal paste. In her two hands she holds a golden lotus and a garland of unfading lotus and in her other two hands she holds *vasupātra* 'pot of grains' and *mātuluṅga* 'citron'.

37. R.E. Enthoven, *Folklore of Bombay*, p. 286

selves for the nectar, Lakṣmī, who rises out of the ocean takes her rest on this tree ; so it is called Śrī-vṛkṣa. Hence it is worshipped on the ninth day of the bright half of Bhādrapada with fruits and cereals (Bhaviṣyottara P. 60, 1f).

In the bright fortnight of Āśvayujā, the festival of the goddess Durgā, a vegetal spirit is observed.[38] During this festival on the sixth day, the *bodhana* wake of the goddess is performed in the Bilva tree. On the seventh day of the month, the nine plants '*navapatrikā*' the personification of the goddess Durgā are worshipped together ; among these plants Bilva is included. The Bilva as a spirit of vegetation gets due worship on different occasions ; so its relation with the divinity.

Now-a-days we find the gods followed by certain animals as carrier '*vāhana*' in the worship and these animals also get a share in the worship together with the deity. We find Garuḍa as the carrier of Viṣṇu, Śiva is followed by his bull Nandī, swan serves the carrier of Brahmā, buffallo of Yama, peacock of Kārttikeya, and mouse of Gaṇeśa.

In Hinduism the anthropomorphic character of gods are quite discernible. As like human beings they are subject to death, decay and rebirth. They carry on certain functions for a temporary period of time. In the Vedic age the animals which are associated with different gods as 'doubles', become their vehicles in later period. The animals so attached to different deities as carriers reflect their very character; they are the menifestations of the divinity in the animal plane and express some important religious ideas before the human eyes.[39] In view of their change of function change of vehicle is marked. Durgā who assumes different forms under different situations takes different vehicles, which reflects her character at that particular situation. As Nandā she rides on an elephant, as Kālarātrī a terrible deity of destruction she is represented as naked and rides on an ass ; but as Śivā she has

38. *Durgotsava Viveka*, p. 7

39. J. Gonda, *Change and Continuity in Indian Religion*, p. 72f; Zimmer, Op. Cit. p. 48ff.

the bull as her carrier, the vehicle of her husband. Thus the vehicle is an indicative of the character of the divinity to whom it is attached.

Though there is rare reference to owl as the vehicle of Lakṣmī in the literature, in the local belief and tradition owl is represented as the carrier of Lakṣmī,[40] the goddess of wealth and prosperity. Some scholars think that as the owls feed on various small animals particularly the squirrels, rats and mice which cause damage to crops they are greatly beneficial to agriculture; but such conjecture does not seem to be appropriate because the birds of the same species who destroy also the above kinds of animals are not connected to the divinity.

In the AtharvaVeda (7, 115, 1-4) we find the description of Pāpī Lakṣmī as well as Pūṇyā Lakṣmī. In the description of Pāpī Lakṣmī, she is also called Nirṛti, a goddess of destruction. The owl, messenger of death is attached to her as a messenger. The Taittirīya Āraṇyaka 4,70—speaks of the owl as *hīraṇyākṣa* having golden eyes, *ayomukha* having the face of iron colour ; it is put as the messenger of the demons. This deity is described as the wife of Mṛtyu and has got owl as her carrier (Mārkaṇḍeya Purāṇa 50,33; 51, 68). This ominous bird is associated with Lilith, the Mesopatamian goddess of evil, the Egyptian ghosts and the spirits of the wailful mothers of the Arabian nation.[41]

Cāmuṇḍā, the same as Devī-Durgā has eight forms.[42] one of which is called Mahālakṣmī, When the goddess Cāmuṇḍā is adored by the Kṣatriyas, she is called Kālī or Mahākālī. In this form she is represented with eight hands holding a trident or sword in one hand and a skull

40. K.W. Morgan, *The Basic Beliefs of Hinduism*, p. 101ff ; *The Vedic Age*, p. 117;

J. Tod, *Annals and Antiquities of Rajasthan* Vol. 1, p, 476; Asis Sen, *Op. Cit.* p. 95ff.

41. Asis Sen, Op. *Cit.*, p. 96

42. N.K. Bhattasali, *Iconography of Buddhist and Brahmanical Sculptures in the* Decca *Museum*, p. 208.

or cup of wine in the other and the owl is put as her vehicle[43]. Her outer description and the animal attached to her express her terrible nature as a deity of destruction.

In the Atharva Veda (7, 115. 1—4) Lakṣmī has the two-sided concept—Pāpī (inauspicious) and *Puṇyā* (auspicious). When the deity Śrī is assimilated with Lākṣmī of auspicious character, Lakṣmī becomes the goddess of prosperity and vegetation and the inauspicious Lakṣmī appears as Alakṣmī. But the owl, who is said to have been associated with her inauspicious form in the past still remains with her as her carrier. Though a divinity of fertility and vegetation, she continues to be attached with the owl which represents the terrible aspects of the mother godddess. The association of owl with the benevolent goddess Lakṣmī[44] reminds us of her old nature. Like the goddess Lakṣmi, in ancient Greece the owl is the vehicle of the goddess Pallas Athene who is described as the protectress of agriculture and the inventress of plough.[45]

Epithet of Lakṣmī

When the goddess becomes popular in the society, like other divinities, she is attributed with different names and epithets. These names and epithets are properly recorded by different lexicographers from time to time. One of the earliest texts of it is Amarkoṣa of Amarasiṁha[46] which belongs probably to the sixth century A.D. This text

43. H.K. Sastri, *South Indian Images of Gods and Goddesses*, p. 197. T.A. Gopinath Rao, *Elements of Hindu Iconography*, p. 386; *Agni Purāṇa*, 50, 30ff.

44. The terrible form of Lakṣmī is still found in the description of the fight between Lalitā and Bhāṇḍāsura. When Lalitā marches in her great chariot to fight with the demon, Bhāṇḍāsura, Lakṣmī with other Śaktis also accompanies her. Like other śaktis Lakṣmī is also represented here as a virgin with eyes red with anger and armed with lance and disc to kill the powerful demon. *Brahmāṇḍa Purāṇa* (*Lalitopākhyāna*) 4, 19, 70ff ; but such description seems to be incompatible in the present form. Cf. *Mbh*. 9, 46, 64ff.

45. S.K. Dixit, *The Mother Goddess*, p. 186.

46. A .B. Keith, *A History of Sanskrit Literature*, p. 413.

enumerates fourteen appelations of Lakṣmī.[47] These names are also given by Sabdakalpadruma which refers to Amarakoṣa.

The epithets like *Kṣirodatanayā* (*Dogdhābdhi tanayā*) *Kṣira-ṣāgarakanyakā* (*jaladhijā*) and *Kṣīrasāgarasutā* clearly refer to her birth from the ocean and her relation with water. Lakṣmī's relation with lotus is quite conspicuous from her different epithets like *Padmā*, *Kamalā*, Padmālyā (*Padmasaṁbhavā*) and her rise from the lotus during the churning of the ocean. And *Haripriyā* (*Hariballabhā*) mentions her position as the wife of Hari (Viṣṇu). She carries the designation Ramā (the delighting one' (Bhāgavata Purāṇa 8, 8, 8), because her very presence brings prosperity and happiness.

In Sabdakalpadruma IV, p. 196 also Indirā is put as one of the synonyms of Lakṣmī. Besides the name is also found in the commentaries of Śrī-Sūkta with the remark—

आनन्द कर्दम चिक्लित इन्दिरासुता ऋषय:

In the Śrī-Sūkta (11-12) Kardama and Ciklita are described as the sons of Lakṣmī. Before finally united with Viṣṇu Lakṣmī is said to have close relation with Indra.[48] In course of time many elements of Indra's characters are taken over by Viṣṇu when he rises to eminence. Lakṣmī who has close association with Indra in the early age is appropriated by Viṣṇu. Therefore Lakṣmī who carries the epithet Indirā due to her relation with Indra is described as the wife of Viṣṇu.[49] and the epithet very well reminds us of her former asso-

47. लक्ष्मी पद्मालया पद्मा कमला श्रीर्हरिप्रिया ।
इन्दिरा लोकमाता मा क्षीरोदतनया रमा ।
भार्गवी लोकजननी क्षीरसागरकन्यका ।।

[Amarakoṣa. 1,1, 27]

48. See Supra,

49. H. Jacobi, *Loc. Cit.*; G. Hartmann, *Op. Cit.*, p. 4f ; J. Gonda, *Op. Cit.*, p. 224f.

ciation with Indra.

Goddess Lakṣmī is stated as the genetrix of the world; she maintains them as a mother ought to do. So she is often called as the *Mātā, Mā* (Śrī-Sūkta 20; Viṣṇu Purāṇa 1, 9 ,126),

लोकमाता सर्वलोकानां जननी (Viṣṇu Purāṇa 1,9,117) mother of the world. The mother goddess in other countries are also given such epithets. The Babylonians designate the mother goddess as Ummu or Umma, the Accadians Ummi and the Greeks as *Mā*. These words can be related to each other and with Umā, the consort of Śiva, the great mother who is related with the universal cult of the mother goddess.[50] The Phrygian mother goddess who is said to be Amma[51] or *Mā* can easily be equated with the name Ambā (Viṣṇu Purāṇa 1, 9, 126).

In popular mythology the mother goddess appears with similar epithets. In Dravidian territories the village goddesses like Sukhalāmmā, the goddess of measles and pox, Mariammā or Marī the goddess of small pox, Suklammā, Peddammā etc. the goddess of epidemic are worshipped.[52] These village goddesses are pre-eminently called 'Mother' as their designations express. They are responsible to protect the inhabitants from such calamities which befall them. It appears that these names are originally associated with Mā or Ammā denoting mother. The Dravidian word for mother is Ammā and the change of Ammā to Mā seems to take place at a very early age. The Śatapatha Brāhmaṇa 8,3,3,5 refers to the mother Earth as Mā deriving it from the root *mā* 'to measure'. In fact the Earth is identified with the goddess in the Aitareya Brāhmaṇa 8,5. In the northern and southern India, the mother goddess is still designated as Mā which may be connected more directly

50. Hopkins, Op. *Cit.*, p. 226.

51. S.K. Dikshit, *Op. Cit,*, p. 59f.

52. H. Whitehead, *Village Gods of South India*, p. 29f.

with Ammā than with *Mātṛ*

Bhārgavī is one of the epithets of Lakṣmī, for she is the daughter of Bhṛgu-Prajāpati. It is told that before her origin from the churning of the ocean, she was born as the daughter of Bhṛgu and Khyāti.[53] The Bhṛgus are a group of Brāhmaṇas. Sukthankar[54], while studying the origin of Mahābhārata contends that the original Mahābhārta which consisted of 24,000 verses in the beginning takes the present form in the hands of the Bhṛguide Brāhmaṇas who had partiality towards Nārāyaṇa-Viṣṇu. The influence of the Bhārgavas are also easily remarkable in the Purāṇa literature. These poets have refashioned the Purāṇa by adding Bhārgava myths and legends according to their own fashion. The legend of Lakṣmī does not escape their redaction ; as a result Lakṣmī has been described as the daughter of Bhṛgu and is given in marriage to Nārāyaṇa.

Lakṣmī's Relation with other Divinities

Apart from her association with male partners Lakṣmī is stated to have relation with different female divinities. One of them is Durgā. In Nṛsiṁhapūrvatāpanī Upaniṣad 3. 4, 2 Durgā is mentioned with Lakṣmī. Here Lakṣmī and Durgā together with other goddesses are designated as *Brahmayoni*. Lakṣmī and Durgā are also described as the daughter of a common parent i.e. Dakṣa and Prasūti.[55] While Lakṣmī is given in marriage to Dharma, Durgā (Satī) gets Rudra as her husband. The Brahmavaivarta Purāṇa 2, 1, 1ff ; 4, 4 and Devī Bhāgavata 9,1, 1ff ; 4, 4 while describing the origin of female divinities speak that the *Mūla prakṛti* (Primordial Nature) assumes five forms at the time of creation of the universe according to the different functions of creation ; Lakṣmī and Durgā are two of them.

53. See Supra,

54. V.S Sukthankar, 'Epic Studies VI', *ABORI*, XVIII, pp. 1-76 ; Suvira Jaiswal, *Op. Cit.*, p. 10.

55. W. Krfel, *Op. Cit.*, p. 40, V.23.

In the Padma Purāṇa (Sr.) 5, 4, there is the description of the birth of Lakṣmī. She is mentioned as Umā born of Menā and Viṣṇu Purāṇa 1, 8, 15ff, while stating the identification of Viṣṇu aud Lakṣmī with different typs of gods and their wives, identifies Lakṣmī with Durgā (Gaurī) and Viṣṇu with Śivā (V-23). On the other hand Viṣṇudharmottara Puraṇa 3,8,4 which recounts the names of Lakṣmī states *Devī* and *Vibhāvarī* among her names, which are generally applied to Durgā. Durgā is called as Nārāyaṇī, Lakṣmī etc. the frequent epithets of her in the Devī Māhātmya 11, 8.

The Devī Māhātmya of Mārkaṇḍeya Purāṇa describes the victroy of Durgā over demons. The divinity is generally designated as the mother-goddess in her terrific character So she is duly adored for victory by the heroes. As such her field of activity is limited to the field of war ; but Lakṣmī, who represents the benevolent aspect of the Mother goddess starts functioning when victory is won. So when Tāraka or Bali wins victory over Indra, Laksmī appears before him. It appears that Durgā and Lakṣmī are very closely related to each other and represent both the aspects—benevolent and awful of the pre-Aryan deity of fertility and later on are united as the spouse of the two prominent gods of Hindu trinity Siva and Viṣṇu respectively.

In the Vedic age Sarasvatī[56] is a goddess of learning and not related to Lakṣmī. But in the purāṇic literature Lakṣmī and Sarasvatī are so closely related that they are sometimes even identified. In the Matsya Purāṇa (64, 9) and Padma Purāṇa (Sr.) 5, 27, 166ff Sarasvatī is called as Lakṣmī and in the Lakṣmī Stotra of Viṣṇu Purāṇa 1, 9, 119 Sarasvatī is mentioned as one of the synonyms of Lakṣmī. Even some parallel slokas containing the same epithets for both the divinities-Lakṣmī and Sarasvatī, are traced out in the above

56. Taking into consideration of different Vedic and Post-Vedic texts N.B. Chaudhury has tried to prove that the Vedic goddess Uṣas has evolved in to two divinities like Lakṣmī and Sarasvatī in later ages ; so these two divinities are so closely related, rather they represent different aspect of the same divinity ; but such hypothesis does not seem to be plausible. N.N. Chaudhury, Goddess Lakṣmī in the Purāṇa had Tantra Poona *Orientalist*, 18, No. 1-2, pp. 1-6.

Sarasvatī Stotra and Lakṣmī Stotra.

The Lalitopākhyāna portion of Brahmāṇḍa Purāṇa (4,40, 5f) gives an account of the birth of Lakṣmī and Sarasvatī from the goddess Mahālakṣmī and their union with different male gods. According to this account Mahālakṣmī produces three eggs. From one egg are born Ambikā and Viṣṇu, from the other egg appear Lakṣmī and Brahmā and from the third egg is produced Sarasvatī (Girā) with Śiva. Then Mahālakṣmī combines Sarasvatī with Brahmā, Durgā with Śiva and Lakṣmī with Viṣṇu. Another account of the goddesses which appears in the Prādhānika Rahasya (p. 121, V,4ff) appended to the Devī Māhātmya of Mārkaṇḍeya Purāṇa though seems parallel still differs a little. Mahālakṣmī endowed with three qualities '*guṇas*' assumes a *tāmasika* form known as Mahākālī and also a *sāttvika* form known as Mahāsarasvatī. The goddesses create three pairs of deities each creating one pair thus —Mahālakṣmī creates Brahmā and Lakṣmī, Mahākālī creates Rudra and Sarasvatī (Trayī) and Mahāsarsavatī creates Viṣṇu and Umā. At last Mahālakṣmī gives Sarasvatī to Brahmā as his wife, Durgā to Rudra and Lakṣmī to Visṇu. But in the Brahmavaivarta Purāṇa (2, 6, 1ff) and DevīBhāgavata (9,6,17) the marriage of Sarasvatī with Viṣṇu is finalised and she is described as the co-wife of Lakṣmi and Gaṅgā. So they all remain with Viṣṇu as his consort.

In the Brahma Purāṇa 122, 71ff there is a description of Viṣṇu with Sarasvatī and Lakṣmī. Visṇu holds Sarasvatī in his mouth and Lakṣmī in his breast ; so he is Sarvajña 'omniscient' and Lakṣmīvān 'prosperous, glorious'. These two qualities are essential for his being as Puruṣottama and Pūrṇa. Sarasvatī, here, symbolises intellectual moral and spiritual advancement or *mukti* and Lakṣmī represents physical or worldly prosperity, well-being or *bhukti*. These two goddesses cover the entire sphere of an individual's life. The harmonious combination of these divine principles leads one to all-round development in life. The greater is the harmony between Sarasvatī and Laksmī in a man's life, that is harmony between *mukti* and *bhukti* or between *jñāna* 'knowledge' and *bhoga* enjoyment, in one's life, the more he advances towards his goal. The redactors of the text always keep it in view, so they represent Sarasvatī and Lakṣmī as the co-wives of Viṣṇu, who are in harmony with each other. This legend also aims at harmonizing and co-ordinating the conflicting forces in nature i.e. Lakṣmī and Sarasvatī.[57]

In popular concept Lakṣmī and Sarasvatī are antagonistic[58] to each other. The Devī Bhāgavata 9, 6, 32ff and Brahmavaivarta Purāṇa 2, 6, 12ff refer to a legend of quarrel between Lakṣmī and Sarasvatī thus : once while Gaṅgā and Sarasvatī are engaged in a quarrel between each other, Lakṣmī dissuades them ; but Sarasvatī becomes furious and curses Lakṣmī to be reborn as a tree and as river. At last Viṣṇu comes to her rescue and sends Gaṅgā to Śiva and Sarasvatī to Brahmā ; as a result Lakṣmī lives with him peacefully. This type of enmity between Sarasvatī and Lakṣmī though not so prominent in earlier literature, becomes an established fact in later texts ; common experience shows that wealth and learning very rarely go together. Like other texts Kalidas also refers to this fact of Lakṣmī and Sarasvatī in Raghuvaṁśa (6, 29) and Vikramorvaśīyam (5, 24),

Viṣṇu is also depicted with Bhūdevī, goddess Earth and Lakṣmī who are his wives (Padma Purāṇa 6, 260, 16). There Lakṣmī is represented with a garland of heavenly flowers on the right side of Viṣṇu and on the left side sits the Earth who holds two *dhānyapātras* 'corn vessels' (Padma Purāṇa 6, 257, 72-74). The Earth goddess is to be made of a light green colour resembling that of the tender sprouts of the paddy. The Viṣṇudharmottara Purāṇa 3, 61, 1-5 states that the goddess Earth should be made of four hands carrying a *ratna-pātra*, 'a jewel vessel', a *sasyapātra* 'a corn vessel, *oṣadhi-pātra* 'a pot full of medicinal herbs' and a lotus respectively. In Mahenjodaro and Harappa we come

57. A.S. Gupta, 'Conception of Sarasvatī in the Purāṇas', *Purāṇa*, Vol. IV, No. 1, January 1962. p. 75.

58. C.V. Davane, 'The Goddess Sarasvatī in Sanskrit Literature', *Journal of the University of Bombay*. Vol. XXXVII, No. 73, October, 1968, pp. 70-77.

across female divinities, which are represented with plants growing from their navel[59]. These deities are accepted as the mother Earth.

When agriculture started, the mother Earth develops into double form—mother and the maiden, and in course of time the mother Earth is identified with young corn spirit. In course of time mother Earth the goddess of prosperity is assimilated with Lakṣmī, the goddess of harvest, then Lakṣmī is regarded as the goddess of fortune and vegetation and attributed with the function of the mother and the maiden.[60] Then only Śrī-Sūkta is prescribed to be used ceremonially to sanctify the earth on the occasion of ceremonial bath (Taittirīya Āraṇyaka 10, 1, 43).

Different aspects of Lakṣmī

Another very pertinent question arises as to what are those Lakṣmīs which reside in the form of Rudrāṇi, consort of Rudra, Svāhā in the fire, as the power and energy of the sun and the moon and Indra, Brahmā, Kubera and other Lokapālas though she has been established on the chest of Viṣṇu as his consort and constant companion (Matsya Purāṇa 82, 11-15). In order to give justification to such concepts, the redactor of the Mahābhārata 13, 11, 3ff probably puts the answer in this way : Lakṣmī lives with Viṣṇu at Vaikuṇṭha in her corporeal form but in others she resides in her manifested form (*prabhāva*)—

नारायणे त्वेकमना वसामि सर्वेण भावेन शरीरभूता । (V19)

59. E. J. H. Mackay, *Further Excavations at Mahenjodaro* Vol. I, p. 265.

60. S.B. Das Gupta has collected enough of materials to show the close relation between the Mother Earth and the goddess Lakṣmī. Though in later stage of development Lakṣmī represents the two aspects of the mother Earth i.e., prosperity and productivity, originally the Earth was attributed with such functions. *The Great Women of India* pp. 52-55.

The idea of her manifested form which expresses prosperity, well-being or good fortune etc. gradually gives rise to different aspects in her character. She is the Svarga Lakṣmī in the heaven, NāgaLakṣmī of the Nāgas, she is RājaLakṣmī of the kings and Gṛhalakṣmī of the householders;[61] Brahmavaivarta Purāṇa 2, 35, 16f tries to elucidate the same concept in course of discussion of the manifestation of Lakṣmī : Mahālakṣmī assumes different forms due to her Yogic power, (St. 16), in Vaikuṇṭha she appears in full form (*paripūrṇatamāparā*) and is endowed with all sorts of wealth and prosperity; she is Svargalakṣmī of heaven, who is the embodiment of the prosperity of Indra (*Śakrasampat svarūpiṇī*), she is Rājalakṣmī of the kings on earth and Nāgalakṣmī of the nether region; she, who resides in the form of the ladies in the houses is the householders' prosperity and the most auspicious of all things :—

> गृहलक्ष्मीः गृहेष्वेव गृहीणांच कलांशतः ।
> सम्पत् स्वरूपा गृहीणां सर्वमंगल मंगला ॥

> she is the beauty and lustre of the moon and the sun and the various objects like ornaments, gems, grains, fruits, etc. (DevīBhāgavata 9, 39, 15—20; BrahmavaivartaPurāṇa 2, 35, 16ff).

Similarly the concepts like Rājaśrī, Brahmaśrī Yajñaśrī appear in different texts (Vidh. 3, 82, 14). Mahābhārata 5, 83, 60 there is the description of Kṛṣṇa's journey where he comes across the ṛṣis who are endued with Brāhmīśrī 'holy lustre, beauty' (Cf. also Mbh. 14, 16, 22—Brāhmīśrī) Brahmāṇḍa, Purāṇa 3,17, 15 states that whoever performs the *śrāddha* on the *daśamī* day gains Brāhmīśrī—

> कुर्वन् दशम्यां तु नरो ब्राह्मीं श्रियं अवाप्नुयात् ।

There is an illuminating story in the Vāmana Purāṇa 49, 16ff; as to her different forms Śrī states before Bali

61. *Devī Bhāgavata* 9, 39, 15-20.

that she assumes four forms at the advice of Viṣṇu ; they are—Śvetāmbarā, Raktāmbarā; Pītambarā and Nīlāmbarā. Śvetāmbarā one with white garments garlanded with white flowers rides on white elephants, the other with red garments, Rāktāmbarā rides on red horse, the yellow attired Devī (Pītāmbarā) climbs on a golden chariot and the blue form rides on the blue Bull. The Devī with white clothes goes to Brahmā; Indra, the kings and the monarchs on earth get the Devī attired with red robes. The Devi who wears the yellow garments and is of golden colour is given to Prajāpati, Śukra and Vaiśyas; but the Devī with blue garments is given to demons and Śudras. The Śri of the king is called Jayaśrī (St.27)

Such concepts have been given concrete form in the Viṣṇudharmottara Purāṇa (3, 82, 14) which lays down instructions for the construction of images of Brāhmī-Lakṣmī, Rājaśrī, Svargalakṣmī and Jayalakṣmī beside the principal image of Lakṣmī.

Out of these concepts, Rājalakṣmī or Rājaśrī seems to be very popular. In the epics and the Purāṇas different episodes have grown round it out of which the legends of the demon Tāraka and others are very interesting. In the Skanda Purāṇa, 1,2,21,1f the account of the victory of Tāraka is mentioned ; when he conquers Indra and other gods and is anointed as the king of the demons, the Lakṣmī of the three worlds appears before him, and being pleased with his chivalry enters into him.

सा चाविवेश तं देवी त्रिजगत् पूजिता रमा ॥231॥

Mahābhārata 3, 229, 51 states that in order to kill the demon Tāraka, when Skanda is anointed by Indra as the chief of the army of gods; and Devasenā is given in marriage to him, Lakṣmī takes resort in him in her bodily form—

यदा स्कन्दः पतिर्लब्धः शाश्वतो देवसेनया ।

तदा तमाश्रयत् लक्ष्मीः स्वयं देवी शरीरिणी ॥

When Skanda marches for a battle Lakṣmī together with other *mātṛs* follows him (Mahābharāta 9, 46, 64). When Lakṣmī is taken as the goddess of fortune and prosperity, the continued prosperity of the king is looked upon as Rājalakṣmī. So long the king practises virtue and protects his subjects, Rājalakṣmī is said to remain there; if the king goes astray or does not look to the interest of his subjects, Rājalakṣmī departs from him. In similar other cases the divinity expresses certain aspect of prosperity and well-being. When Lakṣmī is established as the goddess of wealth and prosperity in the society, the various aspects of wealth or prosperity have been given a concrete shape and name.

Apart from the above concepts, her places of residence have variously been described in different accounts of the epics and the Purāṇas. In the Mahābhārata 13, 11, 6ff when Rukmiṇī asks Śrī about her places of residence, she states that she lives with the virtuous, with the lady who is chaste and serves the husband, the girl, ornament, sacrifice, raincloud, full-blown lotus, the elephant, tank filled with full-blown lotus, and river etc. Brahmavaivarta Purāṇa 2,35, 21f gives an exhaustive list of places of her dwelling: She lives with the king and the queen, in gems, fruits, water, crops, houses, clothes, in icons, the figures drawn for the worship of gods, garlands, milk, sandal, branches of trees, new-clouds etc.

BrahmavaivartaPurāṇa 3, 23, 19f mentions also the dwellings of those persons with whom she is pleased to live with: Lakṣmī does not prefer to live with those who ill-treat their parents, guests, and the preceptor, who take recourse to falsehood and are of misconduct, and who are ungrateful etc. The qualities which are derecognised in the society and which are against good conduct have been taken to incur the displeasure of Lakṣmī. Not even that, even the rules of right conduct have been taken to please Lakṣmī (GaruḍaPurāṇa, 114, 11ff). Lakṣmī does not prefer those who do not clean the body, who wear shabby dresses, who are gluttons, who slumber at sunrise and sunset etc.—

कुचेलिनं दन्तमलोपधारिणं
बह्वाशिनं निष्ठुरवाक्यभाषिणम् ॥
सूर्य्योदये ह्यस्तमयेऽपि शायिनं
विमुंचति श्रीरपि चक्रपाणिम् ॥

"Garuḍa Purāṇa 114, 35.

The same text (V. 37) lays down six ideal rules through which one can recover his lost Śrī (prosperity, glory). Those who wash their head and feet properly, and take a little food, copulate with the wife on days other than festive occasions, who cover their body at the time of sleep, regain their lost Śrī :

शिरः सुधौतं चरणौ सुमार्जितौ
वरांगनासेवनमल्पभोजनम् ।
अनग्नशायित्वमपर्वमैथुनं
चिरप्रनष्टां श्रियमानयन्ति षट् ॥

The redactor of Mārkaṇḍeya Purāṇa 18, 49ff states another account of the significance of her residence : When Lakṣmī resides on the foot of a person she bestows a place of habitation, on the thigh clothes and other types of wealth, in the pudenda a wife ; when she remains in the heart she bestows offspring and fulfills one's desire, on the neck she provides with loving wives, above all if she covers the whole body one attains supremacy over one's fellowmen. But if she covers the head of a person he loses every thing in life because Lakṣmī leaves him for ever. There is allusion to the story of the demons carrying Lakṣmī on their head who lose her for ever due to it.

Once Lakṣmī is accepted as the goddess of wealth and

plenty, various objects, entities and even the norm of good conduct have been attributed to her as favourite and any deviation therefrom is taken to irritate Lakṣmī.

Lakṣmī as Corn Goddess

Lakṣmī is related as the protectress of the field. As the goddess of vegetation who makes land fruitful, she is *ārdrā* and she is rich in cow dung *Karīṣiṇī.* In the Sundanese legends, she is called Devī Śrī or Seri and concerned with the cultivation of crops. The Balinese believe that when she died and was buried, various plants rose out of her body among them rice crops sprang from her navel.[62] In the Sanskrit texts collected from Bali she is described as—

श्री धान्यराज्ञी त्वां देवि प्राणतण्डुलसंज्ञक ।[62]

In India she is worshipped on different occasions. On Śrīpañcamī which falls on the 5th day of the bright half of Mārgaśīrṣa, Lakṣmī is worshipped with—

विरूढ़ान् धान्यसंचयान्

and with fruits and she is put on a bed of seven kinds of crops—

सप्तधान्यसमोपेतं

(Bhaviṣyottara Purāṇa 37, 45, 51). In the month of Mārgaśīrṣa on every Thursday, a corn measure is filled with new ripe corn which represents the goddess Lakṣmī and it is placed on a wooden pedestal. Sheaves of corn stalks are tied together and put on it for the worship. In Rajasthan[64] during Dīpāvalī festival, the agriculturists

62. J. Gonda, *Sanskrit in Indonesia*, p. 132.

63. Sylvain Levi, *Sanskrit Texts from Bali*, p. 62 ff.

64. J. Tod *Op. Cit.*, p. 475.

put corn measures filled with yellow ripe corn and worship Lakṣmī, the corn goddess. In *Viśokadvādaśī Vrata* which falls on the 12th day of the bright half of Āśvayujā, the figure of Lakṣmī is made of river sand, put on a winnowing-fan and covered with a new cloth ; different kinds of food and a golden lotus is offered to her (Bhaviṣyottara Purāṇa 84,1f). Lakṣmī is also ceremonially worshipped on the *Kojāgara pūrṇimā* which falls on Āśvayujā. On Kārttika Amāvasyā on which the *Sukhasuptikā Vrata* falls, Lakṣmī is worshipped in commemoration of her release from the clutches of the demon king Bali, the king of the nether world. These festivals are celebrated after the performance of the festival of the corn mother Gaurī. On *Śuklatṛtīyā* of Bhādrapada, Māgha and Caitra *Gaurī Vrata* is performed where different fruits like *Nārikela*, *Āmalaki*, *Māfuluṅga*, *dāḍima* and other seasonal fruits are offered to her. This is invariably performed by the females for gaining *rūpa* beautiful form, *Saubhāgya* 'good fortune' and *putra* 'sons' (Bhaviṣyottara Purāṇa 28, 1f).

During the vernal equinox the people of Rajasthan observe the *Gaurī Vrata*. This *Vrata* is exclusively observed by females who have their husbands alive. They make an idol of Gaurī made of river sand and a small idol of Śiva by her side. They dig a trench and sow barley seeds in it, it is watered and due heat is provided. When the barley seeds grow, the females dance round the trench in joy. Then the young shoots of barley are collected by the females and brought home, and these shoots are distributed among their husbands who wear it on their turban as a blessing of the corn-spirit Gaurī.[65]

Gaurī is worshipped as the embodiment of seven crops—

सप्तधान्य स्वरुपांच

on a *śūrpa* in Bhādrapada *śuklatṛtīyā* and is regarded as

65. J. Tod, *Op. Cit.*, PP, 454-455.

शूर्पं प्ररूढ नवसस्यमयीं

On Bhādra *śukla ṣaṣṭhī* falls the *Lalitāṣaṣṭhī Vrata* on which females take their ablution in the river and bring sand on a new *śūrpa* or a new basket made of bamboo on which Lalitā-Gaurī is worshipped with seven types of fruits like *Kuṣmāṇḍa, Vārttākī* and other fruits for happiness and good fortune. These seven types of fruits are the embodiment of corn goddess Gaurī, the goddess of fertility. On Bhādrapada *Śuklapakṣa* on the 7th, 8th and the 9th day, a bundle of Agāda plant which is worshipped as Gaurī is carried on a basket to the river, and is thrown away.[66] The winnowing fan on which the goddess is worshipped represents the magical power coming out from the corn and the corn spirit. In Cambodia, certain evil spirits accept the offering provided the offering is brought before them in a winnowing basket.[67] In above *Vratas* Gaurī is regarded as the corn-mother. The yellow colour of the ripe corn represents *gaurī* who is described to be of five kinds—*danta-gaurī, sphuṭacandanagaurī, śaratghanagaurī, candrakagaurī and rukmagaurī*—

रुक्मगौरी दन्तगौरी स्फुटचन्दन गौर्यपि ।

शरद्घन चन्द्रकवत् गौरी पंचविधा स्मृता ।।12।।

(Viṣṇudharmottara Purāṇa 3,27, 12)

The colour *gaurī* signifies yellow and red mixed together or reddish yellow, emblematic of the ripened harvest and conforms to *rukma gaurī* of the above text. In another chapter of the same text (Viṣṇudharmottara Purāṇa 3, 82, 3) Lakṣmī is described as *gaurī* and there it expresses *rukma gaurī*. This goddess Lakṣmī who is the spirit of corn conforms to the colour of yellow-ripe corn. In the

66. Underhill, *Hindu Religious Year*, p. 52

67. Hastings, *ERE*, Vol. III, p. 158.

Vāmana Purāṇa (49, 25) we come across the description of Lakṣmī who is adored by the Vaiśyas, is of yellow colour, yellow-clothed, yellow-wreathed, climbing on a golden chariot, who conforms to the above description of *gaurī*. Gaurī is the beneficient goddess Annapūrṇā, "the goddess who is possessed of plenty of food". Annapūrṇā is represented as a fair woman, standing on a lotus or sitting on a throne; she holds a rice bowl in one hand and in the other a spoon to stir it when boiled (Annapūrṇā Up.1, 9ff).

The other form of Gauri is Durgā who is looked upon as the vegetation spirit and the corn mother. Durgā is worshipped for nine days in her Navarātra festival which commences from the 1st day of the bright half of Āśvayujā. In the beginning of the festival, a pūrṇakalasa 'vase of plenty' made of earthenware is to be placed with different types of corns inside it and worshipped as such as the representative of the corn spirit. On the 6th day of the same festival, the *bodhana* 'awakening' of the corn-goddess Durgā is to be performed on a Bilva tree which is related to Lakṣmī and is called Śrīvṛkṣa as the spirit of vegetation. On the seventh day Navapatrikā, new leaves of nine plants are brought for worship. They are—Kadalī, Sāru, Haridrā, Jayantī, Bilva. Dālimba, Aśoka, Māṇa, Dhānya. Each leaf represents a deity separately. They are all tied together and called plantain-plant lady, which is the personification of vegetation spirit and are invoked as nine forms of Durgā. Durgā as the mother of vegetation is made clear from the statement made in the Devī Māhātmya (Mārkaṇḍeya Purāṇa 91, 43, 44).

ततोऽहं अखिलं लोकं आत्मदेह समुद्भवैः
भरिष्यामि सुराः शाकैराव्रृष्टैः प्राणधारकैः ।।43।।
शाकाम्भरीति विख्यातिं तदा यास्याम्यहं भुवि ।।45a।।

"Next O ye gods, I shall nourish the whole world with the life-sustaining vegetations which shall grow out of my own body during a period of heavy rain. I shall gain fame on the earth then as *śākambharī*". One of the nine plants tied together is Dhānya 'corn' whose presiding deity is Lakṣmī, the goddess of corn. In the Devīmāhātmya of Mārkeṇḍeya Purāṇa 1, 79 Durgā is identified with Lakṣmī—*tvam Śrī.* Thus we find Durgā being identified with Lakṣmī as the goddess of corn.

Lakṣmī as the spirit of corn is worshipped in different countries. In Malaya and Dyaks people think the rice to have possessed soul like human-beings, the rice has got the circle of life like the phenomena of reproduction, growth, decay and death.[68] In Indonesia, the fruit of the corn plant is adored as Śrī, the goddess of crops. Similar is the case in other countries. Like human-beings the corn spirit meets decay to be born once again. The same function is repeated every year. From these accounts we find that the deity of vegetation is originally a goddess not a god. How can it be that a female with a frail structure and limited power at her disposal is to control agricultural operations?

In the long hoary past, when people led the life of nomads, the males were generally engaged in hunting, fighting with the wild animals and fishing, where there was such opportunity, the females were in charge of collecting food for the family. In the primitive state of nature men were just helping the females in agriculture for clearing the forest, but the rest of the operation was performed by the females. This seems to be a common custom throughout the world. Digging of earth and sowing the seed were the functions of the females. So males generally thought it derogatory on their part to dig the earth, to sow the seed or to reap the harvest. Even chastity of the women was better judged through this plantation. They were of opinion that unless one keeps oneself chaste that means when one keeps her power of fertility undisturbed, one can not fertilise others. This is a sympathetic magic. Through action the fertility is transferred from the

68. Frazer, *Golden Bough*, Vol. VII, p. 180ff.
Different examples are cited in support of the adoration of corn spirit in different countries of the world and is spoken of as the goddess of corn.

famales to the seed. In Baganda of central Africa, no woman remains with a male who had no plot of land for cultivation. So a male before marriage had to find out a plot of land for his wife who can work there and produce food for the family. The relation of agriculture . with females is pertinently answered by Frazer thus : 'as women knew how to conceive seed and bear children, so the seeds and roots planted by them bore fruits far more abundantly than if they had been planted by male hands.[69] So the work of food production and collection of the same mainly devolve on women in different parts of the world. In the primitive age man refused to interfere in agriculture because "he thinks it magically depends for success on women connected with child-bearing. When the woman plants maize said the Indian to Gumilla, the stalk produces two or three ears. Why ? Because women know how to produce children. They only know how to plant eorn to ensure its germination."[70] So generally females know how to transfer the power of fertility from one's self to the seed. When anthropomorphism prevailed and man made images after his own fashion, due to the intimate relation of agriculture with female, a female has been selected as presiding deity of vegetation and corn. In different countries of the world, we come across a goddess being worshipped as the corn mother or deity of vegetation and fertility. The corn mother of Egypt is Isiș who wears a wreath of corn and in Rome Ceres is worshipped as the spirit of corn. In Greece Demeter and Kore are worshipped as the vegetation deity.

In the early ages, due to the prevalence of a matriarchal society, the female deities were ruling supreme. Examples are not rare that even prior to the advent of the Aryans India .was peopled by a section who imbibed matriarchal form of society. When the Vedic Aryans came, who belonged to patriarchal family, the old custom gave way to the new

69. Frazer, *Golden Bough*, Vol.,VII, p. 113 ff ; p. 124.

70. J. Harrison, *Prolegomena to the Study of Greek Religion*, p. 272.

one. Aryan conquerors tried to enforce their own system of society on the conquered, that is the pre-Aryans or Dravidians. So in the Vedic age, we find the supremacy of male gods, the female deities like Aditi and others played an insignificant role. But the remnant of the old association of matriarchal family and the worship of the mother goddess can be culled from the excavations at Mahenjodaro and Harappa where different female divinities were found out and they particularly prove to their relation with vegetation. When the Aryans conquered, and colonised the particular area, these people who were pushed out to the southern region settled up there permanently. Even though they are to some extent influenced by the Vedic Aryan, still they retain the old customs, belief and traditions. There the different village goddesses like Mariāmmā, Aṅkāmmā, Gaṅgāmmā etc. are worshipped till now.[71] As agriculture was the most important work of women in the past, throughout the world, the importance of women was felt significant. In the villages which are the seat of agricultural community, the worship of female deities was not improbable.

Women at different stages of life bear different names as divinities. The woman before marriage is called maiden, after marriage a bride, and when bears children she is called mother and when those children produce children, she is called grand mother and so on ; thus the matriarchal form of society reflects the life of woman and gradually this state of affairs gives rise to the growth of the 'Mother' and the maid, Demeter and Kore. In Greece in the early ages, we find the worship of Demeter and Kore as the Mother and maid of corn. Demeter literally speaking—'De' means barley and 'meter' means mother and it means 'Barley Mother.' The mother goddess Demeter was identified with the Earth at that stage and was taken to be the lady of the wild things.[72] This is the period when people used to lead a nomadic life. It is duly attributed by Cicero—"go back

71. Whitehead, Op. *Cit.*, p. 31 ff.

72. J. Harrison *Op. cit*, p. 266.

to earth and rise out of the earth." When agriculture started, the mother of the wild things was gradually converted into corn mother. Then Demeter did not only express the concept of the goddess Earth or 'Lady of the wild things' but expressed the idea of corn mother i.e. one which bears fruits. J. Harrison is right when she states—"it was mainly in connection with agriculture, it would seem that the earth goddess developed her double form as Mother and Maid".[73] It is also remarkable that primarily the two forms of Mother Earth or corn goddess was not Mother and Daughter but it was mother and maiden, and may be named as Demeter and Kore. This relation is well-depicted in a story : Once Kore while wandering in the field saw a beautiful flower and while she tried to get it, was seized by Aidoneus, the king of the nether world and was taken into that nether region. Afterwards she was released at the behest of Zeus, the supreme god of Olympia. During her absence from her mother, the earth became desolate, leaves fell from the trees, there was no fruits and flowers and all the beings suffered for food and they entreated Zeus for the remedy. As Demeter was not able to find out her beloved daughter, she did not glance at others sympathetically. Only when she got back her daughter, she blessed the beings with food and others.[74] This is an allegorical story. When the corn is harvested in the winter, the earth remains deserted and dry. During this period, the young fruit is caught by the lover and is kept detained for a season. When in the spring, the young fruit returns to her mother, the mother is glad at heart to get back her lost daughter. So the earth blossoms with new life then. When Demeter becomes more and more agricultural, more and more actual corn,...the Mother takes the physical side and the Daughter the spiritual, the Mother is more and more of the upper air, the Daughter of the under world. The daughter, the young form of the mother withdraws herself to the kingdom of the nether world, the realm of the spirit. The

73. J. Harrison, *Op. Cit.* p. 272.

74. Cox, *The Mythology of the Aryan Nations.* p. 510 ff.

legend of Sītā's birth from the mother earth represented as Furrow can be alluded to. Sītā, the young cornspirit rises out of the mother Earth. When she has delivered the fruits of her birth to Rāma she again, like the young corn spirit withdraws herself to the realm of the spirit, the mother's womb out of which she came.

Lakṣmī is the goddess of corn, vegetation and fertility. When Bali the demon of vegetation was sent to rule in the under world she followed him as like the young corn spirit entering the under world to enjoy deep slumber for a period. On Kārttika Amāvasyā day, she is said to accompany Bali to the earth and is duly worshipped by one and all for wealth and corn. That is the time when the corn is ripe and is to be harvested. Like the corn mothers Gaurī and Durgā, Lakṣmī is generally worshipped during this period, beginning from the month of Bhādrapada till the end of spring. During this pariod various crops are harvested and the festival in honour of the corn-mother is generally celebrated during this period. So they are duly worshipped in the form of corn as the insignia of the goddess. Not only that, even the corn as her symbol or representative gets due honour and is expected to bring prosperity to the person concerned. In different parts of Europe, it is customary for the bride to be crowned with the ears of corn like goddess Ceres.[76] At the close of the marriage ceremony, the corn is showered on the married couple by those who are present. This act no doubt expresses the showering of blessings on the couple (Hir. G.S. 1, 21, 6). In the same fertility rite, there is *lājāhoma* 'sacrifice of fried corn' in the fire by the bride; then the bride pronounces—I pour these *lājā* which would bring forth my prosperity (Bhr. G.S. 1, 16; 17, 2 ; Par. G.S. 1, 6, 1). Thus we find that the corn or grain used as the symbol of the divinity is a symbol of fruitfulness and prosperity. In different fertility rites the grain is used. Lakṣmī as the spirit of corn or

76. Briffault. Op. Cit., p. 54.
In Bhuvaneśvara, inside the campus of Liṅgarāja temple. the image of Pārvatī the corn-mother is crowned with the sheaves of corn.

as the goddess of corn is worshipped in different parts of the country. In the *dhānyācaladāna* 'donation of heap of rice,' Lakṣmī is identified with *dhānya*—

अन्नमेवयतो लक्ष्मीः

(Bhaviṣyottara p. 196. 44).

The goddess Lakṣmī became very prominent when the nomadic people finally settled up and depended on agriculture. Because of the close relation of the females with agriculture the female deities are conceived to be in charge of agriculture. All the world over a female divinity is generally worshipped as the goddess of corn. Like Demeter or Isis, Lakṣmī is contended as the goddess of corn and is adored by the agricultural community on various occasions especially when the corn grows in the field and during the harvesting season when corn is ripe or brought home.

CHAPTER V

The Concept of Alaksmi

In the tenth Maṇḍala of the ṚgVeda, the term, '*lakṣmī*' appears in the context of sign or mark—*bhadrā eṣā lakṣmīḥ nihitādhivācī* (R. V. 10, 71, 2) "their speech retains the blessed sign imprinted". The epithet applied to *lakṣmī* in this context is *bhadrā*'. When we come to AtharvaVeda we notice Lakṣmī described from two aspects. She is Puṇyā and at the some time she is called Pāpī Lakṣmī. Like most of the mant ras of the AtharvaVeda used for driving off evil spirits by magical device we find reference to different rites in the AtharvaVeda for driving off this Pāpī-Lakṣmī. After the merger of the auspicious Lakṣmi with Śrī, the goddess of beauty, the path became clear for the development of the Pāpī Lakṣmī as a separate and an independent deity.

In the AtharvaVeda which records the customs and traditions of the common people, we come across certain verses as a testimony to this in a propitiatory rite against Pāpī-Lakṣmī—

प्र पतेतः पापि लक्ष्मि नश्येत प्रामुतः पत ।
अयस्मयेनांकेन द्विषते त्वा सजामसि ।। (7, 115, 1)

Fly forth from here O evil sign (Pāpī Lakṣmī), disappear from here, fly forth from yonder ; with a hook of metal (*ayasmaya*) we attach you to him that hates us (A. V. 7, 115, 1). This Pāpī Lakṣmī was taken to be terribly harmful deity to the society. She was thought to be a flying substance sticking to one's body like a creeper to a tree—

या मा लक्ष्मीः पतयालु—

रजुष्टाभिचस्कन्द वन्दनेव वृक्षम् ।

अन्यत्रास्मात् सवितस्तामितो

धा हिरण्यहस्तो वसु नो रराणः ॥

[7, 115, 2]

'The unenjoyable flying Lakṣmī that hath mounted me as a creeper to a tree—that O Savitar may you put hence elsewhere than us, being golden-handed, granting good to us (A. V. 7, 2).

In A. V. 1. 18. 1[1] :—That Lakṣmī which is intended to be driven away and which is at the same time an '*arāti*' is nothing but the same Pāpī Lakṣmī ; she is conceived to be very harmful which frustrates good intentions and disturbs happiness. She is likewise conceived as a demoniac being—

रिश्यपदीं वृषदतीं

गोषेधं विधमामुत ।

विलीढ्यं ललाम्यं ता

अस्मन्नाशयामसि ॥ (A. V. 1, 18, 4)

"Antelope—footed, bull-toothed, the kine-repelling, the outblowing, the licked-out, the pallid (A. V. 1, 18, 4).

1. Depending upon the interpretation of the word '*Vṛṣadaṁśa*' as *biḍāla* in V. S. (24, 31), Geldner takes the meaning of the word *vṛṣadatī* in verse 4 of this hymn as referring to a female cat. Accordingly he interprets the whole hymn as referring to a cat. Because the cat owing to its peculiar features appears as a witch, and because in popular belief cats and witches are always connected, Geldner is inclined to see in this hymn a reference to the cat, a symbol of the witch. Pischel UND Geldner, *Vedische Studien*—Von., pp. 313-315.

Nirṛti

These very mantras of the AtharvaVeda (7, 115, 1-4) which are used to drive away Pāpī Lakṣmī are prescribed by the Kauśika Sūtra (18,16-18) for driving off Nirṛti. In the ṚgVeda (10,95,14) she is mentioned as a malignant deity of death and destruction. In the V.S.(39,13) She is related alongwith Antaka and Mṛtyu.

The Gṛhya Sūtras prescribe a number of rites for propitiation of this malignant deity Nirṛti. When the baby becomes one year old, the Śāṅkhāyana Gṛhya Sūtra (1, 26, 16-17) prescribes sacrifices for Nirṛti alongwith Indra and Jyeṣṭhā.

Like the two-sided development of Lakṣmī-Pāpī-Lakṣmī and Puṇyā Lakṣmī, the T. B. (1, 6, 1, 1) refers to Nirṛti and Anumati. Before the performance of Rājasūya sacrifice two cakes are prepared, one for Nirṛti and the other for Anumati. First of all the offering is made to Nirṛti with the formula—go away *svāhā* rejoicing in the oblations. This is your share, O Nirṛti, the mighty one, you are rich in oblations, free him from anxiety or distress (*aṁhas*). Whereas Nirṛti frees the sacrificer from *aṁhas*, distress and narrowness, Anumati points away the way to the sky.

By the time of the Kauśika Sūtra this malignant deity Nirṛti had already been identified with Pāpī Lakṣmī. This is why the Kauśika Sūtra in prescribing a Śāntikalpa "propitiatory rite" against Nirṛti enjoins the recitation of four mantras of the AtharvaVeda (7, 115, 1-4) which actually speak of Pāpī Lakṣmī. Before the commencement of the *puṣṭika* ceremony, a Śāntikalpa propitiatory rite against Nirṛti is prescribed by the Kauśika Sūtra. The rite is prescribed thus : In order to get rid of Nirṛti's evil influence the sacrificer has to wear black cloth and start the function beside a pool or a lake. He has to offer the old and worn-out shoes and umbrellas in the fire. Then the sacrificer has to pieree an iron nail in the thigh of a black crow which is used as a scape-goat. The same black crow is identified with Nirṛti.

the evil deity. Some cakes are tied to the nail in the thigh of a crow facing towards the Nairṛta (South West) direction and one has to recite the mantra (A. V. 7, 115, 1). Then the crow is allowed to fly away together with it the black Nirṛti and was expected to stick to one's enemies. The sacrificer has to use the black clothes as the under garment, a red garment as the upper dress and a white cloth as a turban. First of all, he has to take out the white turban with a piece of iron and has to throw it into the water with the mantra prescribed in A.V. (7, 115, 2).

While uttering the hymn (A. V. 7, 115, 3) he has to throw away the red clothes by the help of a piece of iron—

एकशतं लक्ष्म्यो मर्त्यस्य साकं
तन्वा जनुषोऽधि जाता ।
तासां पापिष्ठा निरितः प्र हिण्मः
शिवा अस्मभ्यं जातवेदो नि यच्छ ॥

'A hundred and one are the Lakṣmī of a mortal, born from his birth together with his body; the worst of these we send forth out from us, O Jātavedas, confirm propitious (*Śivā*) Lakṣmī. Lastly the sacrificer has to throw away the black clothes by the help of the piece of iron into the water. It was believed that this black Nirṛti was just like an entity sticking to a person like a creeper to a tree. So by this magical rite of throwing away the used-up shoes, umbrellas as well as the clothes worn by one, it was believed that the sacrificer would be immune from the evil influence of the malignant deity, Nirṛti. Thus after propitiating Nirṛti outside near some pool or lake, the sacrificer has to return home to start with the *Puṣṭika* ceremony. By this way the sacrificer has to free himself from the evil spirit Nirṛti.

This Nirṛti, who is no other than Pāpī Lakṣmī, is also found mentioned alongwith a deity Asamṛddhi, an abstract concept deified. For attaining good fortune one has to drive off this oppressive deity. This Nirṛti or Pāpī Lakṣmī for whose propitiation the sacrificer of the Vedic age was so keen, has developed later to be Alakṣmī, the goddess famous for creating misery and misfortune.

Alakṣmī in the ṚgVeda

In the ṚgVeda we come across the hymn 155 in the tenth Maṇḍala. In the verse No.1 of the hymn, an evil spirit called Sadānvā is addressed thus—

अरायि काणे विकटे
गिरिं गच्छ सदान्वे ।

'Go to the hill, O Sadānvā, one-eyed hideous, ever-screaming, (famine) we frighten you away with those heroes (lit. beings) of the 'cloud'. In the third mantra the evil spirit with a wicked looking chin is requested to take recourse to that far-off wood in the sea, that has no connection with human-beings and go to distant lands with it.

अदः यद् दारु प्लवते
सिन्धोः पारे अपुरुषम् ।
तत् आरभस्व दुर्हणो
तेन गच्छ परः तरम् ।।

(R. V. 10, 155, 3)

The Anukramaṇī designates this hymn as Alakṣmīghna sūkta. Yāska in his Nirukta (VI. 30) commenting upon the first mantra says that Śirimbiṭha is the name of the seer Bharadvāja. Endowed with black ears Bharadvāja destroyed Alakṣmī with this mantra—

शिरिम्बिठः भरद्वाजः कालकर्णोपेतः
अलक्ष्मीं निर्नाशयां चकार ।

Śaunaka in his Bṛhaddevatā speaks of this hymn as destructive of Alakṣmī यदरायित्यलक्ष्मीघ्नं (8, 60) Ṛg Vidhāna also speaks of this as Alakṣmīnāśana Sūkta (?). Later commentators following the tradition have traced the concept of Alakṣmī in the hymn (R.V.10,155). Durgācārya (the commentator of Nirukta) who can be placed about the thirteenth century A. D., following the traditional interpretation in commenting on the first mantra of this so-called Alakṣmīghna Sūkta, gives Alakṣmī as one of the meanings of Sadānvā. The great commentator Sāyaṇācārya follows the Niruktakāra and among other meanings of Sadānvā—

सर्वदा आक्रोशकारिणी दुर्भिक्षादि देवता

(The presiding deity of famine, always ready to do mischief) also gives the meaning of Alakṣmī. In the third mantra of this hymn with reference to the log of wood floating in the ocean, though in his first interpretation he connects the wood with the image of Puruṣottama, yet in the second interpretation he brings in the concept of Alakṣmī and interprets the word

दुर्हणो—दुःखेन हननीय (or)
दुष्ट हनुयुक्त अलक्ष्मी

Thus beginning from Yāska to Sāyaṇa all the commentators have tried to find the trace of Alakṣmī in the hymn (R.V.10,155). Because of the use of the expressions like-- *Arāyi* (unholy), *kāṇe* (one.--eyed), *Vikaṭe* (hideous), commentators have been allured to connect all these epithets with Alakṣmī, but when the Lakṣmī concept itself is absent in the ṚgVeda proper we cannot imagine the goddess Alakṣmī to be referred to anywhere. The hymn is really directed against some evil spirit called Sadānvā; the evil spirit is asked to resort to a boat or a log of wood as a scape-goat and to go to a far-off region where there are no human-beings. The witch Sadānvā can be said to represent one of those witches who cause disease and disaster. Like other witches and demons she is driven away to mountains or high lands which lie on the otherside of the ocean. Though she possesses some features of Alakṣmī, but she is not the same as the well- known Alakṣmī, whom we meet so often in the Gṛhya Sūtras and the Purāṇas. But the clear reference to Alakṣmī is noticed not in the ṚgVeda itself but in the appended hymns (Khila Sūkta) which were composed between the period of the Brāhmaṇas and *Upaniṣads*.[2]

Alakṣmī in the Śrī-Sūkta

Śrī-Sūkta occuring in the appended hymns of the ṚgVeda is the earliest record of the goddess Śrī-Lakṣmī ; in this appended hymn we find reference to goddess Alakṣmī. Scheftelowitz[3] who had made a thorough analysis of Śrī-Sūkta rightly designates the three verses (6—8) as related to Alakṣmī. The verse 8 of the hymn[4] says—O Alakṣmī, squalid with hunger and thirst, the elder sister (of fortune), I repel you. Take away from my dwelling all sorts of proverty and misery'. In the verse 6[5] of the hymn —the cryptogamous bilva tree is said to be generated by reason of the austerities of goddess Śrī. The seer

2. *ṚgVeda* (with commt. of Sāyaṇa) Vol. IV, Preface, pp. 901-2.
3. Scheftelowitz, 'Srī Sukta', *ZDMG*, p. 38.
4. क्षुत्पिपासामलां ज्येष्ठां
   अलक्ष्मीर् नाशयाम्यहम् ।
   अभूतिमसमृद्धिं च
   सर्वां निर् नुद मे गृहात् ॥ (V. 8)
5. आदित्यवर्णे तपसोऽधिजातो
   वनस्पतिस्तव वृक्षोऽथ बिल्वः ।
   तस्य फलानि तपसा नुदन्तु
   या अन्तरा याश्च बाह्या अलक्ष्मीः ॥ (Srī Sūkta, Verse 6)

terribly afraid of Alakṣmī prays for her blessings so that through her favour the fruits of the bilva tree may prevent Alakṣmī within and without.

The Bṛhaddevatā (V. 91-2) states that the whole of Śri-Sūkta which is a benediction, can be utilised with profit for driving off Alakṣmī from the house.

श्रीसूक्तं आशीर्वादस्तु··:तत् स्यात् वा अलक्ष्मी अपनुदम्

Origin of Alakṣmī

In the Brāhmaṇas one can notice that the old gods of the ṚgVeda have faded. Some gods like Viṣṇu and Rudra or Śiva have attained far greater prominence in the Brāhmaṇas, but above all stands Prajāpati who is the paramount lord of all creatures. The author of the Brāhmaṇas in glorifying Prajāpati[6] ascribed to him the origin of both the gods and the demons. Likewise Śrī is depicted as coming out of the severe penance of Prajāpati (S. B. 2, 4, 3, 1) and Jyeṣṭhā-Lakṣmī originated from the barren place on the forehead of Prajāpati (T. B. 2, 1, 2, 2).

With the development of Vaiṣṇavism, Viṣṇu became the pre-eminent god. The function of creation ascribed to Prajāpati is found transferred to Viṣṇu. The Liṅga-Purāṇa (2, 6, 3-5) says that Viṣṇu created the universe in two-fold ways. One part consisted of Śrī-Padmā, four Vedas, the rites prescribed by the Vedas and the Brāhmaṇas. And the other part consisted of Alakṣmī, Adharma and the rites deprecated by the Vedas. The same text continues, Viṣṇu created Alakṣmī first and later he created Lakṣmī (Liṅga P. 2. 6, 5). The Brahmavaivarta Purāṇa (1, 8, 10) narrates the birth of Adharma, and Alakṣmī from the back and left side of the creator (Dhātā).

6. M. Winternitz, *History of Indian Literature*, Vol. I, part I, p. 171ff.

The diversity in the description of the origin of Alakṣmī is definitely due to the fact that the Purāṇas are the collection of texts of heterogenous nature. Prof. Kirfel[7] who has made thorough study on Purāṇa literature has given us the real original Purāṇa texts which have been copied and elaborated by the redactors of the later period. In those original texts under the chapter *Sarga* and *Pratisarga* there is found the description of the birth of Lakṣmī. In this description of the primary creation Dakṣa in union with Prasūti gives birth to twenty four daughters like—Śraddhā, Dhṛti, Tuṣṭi. etc. among which Lakṣmī is one.[8] Again in the original text-kernel under the same chapter *Sarga* and *pratisarga*—Lakṣmī is described as the daughter of Bhṛgu and Khyāti.[9] Thus in the Urtext the origin of Lakṣmī is depicted sometimes as the daughter of Dakṣa and Prasūti and sometimes as the daughter of Bhṛgu and Khyāti. But nowhere in the birth account of Lakṣmī there is any mention of Alakṣmī. So it can be very easily concluded that after Alakṣmī attained prominence, and after she was represented as having all the opposite characteristics of Lakṣmī her origin came to be associated with her so-called sister Lakṣmī. Besides making Viṣṇu as the creator of both Lakṣmī and Alakṣmī the interesting legend of the churning of the ocean[10] was also utilised by the redactors of the Purāṇas to trace the account of Alakṣmī.

It is a well known fact that the myth of the churning of the ocean, though first traced to the Rāmāyaṇa (1, 44) has gradually been taken up by later redactors of the Purāṇas. The elaboration has gone to such an extent that whereas in the Rāmāyaṇa the number of entities churned out of the ocean were six, the number of entities has risen up to eighteen in the version of the Skanda Purāṇa. In most of the Purāṇas Lakṣmī was the entity to come out of the ocean. Rather in

7. W. Kirfel, *Das Purāṇa Pancalakṣaṇa*, Introduction, pp. IX-X.
8. *Ibid*, p. 37.
9. *Ibid*, p. 41.
10. For a comparative study of the Legend see *Purāṇa* Journal, Vol. IX, No. 1, January 1967, pp. 7-61.

some of the Purāṇas the churning of the ocean was solely been taken for getting Lakṣmī.[11] Gradually with the spread of Vaiṣṇavism the Purāṇas like Viṣṇu Purāṇa and Bhāgavata Purāṇa have depicted the rise of Lakṣmī from the ocean with more grandeur and imagination. Only when a very close relation developed between Lakṣmī and Alakṣmī, only when it was found that propitiation of Alakṣmī and blessings of Lakṣmī both are necessary for making one's life happy and cheerful, both the birth of Lakṣmī and Alakṣmi were put together in one account. Moreover, sisterly relation though not so cordial, developed between Lakṣmī and Alakṣmī. In consequence the Purāṇakāras depicting the birth of Lakṣmī from the churning of the ocean were enamoured to trace the birth of Alakṣmī from the same source. The Liṅga-Purāṇa (2, 6, 6-7) in referring to the churning of the ocean says that Kālakūṭaviṣa, the all-destroying cosmic poison came out first from the ocean ; then out of that Kālakūṭa poison originated Jyeṣṭhā Devī, otherwise called Alakṣmī, who was very inauspicious. The Padma Purāṇa[12] contains three versions of the churning of the ocean (3, 9 ; 5, 4 ; and 6, 260). Out of these in the two versions only which describe the birth of Alakṣmī from the ocean the first thing to come out of the ocean is the Kālakūṭa and after Kālakūṭa was born Alakṣmī. According to the first version Alakṣmī when born had a black face, red eyes; she looked aged and she had dirty and tawny hairs on her head.[13] The second version depicts her as putting a red garment and decorated with garlands of red flowers

11. उत्पादनार्थं लक्ष्म्याश्च

Padma Purāṇa, 6, 260·6 ; *Padma* p. 5, 4. ; *Viṣṇu* p. 1. 9.

12. *Padma Purāṇa*, 6, 260 ; 5, 4 ; 3, 9 ;

13. ततः अलक्ष्मीः······बिभ्रति तनुं

(Padma p. 3, 9, 9)

ज्येष्ठादेवी समुत्पन्ना
रक्तस्रक् वाससावृता (Padma. p. 6, 260, 23)

and Laksmī was the eleventh entity to be produced. The Linga Purāṇa version[14] of the story traces the origin of Alakṣmī to the churning of the ocean no doubt, but the version differs a little. According to this text first came out the Kālakūṭa poison and from that Kālakūṭa poison was born Alakṣmī. Then after the birth of Alakṣmī was born Lakṣmī. Whereas in the Padmapurāṇa version Alakṣmī originated directly from the churning of the ocean, in the LingaPurāṇa after the Kālakūṭa poison came out Alakṣmī not directly from milky ocean but from the Kālakūṭa poison.

As we have noticed before, the origin of Lakṣmī from the churning of the ocean was never left out either by the authors of the Epics or by the redactors of the Purāṇas. The only development that one can trace by going through the story of the origin of Lakṣmī is that in the earlier verisons Lakṣmī does not become the wife of Viṣṇu.[15] Neither Viṣṇu is anxious to get her as his wife. Only in later version[16] the relation of Viṣṇu with Lakṣmī has come up. Alakṣmī pictured as the elder sister of Lakṣmī had all the evil and inauspicious attributes in con-

14. *Linga* p. 2. 6, 6-7.
ज्येष्ठा तेन समाख्याता अलक्ष्मीर्द्विजसत्तमः ।
अमृतोद्भव वेलायां विषानान्तरं उल्वणात् ।। 6।।
अशुभा सा तथोत्पन्ना ज्येष्ठा इति च वै श्रुतम् ।
ततः श्रीश्च समुत्पन्ना पद्मा विष्णु परिग्रह ।। 7 ।।

15. *Mbh.. Cr. Edn.* 1, 17, 36
श्रीः सुरा चैव सोमश्च तुरगश्च मनोजवः ।
यतो देवाः ततो जग्मुर् आदित्यपथमाश्रितः ।। 36 ।।

16. *Matsya* p., 250.3—
जग्राह कमलां विष्णुः

tradistinction from Lakṣmī who had been endowed with all the noble and auspicious qualities. But Alakṣmī was Jyeṣṭhā. She was born earlier. Once Lakṣmī the younger sister could be brought into union with Viṣṇu it was impossible for the redactors of the Purāṇas to leave Alakṣmī alone without a mate (companion). In the earlier versions where Lakṣmī marries Viṣṇu, there is no mention of the origin of Alakṣmī. But once Alakṣmī was presented as originating earlier than Lakṣmī from the same milky ocean[17] and when following the earlier accounts Viṣṇu becomes anxious to accept her as his wife Lakṣmī revolts against this custom of the marriage of the younger sister before the elder sister, which goes against the law books.[18] In the Padma Purāṇa (6, 118, 4) when Viṣṇu is anxious to accept Lakṣmī as his wife Lakṣmī puts up the objections—O Madhusūdana, how can it be possible for me to get married to you when my elder sister remains unmarried. So please get her married first, then only we shall marry.[19] Then Viṣṇu as the Padma Purāṇa version continues took note of the advice of Lakṣmī and got her elder sister Alakṣmī married to Uddālaka.

Here the Purāṇakāra by bringing together the union of Alakṣmī with Uddālaka, a woman having all the devilish qualities and a reputed sage having all the heavenly virtues has depicted the family feud in the most interesting and humorous manner. Alakṣmī the personification of everything unholy and unrighteous shows the least regard for her husband. She hates everything what her husband likes. She hates to live in her husband's her-

17. *Liṅga* p. 2, 6 ; *Padma* p. 6, 260.

18. *Baudh. D. S.* 2, 1.39 ; *Manusmṛti* 3, 172.

19. असंस्कृत्य कथं ज्येष्ठा कनिष्ठ परिणीयते ।
तस्मात् ममाग्रजां एतां अलक्ष्मीं मधुसूदन ।।
विवाह्य नय मां पश्चात् एप धर्मं सनातनः ।।

(Padm. p. 6, 118, 4)

mitage, made fragrant by sacrifices and resounding with the chanting of the Vedic mantras. She expresses her desire to her husband to take her to a place where everything is inauspicious and evil.[20] Then roaming about here and there in search of a suitable place for Alakṣmī Uddālaka assigned her a temporary residence in the Aśvattha tree and vanished.

The poor Alakṣmī after long waiting for Uddālaka got tired and wept bitterly. Then on the advice of his wife Viṣṇu came with his wife Lakṣmī to Aśvattha tree and consoled her with the words-O, Alakṣmī, let this Aśvattha tree a part and parcel of my ownself be your permanent abode. Your younger sister Lakṣmī will be coming to reside here only on Saturday. So on every Saturday the Aśvattha tree must be worshipped ; but O Alakṣmī, those who worship you every day here, Lakṣmī will continue to live permanently with those house-holders.

Through this anecdote the Purāṇakāra found a clever device for popularising the worship of Aśvattha tree. By making the Aśvattha tree both the abode of Alakṣmī and Lakṣmī (only on Saturday) one could be able to pacify and propitiate the evil and through that one could be able to get the blessings of the other through the worship of Aśvattha tree. Since the Vedic age Aśvattha tree has attained significance and importance.

In the YajurVeda (3. 4. 8) Aśvattha tree is the residence of Gandharvas and Apsarasas. The AtharvaVeda (3, 6, 5) prescribes the use of amulet of Aśvattha for entrapping the enemies and bringing them under control. In order to get relief from demons and to kill one's rivals, along with the wood of the Kṛkaṭasa tree the wood of the Aśvattha tree was

20. The choice of Alakṣmī rests with a residence where there is constant family feud, where the guests are not honoured, where the thieves and scoundrels are in plenty, where people take recourse to illicit love, in other words whatever has been proscribed by lawmakers like Manu, Yajnavalka have been protrayed as the most cherished thing for Alakṣmī (*Padma* P. 5, 118-12-16).

added to the sacrificial fire (A. V. 2, 18, 1-5). For terrifying one's enemy the Samidhas of the Aśvattha tree were offered in the sacrificial fire (A. V. 88, 3.). Even the branches of Aśvattha magically charmed by the Brahmin had the potency of driving away enemies in the battle field (A.V. 3, 6, 8).

The Gṛhya Sūtras connect the Aśvattha tree with different deities. In the Gobhila Gṛhya Sūtra (4, 7, 22) Aśvattha is sacred to the Sungod. In the Mahābhārata (13, 4, 27, ff) there is reference to the story of the mothers of Viśvāmitra and Jamadagni as to how they were blessed with sons by embracing Aśvattha and Udumbara. The tree is believed to be the seat of the dead ancestors (V. S. 25, 4 ; S. B, 13, 8, 3, 1). So by worshipping the Aśvattha tree it was thought that the dead ancestors were honoured. The Bhagavad Gītā (10, 26) gives an exalted position to the Aśvattha tree—

अश्वत्थ सर्व वृक्षाणां

The Brahma Purāṇa identifies Viṣṇu with this tree (Ch. 103,5). And at last here in the Padma Purāṇa Jyeṣṭhā and Lakṣmī both are brought into relation with the Aśvattha tree. The tree which had the potency of making the women fruitful is here pictured as the tree of plenty and prosperity. By worshipping this tree one is able to honour both Lakṣmī and Alakṣmī, because it is the abode of both these deities.

The LingaPurāṇa version (2, 6) of the chapter entitled Alakṣmī vṛtta makes Duḥsaha the husband of Alakṣmī. Like Uddālaka of the Padma Purāṇa Duhsaha finds it difficult to pull on with his spouse. It is because Alakṣmī hates to listen to the chanting of Vedic mantras or recitation of the glory of Hara or Hari. The sage Duḥsaha in the meantime meets Mārkaṇḍeya. He puts the problem before him, the troubles he has faced because of the dirty habits of his wife. Then Mārkaṇḍeya gives him a long list of unholy and inauspicious places which are suitable for the residence of Alakṣmī.

Among the places described as worthy of residence of Alakṣmī are the homes where the preceptor and the guests are offended, where there is constant feud between the wife and husband, where neither Śiva nor Viṣṇu is worshipped, where people are bereft of good conduct, etc. On the whole anything that goes against the sacred laws of our law-makers is favourite of "Alakṣmī. It seems after Alakṣmī, the goddess of poverty and misfortune rose to pre-eminence, the redactor of Liṅga Purāṇa (2, 6, 31-74a) in describing the worthy places of Alakṣmī tried to connect her with those traits and characteristics which according to the Hindu mind are responsible for bringing poverty and misfortune.

When Mārkaṇḍeya after pointing out the places fit for Alakṣmī disappeared, Duhsaha took his wife to those unholy places and specially to the hermitage where people were engaged in reviling Viṣṇu

> विष्णोः निन्दारतात्मनां (V.76). In that hermitage resounding with the calumny of Viṣṇu, Duḥsaha left her, and he himself entered the nether region not to be seen again.

As in the Padma Purāṇa version here also Alaṣkmī left stranded in the hermitage of the revilers of Viṣṇu, complains of her pitiable plight to Viṣṇu. And Viṣṇu for her livelihood apportions to her the residence, the wealth and property, the land and the religious merits of those people who revile Brahmā, Viṣṇu and Śiva.

The Mārkaṇḍeya Purāṇa (50, 33 ff) gives a different turn to the story. In place of Uddālaka of Padma Purāṇa, Duḥsaha of LiṅgaPurāṇa, here Mṛtyu[21] (Death) becomes the

21. Prof. Kirfel in his introduction to *Purāṇa Pancalakṣaṇa* very aptly remarks-in the process of the development of Purāṇa Literature many co-workers have come to the field as a result it has been difficult to arrange the subject matter. Sometimes an individual has himself composed the entire text, or sometimes he is only a redactor, who gathers the text already existing, who arranges and who turns the text into a connected whole through his own contribution, expansion and revision. Because of this we notice such divergent descriptions in the Purāṇa literature. In one version, Uddālaka becomes the husband of Alaksmī. another version makes Duḥsaha her husband ; and in the third version Mrtyu is the husband of Alaksmī and Duḥsaha is her son.

husband of Alakṣmī. Nirṛti appears as the co-wife of Alakṣmī. Alakṣmī gives birth to fourteen sons who are ready to carry out the ccmmand of their father, Mṛtyu. Duhsaha is the foremost among the sons of Alakṣmī, Like Alakṣmī represented as a conglomoration of every thing evil and inauspicious, her son Duhsaha is portrayed as always living with unrighteous persons, influencing the people to be more passionate, more angry. In conformity with his nature Duhsaha is pictured as naked, clothed in rags and having a voice hoarse as a crow's. He is always overtaken by hunger and in consequence he is ready to devour the whole universe.

At last Brahmā comes and requests Duhsaha to be calm and free from passion. When Duhsaha asks Brahmā to tell him his place of refuge and the method of satisfying his hunger and thirst, Brahmā allots to him those places which were very much aspired by her mother Alakṣmī in the LiṅgaPurāṇa. Duhsaha is ordered by Brahmā to remain with the unrighteous people who do not perform sacrifices and other ceremonies, who delight in gambling and women, and who are religious hypocrites. And his food is prescribed to be the remains of a meal, anything uncooked or badly cooked, anything polluted or cooked in broken pots etc.

Duhsaha of LiṅgaPurāṇa who was a great sage, who had great liking for the recitation of Hari and Hara and the chanting of the mantras of the Vedas, had great disappointment to get as wife Alakṣmī endowed with everything ignoble and vicious. But here in Mārkaṇḍeya Purāṇa, Alakṣmī is connected with a husband Mṛtyu having all the evil characteristics as his wife. And Duhsaha becomes the son of Mṛtyu begot by Alakṣmī. Keeping in view of the vicious qualities of both the father and the mother, the son Duhsaha has been pictured as the embodiment of everything devilish. Like Alakṣmī in Padma Purāṇa (6, 260, 25ff) and Liṅga Purāṇa (2, 16, 17 ff) the residence of religious and virtuous people, the worship of divinities, pure and holy conduct become intolerable for Duḥsaha.[22]

Worship of Alakṣmī a sine qua non for attainment of Lakṣmī

Once Alakṣmī became famous for creating poverty and misfortune when she rose into prominence as an independent goddess representing everything evil, it was thought necessary to propitiate her and to appease her so that she may not exert her influence and bring poverty and misery to the people. In the annals of worship it is found that those deities who are malignant by nature and create troubles are generally worshipped (Frazer). In the ṚgVeda the Aryan was very much afraid of the fierce and destructive character of Rudra. He is implored not to slay or injure his worshippers. To avert his great malevolence[23] he is always prayed to be merciful. In the Purāṇa literature we notice that Skanda with[24] his four transformations was the lord or presiding deity of the Grahas i.e. asterisms causing suffering to children. These asterisms known as Skanda grahas exercise their evil influence in the life of a child. The only way to get rid of their evil influence was to give bali, offerings, to them. Many ceremonies observed in honour of Yama,[25] the god of death testify that the divinities

22. *Mārkaṇḍeya Purāṇa,* 50, 33ff.

    According to Eliot 'the evil spirit Duḥsaha described in the Mārkeṇḍeya Purāṇa comes very near the Devil', *Hinduism and Buddhism,* Vol. I, Introduction, LXXIX, Note 1.

23. A. Macdonell, *Vedic Mythology,* p. 75.

24. *Vāyu P.,* 72, 24ff ; *Brahmāṇḍa P.* 2. 55; 3, 11 ;

    Liṅga P. 1, 104, 105 ; *Matsya P.,* 6, 26ff ; 3, 146-160 ;

    Śiva P. Chs. 9-19 ; *Vāmana P.,* Ch. 57 & 58; *Padma P.,* 6, 28 ;

    Skanda P. I, 1. 20-30, I, 2, 20-32.

25. *a. Yama caturthī*

    b. Yama dīpadāna

    c. Yama tarpaṇa

    d. Yama dvitīyā

famous for creating troubles or famous for creating mischief always get the highest honour. The worship of Gaṇeśa, 'lord of troubles', Vighneśa 'disturber of peace' at the beginning of each and every ceremony points to the fact that it was always thought proper to placate him so that there should not be any interference in religious ceremonies.[26] The instance of the goddess Ṣaṣṭhī, a sylvan deity accustomed to live in hills (classed under demons and spirits—*E.R.E.* IV. p. 602) may be taken; she was primarily responsible for causing disease and taking away the life of the mother and the child.[27] Primarily her worship was introduced to appease her, though later on she has adopted auspicious nature and has been represented as the giver and protector of children[28] (Viṣṇudharmottara Purāṇa 2,52,56). That is why in Harśacarita[29] and Kādambarī[30] she is called Jātahāriṇī and Bahuputrikā. Like Ṣaṣṭhī whose malignant nature has so to say been completely overshadowed by all the auspicious traits like protecting children, giving child to childless etc., another Hindu folk-goddess Hāritī,[31] now worshipped in Northern India as the protectress of children was originally a Yakṣiṇī, an ogress, a cannibal demon, who

e. *Yama vrata*

f. *Yama darśanatrayodaśī.*

26. *The Age of Imperial Unity*, p. 469.

27. (*a*) P. K. Agrawala, 'Ṣkanda in the Purāṇas and Classical Literature', *Purāṇa* Vol. VIII, No, 1, Jan., 1966, p. 151ff. Ṣaṣṭhī otherwise called Jātahāriṇī, assimilated in herself all the folk-goddesses concerning the diseases of the mother and the child.

(*b*) A. Bhattacharya in his article 'The Cult of Ṣaṣṭhī in Bengal' refers to an interesting folk tale signifying the malignant aspect of Ṣaṣṭhī, A cat, the carrier of Ṣaṣṭhī carries off the seven children of the youngest daughter-in-law, because of some defect in the worship of Ṣaṣṭhī. *Man in India*, Vol, XXVIII, 1948, pp. 152-162.

28. *Brahmavaivarta* p. 2, 8, 10; *Devī Bhāgavata*, 9, 46.

29. *Harśacarita.* Ch. 4, p. 129.

30. *Kādambarī*, 64.

31. A. Getty, *The gods of Northern Buddhism* pp. 84-85; Also see J N. Banerjee, *The Development of Hindu Iconography*, pp. 380-81.

once devoured all the children in Rājagṛha. In the same line the worship of Alakṣmī came to be a regular feature in Hinduism. The only reason for her worship was to placate and propitiate her.[32]

Vratas for warding Off Alakṣmī

It is well-known fact that *Vratas* occupy the most important position in Hinduism. Most of the *Vratas* practised are *Kāmyā*, that performed for the purpose of securing some result in this world or sometimes in the other world or both. Many of these *Vratas* are really secular though under the garb of religion. And though certain disciplines (fast, worship, etc.) have to be observed yet most of these *Vratas* breathe a frankly materialistic attitude. As heaven and liberation were the things most desired for making the after-life happy alongwith progeny, virtues and fame and learning, wealth or fortune was the most essential thing to make one's life in this world happy and cheerful. Therefore, we notice that many rites and ceremonies are observed in honour of Lakṣmī.[33]

32. In this connection a very interesting stanza may be quoted from the Mahābhārta :

    अकृतोपद्रवः कश्चिन्महान्
    अपि न पूज्यते ।
    पूजयन्ति नरा नागान् न
    तार्क्ष्यं नागघातिनम् ॥ 16 ॥

    Mahābhārata, Vanaparva, 28, 16, Ed. T. R. Krishnamacharya and T. R. Vyasacharya, Bombay 1908.

    'Inspite of all the glory and greatness one is never adored unless one is capable of creating trouble and michief. People are so much zealous in worshipping the serpents ; but they are callous towards Garuḍa, the killer of serpents.'

33. (*a*) *Aśunyaśayana Dvitīyā*
    (*b*) *Viśokadvādaśī*
    (*c*) *Kojāgara Pūrṇimā*
    (*d*) *Dīpāvalī*
    (*e*) *Śrīpañcamī*, etc.

But as without propitiation of Alakṣmī it was difficult to attain Lakṣmī many Vratas are referred to in the Gṛhya Sūtras and the Purāṇa literature refers many Vratas in honour of Alakṣmī.

The Baudhāyana Gṛhya Sūtra dedicates a full chapter on Jyeṣṭhākalpa for the worship of Alakṣmī called Jyeṣṭhā. The Vrata is generally observed in the Prauṣṭhapada (Bhādrapada) in the Anurādhā nakṣatra. On such occasion offerings like til oil, *pāyasa*, curd, *saktu*, *lājā*, rice-gruel and black clothes are offered. In the sacrifice for Jyeṣṭhā tile oil is offered as oblations to Indra, Jyeṣṭhā, and Prajāpati. She is identified with Satyā, Kapilapatnī, Kumbhī, Varadā. Hastimukhī, Vighnapārśadā, Prakumbhī etc.

The Vrata in honour of Jyeṣṭhā called JyeṣṭhāVrata described in Liṅga Purāṇa and Skanda Purāṇa has been quoted in Hemādri (II, 2. pp. 630-633) and NirṇayaSindhu (II. 6, 34). This Jyeṣṭhā Vrata (Also called Nakṣatra Vrata) is to be observed by females on the eighth day of the bright half of the month of Bhādrapada, if it is in conjunction with Jyeṣṭhā *ṇakṣatra.*[34] On this day worship of Jyeṣṭhā Devī (identified with Lakṣmī and Umā) is recommended for removal of Alakṣmī—

अलक्ष्मी विनिवृत्तये

Only women are entitled to perform her worship. Here the offerings prescribed for Jyeṣṭhā are wheat, barley, rice, and such other things. By propitiating Jyeṣṭhā the females are in a position to remove barrenness, the defect of having only one child—

काकवन्ध्यादिदोष and poverty दारिद्र्य विनाशाय.

She is worshipped by gods, demons human beings and if pleased she bestows wealth and offspring. One should

34. Provided there is a Sunday in addition to above, the deity adored is Nīla Jyeṣṭhā.

observe Jyeṣṭhā Vrata, because like salt dissolving in water all the troubles of the devotees vanish for ever

विघ्नास्तस्य प्रणश्यन्ति यथाप्सु लवणं तथा

Besides, Hemadri Vratakhaṇḍa (II. 638-640) quotes from Bhaviṣyottara Purāṇa and prescribes that the Jyeṣṭhā vrata can be observed on any *tithi* of the bright half of Bhādrapada when there is jyeṣṭhānakṣatra. The vrata can be observed by a woman whose children are dead or who has only one child and by a poor man. The vrata can be observed continuously for twelve years or for the whole life. The image of Jyeṣṭhā Devī is to be worshipped and the devotee has to keep awake the whole night.

Alakṣmīnāśaka Snāna

Since the days of the Brāhmaṇas it is noticed that water has played a significant role in all the rites and ceremonies. In prescribing regular bath for the sacrificer and his wife it is only intended to remove the physical impurity. Besides, for warding off demons and goblins, water was invariably used—

आपो हि वै रक्षोघ्नी

(T.B. 3,2,3,12)

Among the different rites necessary for removal of evil effects or their appeasement the Gṛhya Sūtra (Baudhāyana Gr. S. I. 14) recommends *udakaśānti* for mitigating all the troubles caused by the unfavourable position of the planets, for removing the impurity on birth or death in one's family. The Bṛhat Saṁhitā 47 (1-87), Atharvāṇa pariśiṣṭha (V.pp.66-68) Viṣṇudharmottara Purāṇa (2,103,30) refer to a type of *udakaśānti* called Puṣyāśānti for the king for destroying all evil portents. "Water is indeed thunderbolt, he strikes the thunder bolt against enemies". Waters are destroyer of malignant spirits (and it is taken) for destroying evil spirits[35].

The eulogy of a bath in the Ganges or other big rivers like Kṛṣṇā, Godāvarī and Narmadā lies on this aspect of washing off the impurities of both body and mind. Similarily in later digests and commentaries like Smṛti Kaustubha (344-345), Puruṣārtha Cintāmaṇi (307) and Kālasāra (178) a particular *snāna* called *Alakṣmī nāśakasnāna* is prescribed. On full-moon day of Pauṣa where there is Puṣyā nakṣatra, persons should bathe after anointing their bodies with white mustard and drive off Alakṣmī (Misfortune or poverty) and worship images of Nārāyaṇa, Indra, Moon, Bṛhaspati and Puṣya by bathing them in the water in which Sarvauṣadhis are put ; and also he should perform *homa* in honour of these deities. The Brahma Purāṇa (Ch. 137) speaks of the river Ganges as Lakṣmītīrtha. In order to glorify the river Ganges[36] as having the potency of driving off Alakṣmī and endowing one with Lakṣmī the redactor of the Purāṇa depicts a story of quarrel between Lakṣmī and Daridrā (the same as Alakṣmī). Each of them claims one's own superiority ; and at last they go to the river Ganges who gives her verdict in favour of Lakṣmī. Since then a bath in the river Ganges is recommended for *Alakṣmīnāśana* and to make oneself *Lakṣmīvān*.[37]

35. *Vidh.* p. 2, 103, 30.

अलक्ष्मी शमनं पुण्यं रक्षोघ्नं बुद्धि वर्धनम् ।
आरोग्यदं दीप्तिकरं यशस्य शत्रुसूदनम् ।।

36. To most men in India like the Himalayas, the Ganges presents a double aspect—the physical aspect and the spiritual aspect. A great river apart from its volume of water is deemed to have a spiritual or divine life which animates it.

37. ततः प्रभृति तत् तीर्थं अलक्ष्मी नाशनं शुभम् ।
तत्र स्नानेन दानेन लक्ष्मीवान् पुण्यावान् भवेत् ।। 4 ।।

[Brahma Purāṇa 137, 41]

For warding off the evil effects and misfortune we have noticed before how prayers and presents were lavished upon Alakṣmī. Even in Jyeṣṭhā Vrata one can notice that Alakṣmī has been lauded as Lakṣmī and Umā (*tvam Lakṣmī tvam Umā devī*). But besides this propitiation and placation of evil spirits for making oneself free from their malignant influence the method of forcible explusion was also adopted. For banishing the demons of epidemics like cholera and smallpox in Australia, South Africa, Malanesia, China and in our Country, India, people resort to different methods whenever any calamity befalls.[38] But sometimes the expulsion of evils tends to become periodic. It is thought to be desirable to have a general riddance of evil spirits at fixed times, usually once a year in order that people make a fresh start in life, freed from all malignant influences which have been accumulating about them.

This periodic explusion of evil generally took place in the rainy season and in the agricultural season. Because with the first rains there was generally much sickness. In many countries the expulsion was resorted to when the rains begin.[39] At seed time the Khonds of India carry a basket containing each kind of seed donated by the people of the tribe. The basket containing the seeds is taken to a field outside the village by the chief priest of the tribe. The seed thus carried out is called the share of the 'evil spirit, spoilers of the seed'. Thus being driven out with the car the evil spirits do not have any excuse for interfering with the rest of the seed corn[40]. But in some other cases the annual expulsion of devils takes place at harvest time instead of at seed time. At Kiriwina in South Eastern New Guina when the new jams have been harvested people feast and dance for many days. When the festivities are over, all the people gather together and expel the devils from the village by shouting and beating the posts of the houses.[41]

38. Sir 'J. Frazer, 'The occasional expulsion of 'Evil', *Golden Bough*, Vol. IX, pp. 105-123.

39. *Ibid.*, p. 128.

40. *Ibid.*, p. 133.

41. *Ibid.*, p. 134.

The Hos of North Eastern India expel the demons after they have collected the harvest[42]. Among some of Hindookush tribes the expulsion of devils takes place after harvest. When the last crop of autumn has been got in, it is thought necessary to drive away evil-spirits from the granaries. The expulsion of Alakṣmī (goddess of poverty and misfortune) as referred to in the Purāṇa literature takes place in the harvesting season. The Dīpāvalī festival also called Dīpālikā (in colophon to Ch. 140 of Bhaviṣyottara Purāṇa) which falls in the harvesting season spreads over about five days. The whole of festival comprises five principal items, spread over five days—on the thirteenth of the dark half of Āśvina (by the *Pūrṇimānta* reckoning) lighting of lamps in honour of Yama (*Yama-trayodaśī*) the celebration of Viṣṇu's victory over Narakāsura (*Naraka caturdaśī*), on the new moon day worship of Lakṣmī (*Dīpānvitā Lakṣmī pūjā*), on the first day of bright half of Āśvina, victory of Viṣṇu over Bali (*Balipratipadā*) and on the second day of the bright half of Āśvina, the exchange of brotherly and sisterly affection (*Bhātṛ-dvitīyā*). Out of these five days of the festival, on the newmoon day the day singled out for the worship of Lakṣmī the expulsion of Alakṣmī is to be carried out after performing the worship of Lakṣmī,[44] When midnight is past and people's eyes are heavy with approaching sleep, the women in the city should create great noise by beating winnowing baskets and drums and should drive out Alakṣmī from the courtyards of their houses.[45] This custom referred to in the Purāṇa literature

42. *Ibid.*, p. 136.

43. *Ibid.*, p. 137.

44. *Padma* p. 6, 124.

45. एवं गते निशिथे तु

जने निद्रान्धलोचने ॥ 28 ॥

तावत् नगरनारीभिः

शूर्पडिडिमवादनैः ।

is still current among the Hindoos. Crooke[46] refers to this method of expelling Alakṣmī as he noticed in the Punjab. On the morning after Divali the eldest woman of the house takes a corn-sieve or a winnowing basket and broom, beats them in every corner of the house saying "god abide and proverty depart". The sieve is then carried out of the village towards north or east and is thrown away. It is believed that the article thus thrown away bears away with it the poverty and disaster of the house. In general this is the present version of the practice of expelling Alakṣmī referred to in the Purāṇas. In Gujarat[47] this custom of driving away Alakṣmī takes place on the first day of Kārttika which is their new-year's day. On the other hand, the Hindus of Monghyr in Bihar observe this custom on Bhūtacaturdaśī day i. e. on the fourteenth day of the dark fortnight of Kārttika. But their way of expulsion of Alakṣmī is somewhat different. They make an image of Alakṣmī in cowdung and drag her and humiliate her saying—*Lachmighar, dariddar bāhar,* J. N. Banerjea[48] refers to another form of this ritual very much in vogue in several districts of Bengal, where a *Kṣaṇikā* (temporary) image of Alakṣmī is made of cowdung and is worshipped on the newmoon night of Dīpāvalī, then this crude image is taken outside the house with the beating of the winnowing fan and discarded. Whatever may be the method of expelling Alakṣmī, the sound produced by beating winnowing fan is the regular feature every where.

Producing sound is always connected with the expulsion of evil. For expelling the demons of epidemic the Solomn Islanders of Bougainville straits blow conchshells, beat tins, shout and knock on the houses.[49] In Southern China

निष्कास्यते प्रहृष्टाभिः
अलक्ष्मीः स्वगृहांगनात् ।। 29 ।। [*Padma* p. 6, 124, 28-29]

46. *Popular Religion and folk lore of Northern India.* Also quoted by Frazer, *Golden* Bough IX, p. 144 ff.

47. Stevenson, *The rites of the twice born*, p. 265.

48. *Loc. Cit.*

49. *Ibid.*, p. 116

to expel the demon of cholera 'gongs are beaten, guns are fired, crackers are hopped and demon-dispelling trumpets are blown.[50] When cholera breaks out in any Burmese village, the people thump drums, blow trumpets, yell scream, beat floors, walls, tin pans, every thing to make a din, because they think this uproar to be very effective to drive away cholera demon [51].

The Bhaviṣya Purāṇa (12, 43) refers to the custom of attaching bells to the ears of the cattle for the sake of decoration and also for driving off the evil spirit.

घंटा: कर्णेषु बध्नियु: शोभा रक्षार्थमेव च ।

The ringing of a bell at the appearance of dawn is recommended in the Mahābhārata (12,48,20), Manusmṛti (10,33), where two different motives can be attributed —one is for driving off the evil spirits and the other is to invigorate the auspicious power—the newly rising Sun—

घंटा ताड़: अरुणोदये

Though in churches the ringing of bells at funerals is interpreted as a call to the faithful to pray for the departed soul, yet its original motive may be the supposed power of driving away evil spirits lying in wait for the dying man's soul. During the middle ages in Europe bells were chiefly valued for their prophylactic power in scaring the evil spirits from doing harm ghostly and bodily.[52] The Buddhists are also known to have resorted to the ringing of bells to expel the death demon. Therefore, when in place of propitiation and placation of such a malignant deity was not effective, the other

50. *Ibid.*, p, 117.

51. In two chapters of Frazer's *Golden Bough*, Vol. IX, Ch. III & IV, in describing the expulsion of evils either occasional or periodic, the expulsion of embodied evils. we can notice tha noise or uproar is always connected with expulsion of evil.

52. *E.R.E.* VI. p. 315 ff.

means adopted was to ask her to go away. She was threatened and scared off from the house. That is why the Purāṇakāras recommend that a great sound should be produced by the beating of drums and winnowing baskets at the time of expelling Alakṣmī.

The beating of drums is not something uncommon for producing a sound but the sound produced by beating the winnowing fan (*śūrpa*) needs some explanation. Besides, being an emblem of increase and prosperity the winnowing fan has been regarded as possessing magical powers. Among the Kols, when a vacancy occurs in the office of the village priest the winnowing fan with some rice is used, and by its magical power it drags the person who holds it towards the individual on whom the sacred mantle has fallen. The same custom prevails among the Oraons. As in India at present in Europe, too, divination is performed with a pair of shears and a winnowing fan. 'The shears are stuck in a cornsieve or winnowing basket and the maidens hold up the sieve with the tip of their fingers by the handle of the shears, they say 'By St. Peter and St. Paul, he hath not stolen it'[53] After many adjurations the sieve turns at the name of the thief. Even at present in our country this method of divination by rotating the winnowing fan is still prevalent. It is recommended[54] that a man if taken possession of troublesome spirits—the Vināyakas, one has to perform a rite in which offerings put in a winnowing fan are to be placed where four roads meet—

दद्यात् चतुष्पथे शूर्पं.

In Cambodia certain evil spirits accept the offering provided the offering is brought to them in a winnowing basket.[55] The winnowing fan in which the corn is tossed and by means of which the chaff is blown utterly

53. Aubrey, Quoted in *Popular Religion and folk lore of Northern India*, Vol. II, pp. 187-190,

54. *Mānava Gr. S.* 2, 14, 30; *Yājṇavalkya Smṛti* I. 285.

55. *E.R.E.* III, p. 153.

away was to Clement of Alexandria the symbol of utter ruin and destruction. The Egyptians used to burn their scape-goats alive, and their ashes they made away with by winnowing and scattering them.[56] From all these parallel instances cited above, the use of the winnowing fan an instrument endowed wtth magical powers for driving off the evil spirits, the nature of Alakṣmī becomes clear.

Like the winnowing fan the broom used for driving off Alakṣmī is equally endowed with magical potency. For warding off the evil eye the custom of striking the ground with a broom is well-known. Among Bani Israils[57] of Bombay when the midwife drives off the blast of the evil eye she holds in her left hand a shoe, a winnowing fan and a broom. Among the Mirzapur Korwas when a dust-storm comes, the women thrust the house broom, which is a demon-scarer, into the thatch, so that it may not be blown away. Even now the custom of putting the broom near the bed of the child is found where the sole reason is to ward off the evil spirits.[58]

Then we come to the question of the time of expulsion of Alakṣmī. Why does this expulsion occur on the new-moon day of Āśvina—after the worship of Lakṣmī, goddess of corn? The autumn season consisting of Bhādrapada and Āśvina is the harvesting season for *Bhādvi* crops. The cultivator is busy in the reaping and gathering of corn of various kinds. After the gathering in of various harvests all the deities and corn-spirits are offered the first fruits of the year. If we look to the Hindu calendar we notice that all the deities worshipped in this season are somehow or other related to corn. In the month of Bhādrapada on the third day of the bright half seven different varieties of corn are to be put in a winnowing fan; the seven types of corn are taken as the embodiment of the corn goddess Gaurī—

56. J. Harrison, *Prolegommena to the study of Greek Religion*, p. 104.
57. Crooke, *Popular Religion and folk lore of Northern India*, Vol. II, p. 190.
58. Crooke. *Ibid*, Vol. I, p. 81.

शूर्पं प्ररूढा नवसस्यमयीं Bhaviṣyottara Purāṇa (28. 58).

Then comes the celebration of Durgā Pūjā continuing from the first to the ninth day in the bright half of Āśvina. The Goddess Durgā is but a vegetation spirit or corn-mother. This aspect of the deity is evident in her epithet Śākambharī.[59] Then again the new-moon day of Āśvina is very important day for the worship of Lakṣmī, the corn goddess. The same deity is worshipped alongwith Indra riding Airāvata on the full-moon day of Āśvina, the festival is famous as *Kaumudimahotsava*. The explanation of the worship of these corn goddesses like Lakṣmī and Gaurī at this particular period[60] lies in the fact that these two months—Bhādrapada and Āśvina are important for harvest-home; hence the worship of the corn mothers. After the harvest-home one can notice the *Navānnabhakṣaṇa*—partaking

59. (*a*) S.N. Kaviraj, 'Fortility Cult and tree'. *Tree Symbol Worship in India*, pp. 148, 155.

(*b*) R.C. Hazara, Compilation of Purāṇic works or chapters on Sakti Worship', *Our Haritage*, Vol. IV, Part I, January-June 1956, pp. 67-98

(*c*) ततोऽहं अखिलं लोकं
आत्मदेहसमुद्भवैः ।
भरिष्यामि सुराशाकैः
आवृष्टैर्प्राणधारकैः ॥ 43 ॥
शाकंभरीति विख्यातिं
तदा यास्याम्यहं भुवि ॥44a॥

(Mar. p. 91, 43-44)

'Next O' Gods, I shall nourish the whole world with the life sustaining vegetables which shall grow out of my own body during a period of heavy rain. I shall gain fame on the earth then as '*Ś*ākambhari':

60. In Greece in the month of Thargelion, the later part of May and beginning of June, there was the grain harvest. So for the Greeks this month is marked by three important harvest festivals. Jane Harrison in Ch-III. 'Harvest festivals'—very nicely connects celebration of these festivals with reaping and garnering of the various kinds of cereals. pp. 77-119.

of the fresh crops in Mārgaśirṣa. Naturally therefore the day of Dīpāvalī was selected for driving off Alakṣmī, as by this time one was strengthened and fortified oneself by the advent of fresh crops—Lakṣmī incarnate. Presence of Lakṣmī—the newly harvested crop gave sufficient encouragement to throw off Alakṣmī (bad luck, penury, poverty, ill-luck) from one's home and courtyard. Among the Hos of North-Eastern India after the celebration of the great festival—the harvest-home when the granaries are full women and children go in procession in every part of the village with sticks in their hands to drive off the evil-spirit. Among the Hos and Mundaris when the last crop of autumn has been got in, it is thought necessary to drive away evil spirits from the granaries.[61]

Iconographical Representation of Alakṣmī

Lakṣmī, Goddess of fortune or wealth primarily represented goddess of ripe-corn. In the havesting season the agricultural community places a corn-measure filled with ripe-corn, adores it with flowers as the represpentative of Lakṣmī.[62] Naturally, therefore, iconographically Lakṣmī was represented as Gaurī and this Gauri is defined as—

रक्तपीत समायोगात् गौरी इत्यभिधीयते

Nātyaśāstra (23,73)—that which is a mixture of red and yellow colour—is explained as *gaura*. This explanation of *gaura* conforms to the first variety of Gauri[63] as

61. Frazer, *Golden Brough*, IX, pp. 137ff.

62. Todd. *Annals and antiquities of Rajasthan*, pp. 454-455.
Even now in Orissa on every Thursday of the month of Mārgasīrsa, the custom of this type of worship is still prevalent.

63. *Vidh.* p. 3, 27, 11 ff.

गौरी पंचविधा तत्र श्यामा द्वादशधा भवेत् ।। 11 ।।

रुक्मगौरी दन्तगौरी स्फुटचन्दनगौर्यपि ।

शरद्घनचन्द्रकवत् गौरी पञ्चविधा स्मृता ।। 12 ।।

explained in Viṣṇudharmottara Purāṇa. The symbolical representation of Lakṣmī through ripe corn, the recommendation of Viṣṇudharmottara Purāṇa that the image of Lakṣmī should be of *gaura* (a mixture of red and yellow colour) helps us to see in Lakṣmī, the goddess of ripe corn.

Alakṣmī, the deity of misfortune and poverty who came to the picture later and who represented all the evil and inauspicious characteristics unlike the auspicious ones of Lakṣmī, iconographically came to be represented through image made of all types of unholy and inauspicious things. While the Śrī-Sūkta spoke of Lakṣmī as *hiraṇyavarṇā* having golden colour (reminding us of the colour of the ripe wheat or paddy). Alakṣmī's image was recommended to be dark colour like ink.

According to the description of Alakṣmī (referred to as Jyeṣṭhā Devī as given in Aṁśumadbhedāgama, 49th Patala, quoted by Hemadri), she is a goddess with two arms and two eyes with big cheeks and large pendulous breasts descending as far as the navel, with a flabby belly, thick thighs raised nose, hanging lower lips and colour as dark as ink. Her legs have to be hanging down in front of the Bhadrāsana in which she is seated. Her hair is done up in a knot and on the forehead a *tilaka* is marked. She wears a *makuṭa* on her head ; in her right hand she holds a Nīlotpala flower, and the other hand rests upon the seat. One authority however states that she would carry a Nīlotpala in one hand and keep the other in the *abhaya* pose. In actual sculpture she is often seen with the right hand in the *abhaya* pose and the left hand made to rest upon her thigh. Sometimes in the sculptures the right hand holds the Nīlotpala flower and the left hand rests upon the seat.

The ugly features like big cheeks and large pendulous

'Among these colours, the *gauri* (i.e. light shade) should be of five kinds . . . Bright gold, light white, tooth-white, pure sandal white, autumn —cloud-white and autumn moon white— these five traditionally are called the five—fold *Gaurī* (light shade).

breasts, etc. referred to by Hemadri definitely indicate that the goddess has assimilated many non-Aryan aboriginal divinities with her. Gopinath Rao[64] gives a list of names of Jyeṣṭhā as given in the old Tamil *Nighantus*. They are Mugadi Tauvi. Kaladi, Mudevi, Kettai. Like numerous village deities (*Grāma Devatā*) of the aboriginal population—Gaṅgāmmā, the goddess of small pox, Marāmmā the goddess of cholera, Kokkalāmmā, the goddess of cough, Sukhalāmmā the goddess of measles, Udalāmmā, the goddess of swollen necks, godess Jyeṣṭhā has come to be associated with poverty and misfortune with which she is supposed to afflict mankind. The long hanging breasts are everywhere regarded as one of the most unsightly features in a woman's form. Firm upright breasts are characteristics of motherhood and symbols of fertility, That is why when Matsya Purāṇa describing the method of the image of Lakṣmī says that the image of Laṣkmī should be (*pīnonnatastanataṭā, raktoṣṭhī, pīnagaṇḍā*).[65] Alakṣmī's image is to be (*lambamānastanā, lamboṣṭhā*), large pendulous breasts and hanging lower lip.

Lakṣmi originally a corn-goddess later came to represent not only prosperity in grains, but prosperity in every walk of life. That is why the different concepts like Rājalakṣmī, Jayalakṣmī, Vīralakṣmī, etc. Likewise Alakṣmī camc to be regarded in course of time not only as absence of wcalth—penury or poverty but it came to signify every thing inauspicious and evil. Therefore, in contrast to Lakṣmī who came to be regarded as not only a goddess of fourtune but as the goddess of beauty, Alakṣmī developed not only as a goddess of misfortune or ill-luck but as a goddess, symbolising an embodiment of all inauspicious features.

As Lakṣmī became the goddess of prosperity in every sphere of life, those things which are auspicious arc related to her like elephant, lotus etc. Similarly Alakṣmī who is pictured

64. T.A.G. Rao, *Elemeuts of Hindu Iconography*, Vol. I, Part II, p. 395.

65. *Ibid*, pp. 133-135.

as the embodiment of an evil spirit, goddess of ill-luck and poverty, ass was put as her *vāhana* (carrier) *kharārūḍhā*. Ass the carrier of Alakṣmī is regarded to be so much inauspicious that even if seen in a dream, is believed to cause the downfall or death of the person seeing it.[67] If its flesh is taken by a Brahmin he had to undergo a severe penance of Taptakṛchra for the atonement of such sin.[68] Similarly if a Śūdra, or a Vaiśya or a Kṣatriya commits adultery with a higher caste woman the woman so adulterated is made naked and her head being shaved and her body being anointed with butter, she is made to sit on a donkey and conducted along the high road for the atonement of the sin.[69] The ass which is looked upon as an inauspicious or ominous animal is fittingly selected to be the carrier of Alakṣmī, the goddess of misfortune and proverty.

The carrier of Jyeṣṭhā reminds us of another folk goddess Śītalā, goddess of small-pox who is of malignant nature. Śītalā rides on a donkey, has such emblems as a sweeping broom and pitcher, and is adorned with a winnowing fan on her head.[70] Once Jyeṣṭhā who was so popular deity in South India has now become practically obsolete. But the ground lost by Jyeṣthā in her home land was gained by her under another name, Śītalā in eastern and western parts of India.—Bengal, Orissa, Gujurat etc.

66. *Ibid.* p., 158
67. *Rāmāyaṇa*, 5, 27, 19ff.
68. *Manusmṛti*, ii, 157.
69. *Vaśiṣṭha* D.S. 21, 1-5,
70. नमामि शीतलां देवीं

    रासभस्थां दिगम्बरीम् ।

    मार्जनी कलसोपेतां

    शूर्पालंकृतमस्तकाम् ॥

Also quoted by J.N. Banerjee. *Development of Hindu Iconography*. p. 25.

Apart from this carrier ass, Baudhāyana Gṛhya Sūtra [71] while describing Jyeṣṭhā Vrata suggests carriers like lion and tiger in her chariot in Jyeṣṭhā's *dhyāna mantra*[72]— lions are attached to her chariot and tigers follow her.

These carriers show her identification with Durgā who has lion as her carrier. As has been pointed out Alakṣmī is addressed as Umā and Lakṣmī. The *dhyāna mantra* of Durgā

(तामग्निवर्णां तपसा ज्वलन्ती......शरणं अहं प्रपद्ये)

Which is used in the worship of Alakṣmī *corroborates* the same.

To sum up : Lakṣmī who was primarily a corn-goddess when merged with Śrī the Vedic goddess of beauty and brilliance, represented not only as goddess of corn but also the goddess of beauty and well-being. Gradually when she rose to eminence she stood not as a deity of corn only but became a deity representing whole human fortune and well-being. When Lakṣmī became established as the goddess of wealth well-being and prosperity, another deity namely Alakṣmī appeared to represent the other side of human fortune—poverty, misery, misfortune, calamity, etc. When one is in a state of prosperity such state is attributed due to the favour and grace of the goddess Lakṣmī ; but the state of poverty, ill-luck or disaster is taken to be the influence of Alakṣmī, the goddess of ill-luck and poverty. The state of disaster or destruction is taken to be due to the advent of Alakṣmī or her malignance.

In the Mahābhārata (3, 94, 10 ff) the prosperity of Gods is believed to be due to the favour of Lakṣmī, the goddess of prosperity; but the utter destruction and ruin of the demons

71. *Baudhāyana Gr. S.*, pp. 294-296.

72. यस्याः सिंहाः रथे युक्ता

बयाघ्राश्चाप्यनुगामिनः

[Baudh. Gṛ. S.]

was attributed to the evil influence of Alakṣmī the goddess of misfortune. Gradually Alakṣmī became the embodiment of all the evil features—misfortune, disaster and distress. The sad plight of Rāma who was exiled from his kingdom without being coronated, and the loss of Sītā as well as Jaṭāyu in the forest, was attributed to the evil influence of this inauspicious deity, Alakṣmī.[73] She was taken to be so much terrible and dangerous to the society that she was thought to dry the ocean and extinguish fire when furious. So people were terribly afraid of sueh a malignant deity. All the misfortune, ill-luck, ruin or destruction in one's life is generally thought to be due to the influence of Alakṣmī the goddess of ill-luck. So generally Alakṣmī is adored by the people for fear of her terrible influence.

---

73. *Rām* 3. 63, 20-23.

राज्यात् भ्रंशो वनवास: सीता नष्टं द्विजो हत: ।। 20 ।।

ईदृशीयं ममालक्ष्मी: निर्दहेदपि पावकन् ।

सम्पूर्णं चेदद्य प्रतरेयं महोदधिस् ।। 21 ।।

सोऽपि नूनं ममालक्ष्म्या विशुष्येत् सरितां पति: ।। 22a ।।

CHAPTER VI

Religious Observances and Festivities in Honour of Lakṣmi

The religious observances—*Vratas*[1] generally means firstly—the vow or restriction in one's behaviour when one has to take up any religious act; secondly, restrictions and specification of food for it. In the Vedic age, different religious rites were performed and the same old tradition was handed down from generation to generation to perpetuate the old memory in honour of different deities. Moreover, in the Vedic age various fire rituals and sacrifices were performed. But when they became too much expensive and could not suit the purse of the commonfolk, gradually it was on the wane. In the early centuries of the Christian era, the followers of Buddhism and Jainism were very powerful opponents of such ancient sacrificial system. The followers of Vedic system hit upon the idea of glorification of V*ratas.* They gave out the promise that through such vows one could attain heaven and other worldly or spiritual rewards. The procedure of the observance was simplified and made comparatively easier and less expensive than the sacrifices. The exponents of Vedicism went up to the extent of admitting some of the folk observances like *Kukkuṭa-Markaṭī* V*rata* (Bhaviṣyottara Purāṇa 46, 1-43) and the like, into Hinduism to win the heart of the people. They started to extol the V*ratas* instead of sacrifices. So naturally people were attracted towards their religion. The

1. For detail discussion on *Vratas* refer to P. V. Kane, *History of Dharmaśastra*, Vol. V, Part I, p. 1ff.

redactors of the Purāṇas took up this cause and tried to extol the *Vratas* in as many ways as it was possible. Brahma Purāṇa (29, 61) states that the reward that is secured by the worship of the Sun for a single day cannot be secured by hundreds of Vedic sacrifices. Even the redactor of Padma Purāṇa (6, 53, 4-6) went a little further and stated that as the Vedic rites and the rites prescribed by Manu cannot be performed in the Kali Yuga due to excessive expenditure etc., in lieu of them these *Vratas* should be performed by the devotee. By this way various *Vratas* were formulated by the redactors of the Purāṇas. The observances of the *Vratas* were gradually simplified to capture the common mind.

When different religious sects were formed, each sect developed certain *Vratas* for the observance by the followers of their sect. As like different sects, different *Vratas* like *Śaiva Vratas, Vaiṣṇava Vratas. Gāṇapatya Vratas, Śākta Vratas* etc. came to existence to suit the followers of different sects. When Lakṣmī was admitted into the Vaiṣṇava pantheon, different *Vratas* and rituals were formed recommending her worship along with Viṣṇu. There were certain *Vratas* where she is to be worshipped with deities other than Viṣṇu. The antiquity of those *Vratas* can be very well recognised in view of their non-alignment with Vaiṣṇava pantheon.

Due to growing popularity of Lakṣmī the performance of *Vratas* and rituals in her honour were generally considered obligatory. So these festivities are recommended to be observed in certain month of the year with certain paraphernalia as like other observances. As Lakṣmī became the presiding deity of agriculture and fertility, wealth and prosperity she was adored by each and every house-wife for gaining her favour and to attain prosperity.

In the major observances in honour of Lakṣmī, she is not worshipped alone; she is accompained by Viṣṇu or some other gods with whom she had certain alignment. As different festivities are observed at different periods of the year, attempt has been made to deal them serially according to Hindu calendar for convenience.

Aśunyaśayana dvitīyā Vrata[2]

It is the common belief of the Vaiṣṇavas that Viṣṇu retires to deep slumber during the month of Āṣāḍha particularly on the 12th day of the bright fortnight of Āṣāḍha (Vāmana Purāṇa 17, 7-8), when Viṣṇu the chief among the gods retires, other gods, Gandharvas, Yakṣas and the mothers of gods all retire one after the other (St. 4). Subsequently Viśva-karmā goes to sleep on the second day of the dark half of Śrāvaṇa

यस्यां तिथ्यां प्रस्वपिति विश्वकर्मा प्रजापतिः ।
द्वितीया सा शुभा पुण्या अशून्यशयनोदिता ॥

[Vāmana p. 17, 19]

Therefore this day is considered to be auspicious and is called *Aśūnyaśayana dvitīyā*. However Matsya Purāṇa (70, 2) associates Keśava with this day, not with Viśva-karmā as given in the Vāmana Purāṇa. According to Matsya Purāṇa Viṣṇu reposes with Lakṣmī in the milk-ocean on the second day of the dark fortnight in the month of Śrāvaṇa ; one can practise this *Vrata* called *Aśūnyaśayana Vrata* on this day only. Any way, as the day is taken to be auspicious, the *Vrata* is performed on this very day.

In the first day of this *Vrata* Viṣṇu is worshipped along with Lakṣmī with fragrant flowers, sandal paste etc. His image should consist of four arms, he should have *śrīvatsa* mark on his breast and he should be shown lying on a couch with Lakṣmī. In course of worship when fruits are offered to the deity the prayer is uttered thus—"Deva, as you never remain apart from your consort Lakṣmī, similarly let there be

2. *Vāmana Purāṇa* 17, 19ff ; *Matsya Purāṇa* 70, 1-8 ; *Agni Purāṇa* 177, 1-8 ; *Viṣṇudharmottara Purāṇa* 1, 145. 6-20 ; 8, 132, 1-12 ; P. V. Kane, *Op. Cit.*, p. 264.

no aloofness between me and my wife. Madhusūdan, as your household is never bereft of the goddess, so also let not mine be devoid of my wife."[3] After due obeissance and propitiation, the devotee has to take food without oil and salt at night. On the second day he has to distribute fruits to a revered Brāhmaṇa with the formula

लक्ष्मीधर प्रियतां मे

"May Lakṣmīdhara be pleased with me" (Vāmana Purāṇa 17,25). On the day of the festival one has to give away an image of Nārāyaṇa together with a bed equipped with a cushion. But Agni Purāṇa (177, 8) states that such *Vrata* should be continued for a year when beds and fruits should be gifted away.

The *Vrata* seems to have double purpose behind it. This *Vrata* secures *aviyoga* "absence of the loss of wife" to the male devotee, whereas a female devotee secures *avaidhavya* "want of widowhood" (Vāmana Purāṇa 17, 22-23). Like this, each *Vrata* confers a series of merits—material as well as spiritual on the devotees. This type of *Phalaśruti* is enjoined with the *Vrata* generally to attract others for gaining in merit for this life and for the life hereafter.

The *Vrata* falls in Śrāvaṇa (July-August) which is the period of rainy season and the young corn is in a state of slumber and growth. So the *Vrata* might have been contrived for due adoration to Lakṣmī the corn spirit together with

3. यथा हि लक्ष्म्या न वियुज्यसे त्वं
त्रिविक्रमानन्त जगन्निवास ।
तथास्तु अशून्यं शयनं सदैव
अस्माकं एवेह तव प्रसादात् ।। 22 ।।
यथात्वशून्यं तव देव तल्पं
समं हि लक्ष्म्या वरदाच्युतेश ।
सत्येन तेनामितवीर्य विष्णो
गार्हस्थ्यनाशो मम नास्तु देव ।। 23 ।। [Vāmana Purāṇa. 17, 22-23]

Viṣṇu the god of fertility. There may have been another consideration for the worship of Lakṣmī and Viṣṇu. The period when Viṣṇu sleeps together with other gods, is regarded to be inauspicious. So all types of religious activities are to be shunned during such period. During this period, the evil and wicked spirits are believed to be surrounded on every direction to cause harm to the people. In order to be free from their clutches, the worship of Lakṣmī with Viṣṇu might have been planned. Any way the devotees are prone to observe such *Vrata* in a befitting manner.

As to the antiquity of the *Vrata*, it may be presumed that as Lakṣmī was united with Viṣṇu much later, *Vratas* which deal with the joint worship of Lakṣmī with Viṣṇu might have been created in later period of development.

Viśoka dvādaśī Vrata

Out of the *Vratas* where joint worship of Lakṣmī with Viṣṇu are prescribed, the *Viśoka dvādaśi Vrata*[4] is an important one. It is observed for gaining in beauty, health and pleasure which is rightly mentioned by the composer of Padma Purāṇa (5, 21, 47) :

यथा लक्ष्मी नरेश त्वं न परित्यज्य गच्छति ।
तथा सुरूपताऽरोग्यं अशोकं चास्तु मे सदा ।।

"O Lord, as Lakṣmī does not forsake you, similarly beauty, health and pleasure be always mine" (Matsya Purāṇa 80, 25). The Viśokadvādaśī Vrata which is observed on the 12th day of the bright fortnight of Āśvayujā achieves for the devotee his desired end, wealth and prosperity and removes sorrow and distress on this earth (Padma Purāṇa 5, 21, 22).

The presiding deity of the *Vrata* is Lakṣmī who is designated as *Viśokā*' the deity who frees from sorrow. That is why the *Vrata* is so named. Though the worship of the deity starts on the twelfth day of Āśvina (*Śukla*), the

4. *Padma Purāṇa*, 5,21,22-80 ; *Matsya Purāṇa* chs. 81-82 ; P.V. Kane, Op. c.t., Vol. II, pp. 880-881.

ancillary functions start from the 10th day of Āśvina *Śukla*. On the tenth day of Āśvina *Śukla*, the devotee has to resolve to fast on the eleventh day and to worship Keśava and to partake of food the next day. On the 12th day, he has to worship Keśava from head to foot with different names of Viṣṇu. A *maṇḍala* should be made and on it a four cornered altar would be constructed. On this altar the image of Lakṣmī called V*iśokā* made of river sand is to be placed on a winnowing fan for worship. Lakṣmī as V*iśokā* is to be worshipped with the mantra—

नमः देव्यै नम शान्त्यै नमो लक्ष्म्यै नमः श्रियै ।
नमः पुष्ट्यै नमः तुष्ट्यै वृष्ट्यै हृष्ट्यै नमो नमः ॥

(Matsya Purāṇa 80, 16). Then the devotee should say, V*iśokā* goddess, destroy all grief, grant boons, give wealth and fulfil all desires" (St. 17). After this the devotee should wrap up the winnowing-fan in a piece of cloth, and would worship Lakṣmī with fruits and various kinds of clothes and with a golden lotus.

The devotee has to drink water purified by Kuśa grass and spend the whole night singing and dancing; Brāhmaṇa couples are to be honoured duly and are to be duly fed and paid handsomely. At the close of such V*rata*, the devotee has to donate bedstead *śayanasthāna*, *guḍadhenu*, 'a cow made of molasses' and the winnowing fan together with the image of Lakṣmī covered with clothes. The *guḍadhenu dāna* probably was not originally attached with this V*rata*. but later on was joined with it. So the redactor of Matsya Purāṇa puts it in a different chapter altogether (Ch. 81).

This is the period of the advent of new crops. Agriculturists generally make merry and take delight in music and dancing. As Lakṣmī is the presiding deity of corn, and fertility, in honour of her, Brahmin couples are honoured duly. Like goddess Lakṣmī, Gaurī is also regarded as the corn mother. It is interesting to find similarities between the V*iśokadvādaśī* V*rata* of Lakṣmī and *Lalitāṣaṣṭhī* V*rata* of Gaurī.

The *Lalitāṣaṣṭhī* Vrata dedicated to corn mother Gaurī falls on the Bhādrapada on *Śukla Ṣaṣṭhī* day. It is observed by the females for gaining good fortune, happiness, and prosperity. In this *Vrata*, the ladies have to take their bath in the river very early in the morning and bring sand from the river in a new winnowing fan. The image of Gaurī called '*Lalitā*' is to be made of it and to be worshipped duly. The devotee should spend the night in music, dancing and acting. In this *Vrata*, as like *Viśokadvādaśī*, the image of Lalitā together with the winnowing fan should be donated to a Brahmin. At the close of the *Vrata*, a young maiden should be fed with five to ten Brahmins (Bhaviṣyottara Purāṇa 5, 41, 15). The young virgin is the symbol of the power of fertility. So she should be fed during the *Vrata* as the representative of the corn-mother Gaurī or Lalitā.

Kojāgara Pūrṇimā

Out of the different festivals observed in honour of Lakṣmī, *Kojāgara Pūrṇimā*[5] otherwise called *Kaumudī Mahotsava* is very important. It is observed on the full-moon day of Āśvina. The Kāma Sūtra[6] of Vātsyāyana mentions it as *Kaumudijāgara*. Yaśodhara[7] in his commentary, '*Jayamaṅgalā*' on the Kāma Sūtra puts it thus—

कौमुदिजागरः इति—आश्वयुज्यां हि पौर्णमास्यां कौमुद्या
ज्योत्स्नायाः प्रकर्षेण प्रवृत्तेः तत्र दोलाद्यूतप्राया: क्रीड़ाः ।

This is the time when the moonlight is seen in its fullest glory. *Kojāgara* is probably an abbreviation of *Kaumudī jāgara*.

The period of observance of this ritual differs from one text to the other. The redactors of Bhaviṣyottara Purāṇa

5. P. V. Kane, *Op. Cit.*, Vol. V, Part I, pp. 290-291,
6. Vātsyayana, *Kāma Sutra*, 1, 4, 27.
7. *Ibid.*, pp. 152-153.

(140, 4, 60ff) and Padma Purāṇa (6.· 124, 61ff) put the time of the festival of *Kaumudī Mahotsava* on Kārttika *Amāvāsyā* or on *Dīpāvalī* day. Sabdakalapadruma[8] states that *Āśvina Pūrṇimā* is the *Kaumudī Pūrṇimā*—

कोजागर्ति अस्यां पौर्णमास्यां निशायाँ इति लक्ष्म्या

देव्या उक्तिर्यत्र समये आश्विनी पूर्णिमा शरदि द्यूतपूर्णिमा

शरत्प्रभा कौमुदी

In order to substantiate his version, the composer of the lexicon puts the extracts from the two Purāṇas in support of it. In the first extract, which he accepts from the Brahma Purāṇa, he states that people observe this *Vrata* on the fullmoon day of Āśvayujā and worship the demon Nikumbha, who returns after victory from the ocean—

अाश्वयुज्यां पौर्णमास्यां निकुम्भो वालुकार्णवात् ।
आयाति सेनया सार्धं कृत्वा युद्धं सुदारुणम् ॥

The other example he cites from the Liṅga Purāṇa thus—

आश्विने पौर्णमास्यां तु चरेत् जागरणं निशि ।
कौमुदी सा समाख्याता कार्या लीक विभूतये ॥

The concluding words should be *lokaih vibhūtaye* not *loka vibhūtaye*, because it is observed by the people for their prosperity.

Kamalākara Bhaṭṭa[9] while referring to the *Kaumudī Mahotsava* accepts the above example of Liṅga Purāṇa in support of his argument. The fullmoon day of Āśvayujā is observed as *Kaumudī Mahotsava* or the festival of pleasure or merry-making. On this day Lakṣmī and Indra are to be worshipped. The compiler of Sabdakalpadruma[10] puts the text thus—

8. *Subdakalpadruma*, Vol. II, pp. 200-201,

10. *Loc. Cit.*

कौमुद्यां पूजयेत् लक्ष्मीं इन्द्रं ऐरावतं स्थिरं,

but it should be—कौमुद्यां पूजयेत् लक्ष्मीं इन्द्रं ऐरावतस्थितम् ।[11]

Āśvina Pūrṇimā is accepted by majority of the texts[12] as the period of the festival, *Kaumudī Mahotsava, Śāṅkhāyana* Gṛhya Sūtra (4,16. 1,) prescribes Āśvayujā Paurṇamāsyā, for Indra's worship. Viṣṇudharmottara Purāṇa (3, 196, 1—3) designates it as '*Śakravrata*' where Indra with Sacī, Vajra and Airāvata are worshipped.

During this night people are advised to wear beautiful dresses and spend the night in playing on dice—

सुगन्धनिशि सद्वास अक्षैः जागरणं चरेत् ।

It is enjoined that the coconut milk should be drunk at night and the night should be spent in playing dice; probably both these precautions and aids are meant for keeping awake the whole night.[14] The Pitṛs and gods are to be offered coconut. In the said night beneficient Lakṣmī (Varadā Lakṣmī) moves in the world saying- "I shall offer him wealth who is watchful throughout the night playing on dice-

निशिथे वरदा लक्ष्मी को जागर्ती ति भाषिणीम् ।
तस्मै बित्तं प्रयच्छामि अक्षैः क्रीड़ां करोति यः ।।[15]

In this festival, Lakṣmī, the goddess of wealth and vegetation, plays the important role. She is worshipped with Indra, the Vedic god of rain and thunder, who germinates the earth with the fertilising rain.

11. *Nirṇaya Sindhu*, Vol. II, p. 680.

12. For further reference in support of it please refer to *Bhaviṣya, Purāṇa*, 2, 8, 13:ff and *Mudrārākṣasa* edited by K. H. Dhurva, notes in pp. 114-115.

13. *Nirṇaya Sindhu*, Vol. II, p. 680.

14. Under Hill, *The Hindu Religious Year*. pp. 5

15. *Nirṇaya Sindhu*, Vol. 1, p. 681.

The most interesting function during this festival is *Akṣakrīḍā* 'play on dice'. If we look back to the customs and traditions of the people during the period of Ṛg.Veda, we find that the game on dice was looked down upon by the Vedic seers. So such play was forbidden at that time—

अक्षैः मा दीव्य (Ṛg Veda 10, 34, 13)

In the age of the epics, the ṚgVedic custom continued unabated. Vyāsa does not lag behind to depreciate the play as the root of quarrel—

द्यूतं अनर्थमूलम् (Mahābhārata, 2, 52, 11)

So it was regarded as a sin to play on dice.

देवनं पापं (Mahābhārata 2, 53, 2)

But gradually old order changed. When we come across Kāma Sūtra, we find that the custom which was so much disparaged by the seers of the Ṛg.Veda or by the epic has been accepted as a regular pastime of the citizens on a certain auspicious festive occasion like *Kojāgara Pūrṇimā* etc. An Ākhyāyikā of Vratarāja[16] mentions how a poor Brahmin named Balita became rich by playing on dice on *Kojāgara Pūrṇimā* night which is sacred to goddess Lakṣmī. This shows how playing on dice was accepted as a part of the ritual of Lakṣmi worship, as it is believed that Lakṣmī will be pleased with those who play on dice on Āśvina Pūrṇīmā night—

इषस्य शुक्लपूर्णायां द्यूतात् लक्ष्मीः प्रसीदति । 42a

This festival is preeminently a Lakṣmī V*rata*. Those who observe such V*rata* are never afflicted by poverty, rather they are blessed with offspring, wealth, long and prosperious life—

इह चायुष्यं आरोग्यं पुत्रपौत्रादि सम्पदम् ।

16, *Vratarāja*, p. 628f.

अप्सराभिः परिवृतः स्वर्गलोके महीयते ।।

× × × ×

एवं लक्ष्मीव्रतं कृत्वा न दरिद्रो नो दुःखभाक् ।।[17]

The choice of Āśvina Pūrṇimā for the worship of Lakṣmī is significant. The autumn season which consists of Bhādrapada and Āśvina marks the beginning of the harvest of Kharif crops. During this period the earth is covered with ripe crops—

आपक्वशालिरुचिरा तनुगात्रयष्टिः [18]

When the fields lay full of the ripe corn, it was a signal for holding *Kojāgara*[19] *Pūrṇimā* in honour of Lakṣmī, the goddess of harvest and fortune, to propitiate her, without whose favour the cultivators will not be able to have a good harvest. Therefore, this is the right time for the adoration of the corn-goddess who is to bless the agriculturist at the time of harvest. So Lakṣmī, the goddess of corn and prosperity is duly propitiated for prosperity and wealth at the right time.

Dīpāvalī

One of the most joyful of all festivals of the goddess Lakṣmī is *Dīpāvalī*,[20] which is observed throughout the length

17. *Ibid.*, p. 630.

18. Kalidasa, *Ritusaṁhāra*, Ch. 3, 1.

19. While studying the social and economic history of Northern India, B.P. Mazumdar tries to discuss the different festivals of the Hindus current in that region ; in course of discussion on *Kojāgara Purṇimā* he has tried to show the intimate connection of the rice plant with our religious life and in that context he has mentioned the intimate relation of Lakṣmī with rice plants ; *Socio-Economic History of Northern India*, Calcutta, 1960, p. 295 ; 303.

20. P. K. Gode contributed three papers on *Dīpāvalī* and has tried to prove the historicity of the festival and its significance. *Studies in Indian Cultural History*, Vol. II, Poona, 1960, pp. 186-260 P.V. Kane, *Op. Cit.*, pp. 194-207; *Padma Purāṇa* 6,124; *Bhaviṣyottara Purāṇa* 140, 1ff. *Nirnaya Sindhu*, Vol. II, p. 197 ; *Vratarāja* ; p. 563.

and breadth of the country. This is a festival of lights, illuminations and fire works. The period of its observance extends from three to five days according to different authorities. According to Padma Purāṇa (6, 124, 4f) the festival lasts for five days which starts from the thirteenth day of the dark fortnight of Kārttika and ends on the second day of the bright half of Kārttika, and the illumination has to be started from the same day. But Nirṇaya Sindhu (Vol.II,p.709.

दीपोत्सवः दिनत्रयम्)

and Skanda Purāṇa (2,4,9, 49) mention that the festival should be observed for three days. The demon king Bali gave *tripāda dāna* to Vāmana-Viṣṇu, who was ultimately pleased to allow Bali to rule in the Sutala -'nether world'. However he was permitted to enjoy his kingdom on earth for three days in view of his *tripāda dāna* 'gift of three steps measured earth.' Those three days are the fourteenth day of the dark fortnight of Kārttika, *Amāvāsyā* and Kārttika *Śuklapratipadā*. On these three days the earth is designated as the kingdom of Bali. Therefore, the Dīpāvalī festival is observed for three days.

Out of the three days of Bali's kingdom on earth the first day which falls on the fourteenth day of the dark fortnight of Kārttika is variously called as *Narakacaturdaśī, Bhūtacaturdaśī* or *Pretacaturdaśī.*

Naraka was a demon who was born due to the union of Bhūmi 'Earth' and Viṣṇu in his Varāha incarnation. But as he oppressed the gods in heaven he was ultimately killed by Kṛṣṇa-Viṣṇu. In commemoration of the extirpation of the demon, the day is observed on earth. Like the Christian's All soul's day *Narakacaturdaśī* was the day on which all the spirits of Pitṛs who are freed to receive the offerings made by their descendants on the *Mahālayā śrāddha* (*Āśvina Amāvāsyā*) and were wandering on earth return to *Naraka* 'hell'.

> In the morning on *Narakacaturdaśī* persons afraid of hell should take an oil bath at the time of day-break, because Lakṣmī dwells in the oil and the Ganges in water on that day—

तैले लक्ष्मीर्जले गङ्गा दीपावल्यां चतुर्दश्यां

(Padma Purāṇa (6,124,9). After the oil bath and bath in water one has to offer *tarpaṇa* satiation with handful of water etc. mixed with sesame to Yama who is the lord of the spirits. In the evening a lamp should be offered to Naraka and illumination with lamps should be provided in the temples of Brahmā, Viṣṇu, Śiva and others and in monasteries, in rooms for implements, on *Caityas*, in assembly halls etc. The ancestral spirits who wander on the earth when pleased with their ancestors, grant boons for the welfare of their offspring ; in the same evening men with fire brands in their hands are advised to show the way to their deceased ancestors who find their way by the bright light and reach their world.

During this day the cultivators go in procession and pay due respect to the crop and offer sacrifices of ram or goat in order to express their obligation to the crop ready for harvest. Moreover they visit the dunghill which is collected for manuring the field for future crops and fall prostrate and beg to fertilise their lands and to procure abundant crops.[21] In the Deccan and in Orissa the heap of cowdung is also worshipped by every householder on this day.[22] The dungheap which is so adored as the emblematic of Naraka is the spirit of vegetation which fertilizes the field.

The second day of the festival is the Kārttika *amāvāsyā*. The day is designated as *Yakṣarātri* by Vātsyāyana in his Kāma Sūtra (I ; 4, 27) ; Yaśodhara in his commentary—*Jayamaṅgalā* on the Kāma Sūtra explains it thus

सुखरात्रिः यक्षाणां तत्र सन्निधानात् ।

तत्र प्रायशो लोकस्य द्यूतक्रीड़ा

Thus he equates *Yakṣarātri* with *Sukhasuptikā* and it is popularly called Dīpāvalī amāvāsyā,

21. Dubois, *Loc. Cit.*

22. R.E. Enthoven, *Op. Cit.*, p. 95.

This day is significant in two ways; firstly Lakṣmī the consort of Viṣṇu rises from her slumber before Viṣṇu on this day for it is imperative on the part of a Hindu woman to rise before her husband and to look to his comforts (Skanda P. 2, 4, 9, 86), so it is called *Sukhasuptikā* ; secondly, this is the day on which Lakṣmī is said to have been released from the prison of Bali by Viṣṇu together with other gods (Skanda Purāṇa 2, 4, 9, 77). In commemoration of this incident, the *Sukhasuptikā Vrata* is observed on this day.

The presiding deity of this festival is Lakṣmī. Early in the morning one has to take oil bath and worship the gods and *pītṛs* and perform the *pārvaṇa śrāddha* with curds, milk, ghee and feed the Brahmins with various foods. In the afternoon, the king proclaims in his capital, the day of sovereignty of Bali and asks people to enjoy life to the lees. So people in their houses make merry with music and dance, offer *tāmbula* to each other, anoint their body with saffron powder and dress themselves with silken robes and wear different types of ornaments. Young women move in groups wearing bright clothes and cast rice grains about and the houses are decorated with rows of lamps. In the midnight the king moves round his capital on foot to see the fun and charm of the festival.

In the evening people illuminate their houses, shrines of gods, squares where four roads meet, cemeteries, rivers, mountains, bottoms of trees, cowpens, caves etc. The shops are decorated with cloth and flowers.

Thus people illuminate different places with the belief that the lighting of lamps during Bali's domination would make Lakṣmī stable in their houses. But those who do not illuminate their houses during this festival, cannot enjoy prosperity and plenty during that year. In this night the image of Lakṣmī is to be made of five colours together with Brahmā, Viṣṇu, Śiva and others. A couch made of cotton is to be prepared for Lakṣmī and clothes as soft as the foam of milk is to be spread over and there the gods and Lakṣmī are to be placed on it. Those who prepare the bed of lotus for Lakṣmī are never bereft of wealth (Skanda Purāṇa 2,9,79,-82). At midnight of new-moon, the expulsion of Alakṣmī is done in a befitting manner by the women of the city by beating the winnowing fans. On the other hand Nīlamata Purāṇa[23] (p. 42 verses 50) prescribes the worship of *Karīṣiṇī* cowdung as an emblemmatic of Lakṣmī. This also reminds us of her former relation with cowdung. In the Śrī Sūkta she is described as ever nourished in cowdung and in the Mahābhārat (13,82,24ff) there is a legend how Lakṣmī came to live in the cowdung. The cowdung is an element of fertility which adds fertility to the soil, so she is worshipped in such a form. Only the females observe this *Vrata* after due permission from their husbands. Different kinds of sweets are prepared for Lakṣmī and with other four kinds of foods the sweets are offered to her. In the house ripe crops and fruits are to be kept. Wreath made of betel leaves are to be hanged in the house and the main road is to be decorated with lotus, and the lamps are to be waved round (*nirājanā*) the head of a person.

The *nirājanā*[24] or waving of light round one's head is very important on this occasion. It is aimed at driving away ghosts and evil spirits from the person concerned (Skanda Purāṇa 2,4,9,8). This waving of lamp (*nirājanā*) of the king bestows victory on him and it scares away demons and other evil spirits from the person concerned and removes all types of dangers and difficulties (Bhaviṣyottara Purāṇa, 140, 24-25).

During the kingdom of Bali, Yakṣas, Gandharvas, Piśācas etc. are happy. Young children are given toys to play; from their performance, the sign of future happiness or misery is well known. If the boys are unhappy on those days it is anticipated that the king would not enjoy better future and if the boys are happy, it tells upon the future happiness of

23 The Nīlamata Purāṇa as referred to by P.K. Gode, *Op. Cit.*, p. 229.

24 *Viṣṇudharmottara Purāṇa* 2, 159, 1ff; *Agni Purāṇa* 268, 15ff; *Nirṇaya Sindhu*, Vol. II, p. 169.

the king. If the boys fight between themselves, there is an anticipation of wars ; if they weep, there is fear of destruction of the kingdom. From the play of boys using sticks as horses, the victory of the king and the destruction of other kingdoms are expected. If boys play holding their penis, there is fear of lasciviousness among females in future time and if they hide rice inside water, it is sure indication of famine.[25]

During this night females are directed to take recourse to gambling and to play on dice with their husbands for victory. Those who win victory, have to enjoy that state during that year but those who meet defeat, has to suffer the whole year. It is said that Pārvatī[26] worshipped Lakṣmī on this day and then she won victory over Śiva in the play of dice, as a consequence Śiva has to lose everything including his very garments and has to remain naked (Padma Purāṇa 6,124, 26-28a). The win or loss in the gambie portends good or bad fortune for the year. The dice-play and gambling are advised on this night as they incur the pleasure of Lakṣmī. In Siam also the new year is observed for three days beginning from the 1st of April when women and children visit temples and make offerings, which is followed by numerous charitable and religious deeds. The rich entertain monks. The departed souls return to the heart of their family freed from the fetters of the under world. On these days gambling is not confined to the licensed houses but every body is at liberty to indulge in it which holds powerful sway over every householder.[27] Gambling on these three days is always welcome because it is a pastime for spending the period of happiness and luxury.

Another feature of this day is the worship of Kubera, the god of wealth (Nirṇaya Sindhu, IIp. 714) after sunset. It is as

25. *Vratarāja.* p. 650.

26. The play of dice between Śiva and Pārvatī is well represented in the sculptures of Ellora Cave No. 21 which is corroborated by this text. P.V. Kane, *Op. Cit.*, p. 203.

27. Frazer, *Op. Cit.*. Vol., IX, pp. 149-150.

important as the worship of Lakṣmī. Kubera is the lord of Yakṣas and related with this night—*Yakṣarātri*. So his worship is desirable as the god of riches and a genius of vegetation and fecundity. Now-a-days this day is specially important for the merchants and traders. They invite their friends, customers and other traders and give them sweets etc; they close the old accounts and open new ones. There is a popular belief that Brahmā gave *Rakṣābandhana* (Śrāvaṇa full-moon day) to Brhmins as their festival, *Daśarā* to Kṣatriyas and *Dīpāvalī* to Vaiśyas and *Holikā* to *Śūdras*.[28]

On the last day of the festival falls the *Balipratipadā* or *Balirājyapravartinī* on the first day of the bright fortnight of Kārttika. Lakṣmī comes out of the underworld with Bali, who is expected to rule the world for these days.

This day is exclusively set apart for the worship of Bali. When the king has to worship him, he has to make the image of Bali with the powder of five colours on a *maṅḍala* (Padma Purāṇa 6, 124, 47ff) ; his wife Vindhyāvalī is to be made well decorated with ornaments and beside them are to be put the images of other demons like Kuṣmāṇḍa, Maya, Jambhoru etc. In the middle of the house these images are to be put and duly adored with flowers, incense etc. Along with wine, meat etc. rice and porridge are to be offered to Bali and the night should be spent in music, dancing and dialogue. The worship of Bali during this day brings happiness, and joy for the whole family (Padma Purāṇa 6, 124, 5ff) throughout the year.

But common people worship Bali in a different manner. They make a couch for Bali inside their house and establish the image of Bali made with white rice grains and worship him with fruits and flowers. But those who like to worship Bali in their courtyard make his image of cowdung (*gomayena*) sprinkle curd before it and pay due homage (Skanda Purāṇa 2, 4, 10, 15). Those who give away donation according to their capacity on this day proper their wealth increases and

28. P. V. Kane, *Op. Cit.*, p. 200.

such gift also pleases Viṣṇu. Those who worship Bali on this day, are freed from diseases ; they enjoy plenty and prosperity and are freed from dangers and difficulties. In a nutshell people spend the year in the same manner as they enjoy life during Bali's kingdom on earth (Padma Purāṇa 6, 124, 65-66). So it is desirable on the part of the common people to spend the period in pomp and grandeur, so that the year round they would enjoy their life without any trouble.

In Malabar, during their great national festival *onam*, (August-September), people worship Bali, the demon king. But the preliminaries of the festival starts in the previous month (Śrāvaṇa). During this month they bring the first bunch of paddy in a ceremonial manner through young boys and girls. A girl holds a lamp in front of the procession and enters into the interior chamber dedicated to the mother goddess of corn and shout *Nirā* (fill), plenty, fill etc. Thus propitiating the first bunch of paddy they believe to be saved from famine during the year. At the end of the month of Śrāvaṇa, they remove all rubbish of the house by a ceremony which, they believe drives away Alakṣmī, the goddess of dirt'. After this begins the *Onam* month (Bhādrapada). Among the different paraphernalia of the festival, the worship of Bali is most important. They make an image of Bali out of mud and propitiate.[29]

Bali is a spirit of Vegetation.[30] During his festival he is worshipped by agriculturist preparing his image with white rice grains. In *Aviyogatṛtīyā* *Vrata* which falls on the 3rd day of bright half of Mārgaśirṣa the image of Śiva and Gaurī are made of a powder of corn *śālipiṣṭa* ; they are enjoined to be worshipped for bestowing beauty, wealth, off-spring etc. (Bhaviṣyottara Purāṇa 22, 8-9). Towards the last part of the festival of Gaurī (which falls in September) the image of Gaurī is to be moulded in the rice dough and placed in a shrine for worship.[31]

29. *Bhārata Kaumudī*, pp. 427-432.
30. For a detail discussion on Bali as a spirit of Vegetation refer to J.J. Meyer, *Trilogie*.
31. Dubois, *Op. Cit.*, p. 568.

Nikṣubhā, the other wife of the sun is also identified with the Mother-Earth (Bhaviṣya Purāṇa 1, 79, 4ff). She is a goddess of fertility who in union with the sun bears crops for the maintenance of created beings. The image of Nikṣubhā and the sun is also prescribed to be made of powdered rice and among other offerings different types of paddy are included (Bhaviṣya Purāṇa 1,169,2ff). In the month of Māgha the image of sun is to be made of powdered rice (Bhaviṣya Purāṇa 1, 169, 4ff). The sun is a god of fertility without whose blessings no crop thrives. So tne sun is also related with Bali who is an underworld spirit of corn.

Bali visits the world when the crop is ripe and is ready for harvest ; he is especially worshipped when different crops are ripe. So his kingdom on earth is observed in those days (Bhaviṣya Purāṇa 1, 18, 28). Those who adore Bali during those days enjoy happiness and prosperity.

Dīpāvalī is a compound festival which consists of honouring the ancestors, worship of cowdung, the worship of Lākṣmī, the goddess of bounty and Bali the spirit of vegetation. This is the time when the fields are filled with ripe corn and it is the ripe time to worship Bali and Lakṣmī as the divinities of vegetation and fertility and cowdung, the factor serving the purpose of fecundity, which would fertilize the field for future crops. When the agriculturists are ready to harvest, it is but natural on their part to honour those who would bless them with plenty and prosperity. So the festival is rightly chosen for the worship of Lakṣmī and Bali who are responsible for better harvest ; therefore they are duly propitiated.

Guruvāra Vrata

Unlike other *Vrata* which are observed on particular *tithis* in certain months, we come across a particular observance namely *Guruvāra* V*ratas* which is observed in honour of Lakṣmī. This V*rata* is practised throughout, Orissa and some parts of Bengal till now as a particular observance in the month of Mārgśirṣa on every *Guruvāra* 'Thursday'. In the northern part of Orissa it is popularly called '*Māṇavasā*' placing of the corn measure' and on this day a corn measure filled with new-corn is put on a pedestal and adored duly as emblematic of Lakṣmī, goddess of corn; but in the Purāṇas the description does not tally with the local customs.

The Padma Purāṇa (3, 11, 34ff) in order to magnify this *Vrata* appends a legend to it and states the procedure of her worship in different manner thus: On the first Thursday of Mārgaśīrṣa, Lakṣmī with Viṣṇu is installed and worshipped. Sweets and *pāyasa* 'rice gruel' etc. are offered to Lakṣmī and is prayed for her blessing; The offerings are to be distributed among Brahmins and among the family members. On the second Thursday of the month—

(द्वितीये तु गुरोर्वारे—Verse 40)

> cakes made of wheat etc. are to be offered to Lakṣmī; but on the third Thursday one has to offer rice mixed with curd and on the fourth Thursday, *śyāmaka* and *śāli* paddy are offered and Brahmins are honoured for her sake with clothes, ornaments and different types of fruits etc.

This is the month when harvesting is done in full swing. The paddy crop collected and stored in the house represents Lakṣmī, the goddess of corn. So it is befitting on the part of the agriculturists to worship her with due pomp and grandeur and without whose blessing, he will not be able to attain plenty and prosperity.

Śrīpañcamī Vrata

The *Śrīpañcamī Vrata* is observed now-a-days in honour of Sarasvatī, the goddess of learning during the month of Māgha on the fifth day of the bright fortnight; but originally this *Vrata* was observed on the fifth day of bright half of Mārgaśīrṣa and was sacred to Lakṣmī ; later on it has been changed and shifted to other month and the presiding deity is also altered. The Bhaviṣyottara Purāṇa (37, 1ff) dedicates a chapter on its observance in honour of Lakṣmī.[32]

On this day one has to make an image of Lakṣmī of gold, silver, copper, wood or clay or draw her figure on a piece of cloth for her worship. She is to be represented with lotus in her hands and of lotus colour and bathed by the elephants of the quarters with golden pitchers. On the third part of the day, one has to take bath and worship her after due adoration to other gods and dead ancestors.

The special characteristic of her worship, as a spirit of corn is very important. Though fruits are offered to her but chief of the offerings are the sprouted grain (Bhaviṣyottara Purāṇa 37, 45), sweetened rice is also dedicated in her honour. A pot of rice grains with a vessel full of ghee is to be donated in her honour. Every month on the same day (*Śukla pañcamī*) Lākṣmī is to be worshipped taking a different name of Lakṣmī. At the end of worship, a *maṇḍapa* is to be made and on it clothes are to be spread as a couch on which Lakṣmī has to be placed for worship ; seven kinds of rice grains are to be placed beside Lakṣmī for her worship, which clearly express her character as a goddess of corn.

32. P.V. Kane, *Op. Cit.*, pp. 432-433.

CHAPTER VII

Laksmi in The Pancaratra

In the annals of early Viṣṇuism, the Pāñcarātra is accepted as the oldest surviving Viṣṇuite sect Though the theological and ritualistic aspects of Pāñcarātra system attracted the scholars in the past, only a few texts[1] have been edited so far, F. O. Schrader,[2] while editing the Ahirbudhnya Saṁhitā, gives an illuminating introduction to the Pāñcarātra literature and mentions an exhaustive list of Pāñcarātra Saṁhitās which are 210 in number. In view of its popular practice in certain areas, it is attracting the attention of the scholars of present generation.

These Saṁhitās are sacred to the Viṣṇuite sect and are taken to be the first mannual to express the belief and observances of the Vaiṣṇavas. Instead of laying enough of importance on Nārāyaṇa—Viṣṇu as the cult-deity they have given the foremost position to his Śakti i.e. Lakṣmī. The importance of Śakti in the Pāñcarātra system marks the emergence of Śākta principle in the Vaiṣṇava sect.[3] Like the Tantras of the Śāktas the Pāñearātra Saṁhitās lay enough of importance on *Mantra, Maṇḍala, Yantra* etc. for the worship of the cult deities.[4] The influence of tantric ideas and practices are quite

1. In the introduction to Sanat KumāraSaṁhitā, V. Raghavan presents an exhaustive report on the name of Samhitās so far published then. Vide *Sanat KumāraSamhita*, Intro. p, vff ; and after the same other Saṁhitās have already come to the market.
2. F.O. Schrader. *Introduction to the Pāṇcarātra and the* Ahirbudhnya Saṁhitā, pp. 6,12.
3. For further information on the introduction of Śaktī in Pāṇcarātra literature, refer to Sanjukta Gupta, *Lakṣmī Tantra* (Translation and Notes) Introduction, p. xxxv.

dominant in the extant Saṁhitās which are taken to be the earlier record of the tantric influence.[4]

The followers of Pāñcarātra believe in one ultimate non-dual reality which possesses in its fundamental nature two aspects viz. *nivṛtti* 'static' and *pravṛtti* 'dynamic' aspects and these two aspects of the cult-deity represent the Brahman and his Śakti respectively. The dynamic aspect or Śakti of the supreme being is Lakṣmī who is instrumental cause of all creation. The Supreme being is Nārāyaṇa and the Pāñcarātrins worship him in his four *Vyūha* forms—Vāsudeva, Saṅkarṣaṇa, Pradyumna and Aniruddha. The devotional attitude of the Pāñcarātrins have further deified many aspects of his Śakti i.e. Lakṣmī and have also connected various powers—small and great with manifestations and sub-manifestations of the lord. Lakṣmī, Kīrti, Jayā and Māyā are the four powers which act as the consorts of Vāsudeva, Saṅkarsaṇa, Pradyumna and Aniruddha respectively.

Lakṣmī, Śakti of Nārāyaṇa

Lakṣmī is accepted as the Śakti of the supreme being Nārāyaṇa, The concept of Śakti in case of a Vaiṣṇava sect seems very baffling. So in order to justify the introduction of Śakti and her role in different spheres of life, the Pāñcarātrins contend that the supreme being dwells for timeless ages in his transcendent form, but this transcendent nature of the supreme being is incompatible in relation to the changing world. The desire to preserve the purity and unchanged nature of the supreme being in relation to the changing universe gives rise to the view that it is not the supreme being who is responsible for creation, sustenance and destruction of the universe, but his Śakti.

This work of creation is assigned to his Śakti who practi–

4. J.N. Farquhar, *Op. Cit.*, p. 183; S.R. Bhatt, *The Philosophy of Pāñcarātra*, p. 10.

cally usurps the place of the lord in relation to the world. If the supreme deity were the only reality and were not related to the changing world, naturally one would conclude that the supreme being is only real and the world is not real, but only phenomenal. In order to avoid complicacies they try to maintain that the Śakti is an aspect of the supreme being in his immanent form ; that Śakti 'divine power' of the lord, is called *svātantrya śakti* which forms his own self '*atmabhūta*' and reveals itself or becomes determinate at the hour of need.

The relation of the supreme reality with Lakṣmī is variously put by the Pāñcarātrins. The Brahman possesses the highest power and this power aspect is deified in the goddess Lakṣmī. The relation between god and his Śakti is that of total inseparable, non-distinguishable absolute unity ; this Śakti can neither be affirmed nor negated ; it is regarded as neither real nor unreal, neither *śānta* 'unmanifest' nor *udita* 'manifest' nor *madhyma* 'middle' position among the two

न शान्ता नोदिता नापि मध्यमाहं चिदात्मिका ।

[Lakṣmī Tantra 4, 2]

They also mean to say that it has *bhāva* 'subsistence' but not *sattā* 'existence'. The idea of her subsistence without existence can be marked from the comment of *Ahirbudhnya Saṁhitā* (3, 2)

स्वरूपे नैव दृश्यन्ते दृश्यन्ते कार्यतस्तु ताः ।।

The mutual relation between the ultimate reality and Lakṣmī is described to be one of inseparable connection or inherence like that of an attribute and its bearer, substance and that which subsists, 'I' ness and 'I' etc. ; because of their *avinābhāva* 'unbroken association' and *ṣamavāya* 'inherence' the relation between them is regarded as identical. The relation of Lakṣmī with the lord is better illustrated in the Jayākhya Saṁhitā (6, 78) where it is said that Lakṣmī is inseparably connected with the lord as the rays with the sun and the waves with the ocean—

सूर्यस्य रश्मयो यद्वत ऊर्मयोश्चाम्वुधेरिव ।
सर्वैश्वर्य प्रभावेन कमला श्रीपतेः तथा ॥

In the Lakṣmī Tantra (2, 17ff) she describes herself in this way, 'I am its supreme Śakti, *Ahaṁtā*, eternal and unchanging. My activity is of the nature of desire to create (*Sisṛkṣā*). I create of my own independent power, by means of a myriad part of myself. I become two kinds of beings, the knower and the known, *citśakti* being the enlightener of both[5]. The Ahirbudhnya Saṁhitā states that Lakṣmī and Brahman are said to be one, who do not differ in denotation rather in connotation ; they stand in relation between Śakti and *Śaktimat*, and hence one cannot be conceived without the other.

Lakṣmī, who is conceived to be the creative principle, is called *ānanda* 'bliss' which does not depend on anything (*nirapekṣatayānanda*) ; as it is not limited to time, it is eternal (*nitya*) ; because it is not limited by any form, it is complete (*pūrṇa*) and because it manifests itself as the world it is called Lakṣmī—

जगत्तया लक्ष्यमाणा सा लक्ष्मीरिति गीयते ।

(Ahirbudhnya Saṁhitā 3, 9)

As it contracts itself into the form of the world, it is called *Kuṇḍalinī* (st. 12) as the supreme power of Viṣṇu it is V*iṣṇuśakti* (st. 11). Though the power in reality is different from Brahman, still it appears as one with it. It is this *Viṣṇu Śakti* or Lakṣmī which impels the *avyakta* 'unmanifest' in to the course of evolution and the *puruṣa* to face the products of *prakṛti* and move through their experiences.[6]

5. *Ahirbudhnya Saṁhitā*, Ch. 3, 7ff.

6. S.N. Dasgupta, *A History of Indian Philosophy*, Vol. III, p. 36.

Lakṣmī is never pictured as a deity having independent existence from her lord, rather she is understood only as an aspect of the supreme Brahman and not as a distinct deity for she is related to the deity as an attribute '*dharma*' to its bearer '*dharmin*' or as sunshine to the sun (Ahirbudhnya Saṁhitā 6, 1ff) and still in order to preserve the transcendent character of the supreme being, Lakṣmī is regarded as the Śakti eternally distinct from the lord. As Schrader[7] rightly remarks, 'inspite of frequent assurances as to the real identity of Lakṣmī and Viṣṇu, the two are actually regarded as distinct : even in *Pralaya* they do not completely coalesce, but become only 'as it were' a single principle (Ahirbudhnya Saṁhitā 4, 78), the Lakṣmī eventually emerging from the Great Night being the old Lakṣmī not a new one. Still he comes to the conclusion, "the dualism is strictly speaking, a makeshift for preserving the transcendent character of Viṣṇu : Lakṣmī alone acts, but everything she does is the mere expression of the Lord's wishes". Thus it seems that the supreme being is related to the world through his Śakti, which is so distinct from its own nature that though she is engaged in creation, sustenance and absorption of the world, its essential nature always remains unchanged.

This Śakti, is said to have two-fold nature as *Kriyā*, 'dynamic activity' and *bhūti* 'determining being'—

लक्ष्मीमयः समुन्मेषः सा द्विधा व्यवतिष्ठते ।

क्रियाभूतिविभेदेन······ (Ahirbudhnya Saṁhitā 3, 28)

the latter being the result of the former, This dynamic activity is variously designated like Lakṣmī, *Saṁkalpa* 'desire' or *Svātantrya mūla icchā* ; this activity which is also called *vidyā*, at the time of creation showers itself as rain and produces foodstuff and during dissolution expresses itself as a drying force.[8] This energy is differently designated like Gaurī, Sarasvatī, Dhenu etc. (Ahirbudhnya saṁhitā 3,13f).

7. Schrader, Op. Cit., p, 30f.
8. Dasgupta, Op. Cit., p. 49ff ; *Ahirbudhnya Saṁhitā*, 7, 60-61.

Lakṣmī and the Creation

The essental part of the Pāñcarātra theology centers round the ideology of the creation which includes three phases viz., Pure or Higher, Impure or Intermediate, and the Secondary creation. As it is closely knit with the story of creation where Lakṣmī plays the vital role, it is desirable to deal with it to trace the part played by her.

The cause of creation according to Lakṣmī Tantra (2,11f) is '*sisṛkṣā*' his will to be or the desire to create. In the last part of the cosmic night '*Pauruṣī rātri* (Lakṣmī Tantra 4,5) the great śakti of the lord which was existing in a form of 'darkness or emptiness' awakens as it were at his command, opens her eyes '*unmeṣa*' is like the appearance of lightning in the sky; this *unmeṣa* 'opening of eyes' flashes out from the motionless ocean suddenly by some independent resolve (*kasmāccit svātantryāt*) by means of a myriad part of herself in her dual aspect of *Kriyā* 'acting', and *bhūti* 'becoming' i.e. Force and Matter—

या सा शक्तिर्महासत्ता विष्णोस्तद्धर्मधर्मिणी ।
तस्याः कोट्यर्बुदांशेन शक्ती द्वे कथिते तव ।। 7 ।।
भूतिश्चेति क्रिया चेति भाव्यभावकसंज्ञिते ।। 8a ।।

(Ahirbudhnya Saṁhitā 14,7-8a)

The *kriyā śakti* of Lakṣmī is the *sudarśana*

······या क्रियाशक्तिर्लक्ष्म्याः सौदर्शनी कला ।।

(Ahirbudhnya Saṁhitā 3,45b; cf.5,12).

It is identical with Viṣṇu's 'Will to be'. The *Kriyā śakti* is independent of space and time in contrast to the *bhūti śakti* which is limited by space and time is divided in many ways. So Viṣṇu, *kriyāśakti* and *bhūtiśakti* are respectively the 'causa efficiens', 'causa instrumentalis; and the 'causa materialis of the world. As the transcendent aspect of the Lord remains in the back ground in the matter of creation, the practical part, however is played by Lakṣmī who as *bhūtiśakti* appears as the universe and as *kriyāśaktī* vitalises and governs it. This *kriyā śakti* or *Sudarśana* is called Viṣṇu's resolve consisting of life—

प्राणरूपो विष्णोः संकल्प (Ahirbudhnya Saṁhitā 3, 30)

> 'that which keeps existence a-going', '*bhūti parivartaka*—(3,29) 'makes becoming possible', *bhūtim sambhāvayati* (3,32), at the time of creation it joins primordial matter to the faculty of evolving, time to the work of counting and the soul to the effort for enjoyment; preserves all these as long as the world lasts; and withdraws the said faculties at the time of dissolution. "just as a fire or a cloud is kept moving by the wind, even so is the *vibhūti* part of Śakti impelled by *Sudarśana*".[9]

In the first phase of the manifestation, *Śuddhasṛṣṭi* 'pure creation' in association with Lakṣmī who is said to be lying in dormant before creation, Nārāyaṇa the Supreme being passes from its transcendent and undifferentiated form to the personal form characterised by six *guṇas* 'ideal qualities' viz; *jñāna*, 'knowledge', *aiśvarya* 'sovereignty', *śakti* 'potency', *bala* 'strength', *vīrya* 'virility' and *tejas* 'splendour or might.' These ideal qualities do not belong to nature but in their totality make up the body of Lakṣmi and also of the immanent aspect of the supreme being Para—Vāsudeva the highest personal God. These qualities express the Pāñcarātra concept of a supreme God-

षाड्गुण्यविग्रहं देवं तादृश्या च श्रिया युतम् ।

[Ahirbudhnya Saṁhita. 6, 25a]

> These six ideal qualities fall under two main groups; the first three *guṇas-jñāna, aiśvarya* and *śakti* form the group of *viśrāmbhūmayaḥ* 'stages of rest' which are innate in the being and the rest three- *bala, vīrya* and

9. *Sudarśana*, which represents the *kriyā śakti of* Lakṣmī is well-illustrated in the Ch. 3 of *Ahirbudhnya Saṁhitā* and its role in the creation of the world is described; it is defined in a nut-shell as the 'will embodied in wisdom and resulting in action'. F.O. Schrader. Op. Cit. p. 102.

tejas make up the *śramabhumayaḥ* 'stages of action' which impells others to act. However the evolution of these qualities does not affect the 'being' or essence of the transcendent being, for it merely concerns its 'becoming' or 'manifestation' i.e. its *śakti*. The six qualities in their totality are the material or instruments, as it were of pure creation.

The Pāñcarātra teachers try to explain the evolution of the 3 *Vyūhas* 'emanations' (including Vāsudeva, four) through these three pairs of *Guṇas*; these *Vyūhas* are designated after the elder brother, the son and the grandson of Kṛṣṇa respectively, namely—Saṁkarṣaṇa(or Balarāma, *Baladeva*), Pradyumna and Aniruddha and the pairs of *Guṇas* connected with these are—*jñana* and *bala* ; *aiśarya* and *Vīrya*. *śakti* and *tejas* respectively. Thus these separate powers of the Lord are observable only when they manifest themselves, but when they do not manifest, they exist in the supreme being as its śakti, Lakṣmī.

The universe is a manifestation of Lakṣmī and she is absolutely independent in converting her will into action. Lakṣmī has also fivefold[10] functions (*Karmapañcakam*) namely *sṛṣṭi* 'creation' *sthiti* 'preservation', *saṁhṛti* 'destruction' *anugraha* 'favour, grace' and *tirobhāva* 'disfavour'.

तिरोभावस्तथा सृष्टिः स्थितिः संहृतिरेव च ।। 13b
अनुग्रह इति प्रोक्तं मदीयं कर्मपंचकम् ।14a

Lakṣmī Tantra 12. 13b-14b

(Cf. Ahirbudhnya Saṁhitā 21, 12-13), through which she prepares and predetermines the fate of the soul. These are also called her five śaktis as they sum up in different ways in which she exercises her power of action. The Brahman as associated with its Śakti is called the highest Viṣṇu as distinguished from the lower Viṣṇu the god of maintenance. This Śakti of the Lord is always in a state of internal agitation, though it may not be observed

10. Sanjukta Gupta has explained these five functions of Lakṣmī in a clear-cut manner, Op. Cit., Introduction p. xxviff.

from its outward appearance; such internal agitation is so subtle that it appears to be in a state of absolute calmness like that of the ocean (Ahirbudhnya Saṁhitā 51, 49-50). This Śakti is also called the *Māyā* of Viṣṇu (Ahirbudhnya Saṁhitā 51, 58). At the time of great dissolution all effects are reduced to a dormant stage without the movement of any kind. All the six divine qualities of the Lord are in a state of absolute calmness like the sky without a puff of air. This collection of power in a state of calmness is Lakṣmī which exists as it were like the very void indistinguishable from the Lord[11] and these six qualities form her body at the time of creation.

Lakṣmī and her Incarnations

Apart from her relation with the Lord as the active principle of creation there are different accounts of Lakṣmī's incarnations for the fulfilment of her purpose. These incarnations are of two kinds; firstly Lakṣmī assumes incarnations which follow the Lord in his different forms or in his corresponding incarnations; but there are exclusive incarnations of Lakṣmī unaccompanied by God's manifested descent on earth as his spouse or partner.

Different Saṁhitās speak of different manifestations of Lakṣmī, the Śakti of Viṣṇu—Jayākhya Saṁhitā (6, 77), Lakṣmī Tantra (8, 22) and Śrīpraśna Saṁhitā (50, 60) mention four manifestations of Lakṣmī; they are Śrī, Kīrti, Jayā and Māyā; these four forms of Lakṣmi act as consorts of the *Vyūhas* viz., Vāsudeva, Saṅkarṣaṇa, Pradyumna and Aniruddha respectively. The eight incarnations of Lakṣmī as described in the Vihagendra Saṁhitā (3,5) are—Śrī, Kīrti, Vijayā, Śraddhā, Smṛti, Medhā, Dhṛti and Karuṇā. The twelve forms of the Śakti as enumerated in the Lakṣmī Tantra (8, 26, 27) are Śrī, Kāmeśvarī, Kānti, Kriyā, Śakti,

11. Schrader, Op. Cit., p. 50.

Vibhūti, Icchā, Prīti, Rati, Māyā, Dhī and Mahīman and follow the Lord as usual.

Apart from her different incarnations followed by Nārāyaṇa, Lakṣmī had her own exclusive incarnations which are described in Lakṣmī Tantra (Ch. 9,1) in an exhaustive manner. In the beginning of creation Lakṣmī manifests herself as Mahālakṣmī and then she becomes two by assuming two forms—Kṛṣṇā and Brāhmī. These three forms—mahālakṣmī, Kṛṣṇā and Brāhmī are her supreme manifestations according to her three *guṇas—sattva*, *rajas* and *tamas* (Vs. 7-8). Later on Mahālakṣmī appears in different forms for the destruction of different demons or wicked spirits who cause concern to the gods and others.

As like the Devī Māhātmya of Mārkaṇḍeya Purāṇa (9, 50ff) describing the nine incarnations of Devī, the enumeration of these very nine incarnations of Lakṣmī in her manifested form appears in the Lakṣmī Tantra. Out of these nine incarnations described in both the texts, the three incarnations —Mahiṣāmardinī, Yogindrā (Mahākāli) and Kauṣikī appeared in the past and the other six manifestations of Lakṣmī to appear in the future years to come are—Sunandā (Vindhyavāsinī), Raktadantikā, Śākambharī, Durgā, Bhīmā and Bhrāmarī. In the Devī Māhātmya, the appropriate details of different episodes connected with her different manifestations are related, but in the Lakṣmī Tantra, the episodes are simply hinted at without going into detail. The four Stutis[12]—*Brahmā Stuti, Śakrādi Stuti, Viṣṇumāyā Stuti* and *Nārāyaṇī Stuti*, which help us to know much about the nature of the Sakti worship in the purāṇic age are simply mentioned here. The story of Svāroci and Suratha of Devī Māhātmya (9, 50) is also referred to here. The present text seems to be a later adaptation of Devī Māhātmya of Mārkeṇḍeya Purāṇa by the redactor of Lakṣmī Tantra when the worship of Mahālakṣmī came into vogue.

12. While delivering his speech on Śākta cult, J.N. Banerjee has tried to discuss the importance of Devī Mahātmya through these Stutis and has shown their contribution towards the development of Śākta cult. *Purāṇic and Tantric Religion* (Early phase), p. 121ff.

Like the Devī Māhātmya, the Lakṣmī Tantra 9, 8ff describes the individual incarnations of Lakṣmī thus: During the reign of Svāyambhuva (Manu) for the destruction of the demon Mahiṣa, Mahālakṣmī appeared as Mahiṣāmardinī. The elements of her Śakti inherent in each god combined to constitute her form and the Śaktis belonging to the special weapons of each god turned into her weapon and in that form she slew the demon Mahiṣa (Vs. 9-14). Yoganidrā is that Śakti in the form of Mahākālī. When Madhu and Kaiṭabha oppressed Brahmā they were killed by Lakṣmī in the form of Yoganidrā (Vs. 15-19) In the period of Tāmasa (Manu), she, the supreme Mahāvidyā was Kauṣikī, who sprang from Gaurī to slay all those notorious demons including Śumbha and Niśumbha and rescued the worlds and the gods from their oppression (Vs. 20-27).

During the period of Vaivaśvata (Manu), when these demons, Śumbha and Niśumbha will be reborn and will torment the gods, she in the form of Sunandā, daughter of Yaśodā in the family of the cowherd Nanda will slay them while residing in the Vindhya mountain. When she will kill the mighty demons of Vipracitta lineage, and will devour these, her teeth will become red as the flowers of the pomegranate tree. Then she will be called as Raktadantikā (the Red-toothed one) (Vs. 29-32). In the shape of the goddess Durgā, she will slay the demon (Vs. 36) Durga. In the fiftieth era when she will be born as Bhimā on the Himalayas, she will devour the demons and will protect the sages from them (Vs. 39-41). During the sixtieth era, when the demon, Aruṇa will oppress the sages and other people, she will then appear in bee-form incorporating inumerable bees and will slay the demon. So she will be renowned as Bhrāmarī (Vs. 41-43).

Apart from her terrible form, she also assumed blissful forms to nourish the whole world. During fortieth era, when drought and scarcity of water will prevail all over the earth causing the loss of life, she will assume the form of Śākambharī (the embodiment of vegetation) and save the world with wonderful life-sustaining plants issuing from her own body.

In the above account, we come across her peaceful and awful forms, her saviour aspects as well as of her other features. In the Lakṣmī Tantra (Ch. 9, 28f) Śrī narrates her various future manifestations in different ages for destroying the evil-doers and for sustaining the world. In course of her assurance in the Bhagavadgītā vein she states the purpose of her incarnations thus :

इत्थं यदा यदा बाधा दानवोत्था भविष्यति ।
तदा तदावतीर्याहं हनिष्यामि महासुरान् ॥ 44॥

[Lakṣmī Tantra 9, 44]

"Thus on each occasion the demons disturb the earth, I shall descend (on the earth) to kill these powerful demons."

Bibliography

A. Texts and Translation

1. Vedic Works

(a) *Saṁhitās*

ṚgVeda Saṁhītā : Ṛg Veda Saṁhitā with the commentary of Sāyaṇācārya, ed. N. S. Sontakke, C.G. Kasikar and others, 5 Volumes, Vaidika Saṁśodhana Mandal, Poona, 1933-51.

Ṛg Veda Saṁhitā ed. by MaxMuller, 6 Volumes, London, 1849-74. Die Hymen Des Rigveda, ed. Theodor Aufrecht, 2 volumes, Wiesbaden, 1955.

Der RigVeda, by Karl Friedrich Geldner, 3 Volumes, Harvard Oriental Series, 33-35, Camb.-Mass. 1951.

The Hymns of the ṚgVeda, Tr. Ralph T. H. Griffith, 2 Volumes, Fourth Edn., Varanasi, 1963.

Sāma Veda Saṁhitā: SāmaVeda Ed. Bhattacharya Srīpada Sharma Santavalekara, Bombay, 1956.

The Sama Veda Saṁhitā (English translation) by Rev. J. Stevenson, Varanasi, 1961.

Kopiṣṭala-Kaṭha Saṁhitā : Ed. Raghuvira, Delhi, 1968.

Kāṭhaka Saṁhītā Ed. D. Santavalekar Bombay, 1946.

Maitrāyaṇī Saṁhitā — Yajurvedīya-Maitrāyaṇī-Saṁhitā, ed. S. Sharma Satavalekar, Aundh, 1942 (Vs 1998)

Taittirīya Saṁhitā : — Kṛṣṇa—Yajurvedīya Taittirīya Saṁhitā ed. S. Sharma Satavalekar, 2nd Edn., Bombay, 1957 (Vs 2013).

The Veda of the Block Yajus school entitled Taittirīya Saṁhitā. Translated by A. B. Keith Harvard Oriental Series, 18-19, Camb.—Mass. 1914 Delhi 1967.

Kāṇva Saṁhitā : — Śukla Yajurvedīya-Kāṇva-Saṁhitā ed. by S. Sharma Satavalekar, Aundh 1941 (Vs 1997).

Vājosaneyī Saṁhitā : — Vājasaneyī— Mādhyandina— Śukla Yajurveda Saṁhitā, ed. by Satavalekar, Paradi 1957 (Vs 2013).

The Texts of the white Yajurveda, by Ralph T. R. Griffith, third edition, Banaras, 1957.

Atharva Veda : — Atharva Veda Saṁhitā published by Arya Sahitya Mandala, Ajmer, 1957. Atharva Veda Saṁhitā, Translated by W. D. Whitney and edited by C. R. Lanman, 2 Volumes, Harvard Oriental Series 7-8, Camb.-Mass, 1905.

(b) Brāhmaṇas, Āraṇyakas and Upaniṣds

Aitareya-Brāhmaṇa — Aitareya Brāhmaṇa with the commentary of Sāyaṇa, ed. V. G. Apte, Ānandāsharma Sanskrit Series, .32, Poona, 1930-31.

Ṛg Veda Brāhmaṇas : the Aitareya and Kauṣitakī Brahmaṇas of the Ṛg-

Veda, Tr. By A. B, Keith, Harvard Oriental Series, 25, Camb.-Mass, 1920.

Jāiminīya Brāhmaṇa ; Jaiminīya Brāhmaṇa of Sāma Veda ed. Raghuvira and Lokesh Chandra, Nagpur, 1954.

Tāṇdya-Mahābrāhmaṇa: Sāmavedīya-Tāṇḍya (Pañcaviṁśa) Brāhmaṇa with the commentary of Sāyaṇa ed. Chinnaswami Sastri, 2 Volumes, Kasi Sanskrit Series, 105, Banaras, 1935-36.

Pañcaviṁśa Brāhmaṇa Tr. W. Caland. Calcutta. 1931.

Taittirīya-Brāhmaṇa : Kṛṣṇa - Yajurvedīya Taittirīya-Brāhmaṇa with the commentary of Sāyaṇācārya, ed. H. N. Apte, 3 Volumes, Ānandāshrama Saskrit Series, 37, Poona, 1898.

Śatapatha-Brāhmaṇa: Srimad - Vājasaneyī - Mādhyandina-Śatapatha - Brāhmaṇa with the commentary of Sāyaṇa, ed. A. Weber, 2nd edn. Varanasi, 1964.

The Śatapatha Brāhmaṇa, Tr. by Julious Eggeling, 5 Volumes, Sacred Books of the East, 12, 26,41, 43, 44, Delhi, 1963.

Gapatha-Brāhmaṇa: Gopatha Brāhmaṇa of AtharvaVeda ed. by Rajendra Lal Mitra, Delhi, 1972.

Aitareya-Āraṇyaka : Aitareya-Āraṇyaka, Ānandashrama Sanskrit Series, 38 Poona, 1959.

Śankhāyaṇa-Āraṇyaka : Śāṇkhāyana-Āraṇyaka,Ānandāsharma Sanskrit Series, Poona, 1922, Tr. A.

B. Keith, The Royal Asiatic Society, London, 1908.

Taittirīya-Āraṇyaka : Taittirīya Āraṇyaka with the commentary of Sāyaṇa, ed. V.G. Apte-Ānandāshrama Sanskrit Series, 36,2 Volumes, Poona, 1927.

Iśādyaṣṭottaraśatopaniṣad: Nirnaya Sagar Press, Bombay 1927. The Śākta Upanisads, Translated into English by A. G. Krishna Warrier, Adyar, 1967.

(c) *Sūtras*

Āpastamba-Śrauta-Sūtra : Ed. A. Chinnaswami Sastri, Oriental Institute, Baroda, 1955.

Śaṅkhayana-Śrouta-Sūtra : With the commentary of Varadattasuta Anartiya, Ed. Alfred Hille brandt in Bibliotheca Indica, Calcutta, 1888.

Agniveśya Gṛhya-Sūtra : Ed. L. R. Ravivarma, Trivandram, 1940.

Bhāradvāja-Gṛhya-Sūtra : Ed. H. J. W. Salomons, Leyden, 1913.

Bodhāyana-Gṛhya Sūtra: Ed. Sharma Sastri, Mysore, 1926.

Drāhyāyana-Gṛhya-Sūtra : Ed. H. N. Apte Anandsharma Sanskrit Series, Poona, 1914.

Gobhila-Gṛhya-Sutra . Ed, Chintamani Bhattachrya, Calcutta, 1936.

Kāṭhaka-Gṛhya-Sūtra : Ed. W. Calend, Utrechi, 1925.

Kauśika-Sūtra : Ed. Thankur Udaya Narayana Singh, Muzaffarpur, 1942.

Kauṣitaka-Gṛhya-Sūtra : With the commentary of Bhavatrāta, ed. T. R. Chintamani, Madras 1944.

Mānava Gṛhya-Sūtra : Ed. Ramkrishna Harshaji, Gaekawad's Oriental Series, Vol. XXXV, Baroda 1926.

Pāraskara-Gṛhya-Sūtra : Venkateshwar Press, 1938.

Śāṅkhāyana-Gṛhya-Sūtra : Ed. S. K. Sehgal, Delhi, 1960

Vaikhānasa-Gṛhya Sūtra : Ed. W. Caland, Utrecht 1926

The Grihya Sutra, Tr. by H. Oldenberg, Part I & II, Sacred Books, of the East, 29, 30 Motilal Banarsidas, Delhi, 1967.

Baudhayāna-Dharma-Sūtra: With the commentary of Govinda Swamin, ed. by L. Srinivasacharya, Mysore 1907.

Viṣṇu Smṛti : With the Sanskrit commentary of Nanda Pandit called Vaijayanti, ed. Julius Jolly, Calcutta 1881 reprinted Chowkhamba Sanskrit Series 95 Varanasi 1962. The Institutes of Viṣṇu Tr. Julius Jolly, Sacred Books of the East, 7, Delhi 1970.

(d) *Other Works of Vedic Literature*

Bṛhaddevatā: The Bṛhaddevatā of Śaunaka, critically edited and translated by A.A. Macdonell, Part I: Introduction, Text and Appendices, Part II: Translation and Notes, Harvard Oriental Series. 4,6, Camb.- Mass. 1904, New Delhi 1956.

Nighanṭu and Nirukta : Edited and translated by Laksman Sarup, 2 parts University of Punjab, 1927.

Ṛgvidhāna : The Ṛgvidhāna, Tr. by J. Gonda, Utrecht 1951.

2. *Epics and Purāṇas*

a) *Epics*

Mahābhārata; The Mahābhārata, critically edited by V.S. Sukthankar, S.K. Belvalkar, Poona 1933 ff.

Rāmāyaṇa: The Vālmikī Rāmāyaṇa critically edited by G.H. Bhatt, G.C. Jhala & others, Vols. 1-5, Oriental Institute, Baroda 1960ff.

for Vols. 6-7 references are made to the Gita Press edition, Gorakhpur Vs 2017.

b) Purāṇa

Agni-Purāṇa: Ed. M. C. Apte, Ānandāshrama Sanskrit Series, 41, Poona 1957. Prose English translation of Agni Purana, by M.N. Dutta, 2 Volumes Calcutta 1903-4

Bhāgavata Purāṇa: With the commentary of Śrīdhara, P. Ramateja Sastri, Pandita-Pustakā laya, Varanasi Vs 2019 (1963).

Bhaviṣya-Purāṇa Venkateshwar Press, Bombay 1959.

Brahma-Purāṇa: Ed. H. N. Apte, Ānandāshrama Sanskrit Series 28, Poona 1895.

Brahmavaivarta-Purāṇa: Ed. V.G. Apte, 2 Volumes, Ānandāshrama Sanskrit Series 102, Poona 1935.

Brahmāṇḍa-Purāṇa: Venkateshwar Press Bombay Vs 1992 (1936)

Dev*ībhāgavata-Purāṇa* : Pandita-Pustakalaya, Kasi 2026 (1969).

Garuḍa-Purāṇa : Ed. Ramshankar Bhattāchārya, Varanasi 1964.

Prose English translation of Garuḍa Purāṇa, by M. N. Dutta, Calcutta 1908.

Harivaṁśa : The Harivaṁśa critically edited by P. L. Vaidya, 2 volumes, Bhandarkar Oriental Research Institute, Poona 1969ff.

Kālikā-Purāṇa : Ed. Biswanarayan Sastri, Varanasi 1972.

Kūrma-Pūrāṇa ; Venkateshwar Press, Bombay, VS 1962 (1906).

Liṅga-Purāṇa : Ed. Jivānanda Vidyāsāgara Bhattācharya, Calcultta 1885.

Mārkaṇḍeya-Purāṇa : Ed. Jivānanda Vidyāsāgara Bhattāchārya, Calcutta. 1879.

The Mārkaṇḍeya Purāṇa—Translated by F. E. Pargiter, Indological Book House, Varanasi 1969.

Matsya-Purāṇa : Ed. Jivānanda Vidyāsāgara Bhattāchārya, Calculta 1876.

The Matsya Purāṇa—Translated by Taluqdar of Oudh, Allahabad 1916.

Devī *Māhātmya* : Durgāsaptaśati of Mārkaṇḍeya-Purāṇa, Gita Press, Gorakhapur Vs 2027.

Nārada-Purāṇa : Venkateshwar Press, Bombay VS 1962 (1906).

Padma-Purāṇa Ed. M.C. Apte, 4 Volumes, Ānandāshrama Sanskrit Series, 131. Poona 1893-4.

Purāṇa-Pañcalakṣaṇa : Das Purāṇa Pañcalakṣaṇa by Willibald Kirfel, Leiden 1927.

Śiva-Purāṇa : Ed. Ramateja Sastri, Pandita Pustakalaya, Kasi, Samvat 2020.

Skanda-Puraṇa : Venkateshwar Press, Bombay VS 1966 (1910).

Vāmaṇa-Purāṇa : Critically edited with English translation by A. S. Gupta, All India Kashiraja Trust, Varanasi 1968.

Vārāha-Purāṇa : Venkateshwar Press, Bombay VS 1959 (1903).

Vāyu-Purāṇa : Venkateshwar Press, Bombay.

Viṣṇu Purāṇa: Gita Press, Gorkhapur VS 2026 (1969).

The 'Vishnu Purāṇa-Translated by H.H. Wilson, third edn., Calcutta 1961.

Viṣṇudharmottara Purāṇa: Venkateshwar Press, Bombay Vs 1969 (1913).

The Viṣṇudharmottara (Part III) A Treatise on Indian Painting and Image-making, by Stella Kramrisch, second revised and enlarged edn., Calcutta University, Calcutta 1928.

3. *Other Texts*

a) Secular Literature

Arthaśāstra: Arthaśāstra of Kautilya Ed. by J. Jolly and R. Schmidt, 2 volumes, Lahore 1923-24

Kāmasūtra : The Kāma Sūtra of Vātsyāyana

with the Jayamaṅgalā Sanskrit Commentary of Yaśodhara, Varanasi 1964.

Nāṭya-Śāstra: Nātya Śastra of Bharata, with the commentary of Abhinavagupta, 3 vols., M.R. Kavi, Gaekwad's Oriental Series 36, 68, 124, Baroda 1956, 1934 and 1954. Tr. Manmohan Ghosh, Asiatic Society of Bengal, Calcutta, 1951.

(*b*) *Smṛtis*

Durgotsava-Viveka : Durgotsavaviveka of Śūlapāṇi, Sanskrit Sahitya Parisad, Calcutta 1331 (1924).

Kālasāra : Kālasāra of Gadādhara Rājaguru, Bamanda, 1898.

Manusmṛti : Manusmṛti with the 'Manubhāṣya' of Medhātithi, Ed. by Ganganatha Jha, Bibliotheca Indica, 256, Calcutta 1932 ff.

Tr. G. Buhler, Sacred Books of the East 25, Delhi 1967.

Nirṇaya Sindhu : Nirṇaya Sindhu of Kamalākara Bhatta ed. G. Sastri Nene, 3 volumes, Varanasi 1921 ff.

Rājamārtaṇḍa : Rājamārtaṇḍa of Bhoja, ed. P. V. Kane, Annals of the Bhandarkar Oriental Research Institute 36(1955) pp. 306-339.

Śrī *Vratarāja* : Ed. Viśvanātha Sharma, Venkateshwar Press, Bombay Vs 2010.

(c) *Philosophical works*

Ahirbudhnya Saṁhitā : Ahirbudhnya Saṁhita of Pāñcarātrāgama, Ed. M. D. Ramanujācharya, 2 volumes, 2nd edn., Adyar 1966.

Jayākhya Saṁhitā : Critically ed. by E. Krishnamacharya, Gaekawad's Oriental Series, 54, Baroda 103.

Lakṣmī Tantra : Lakṣmī Tantra, A Pāñcarātra Āgama, ed. by V. Krishnamacharya, Adyar, 1959.

Lakṣmī Tantra, A Pāñcarātra Text, Translation and Notes by Sanjukta Gupta, Leiden 1972.

Sanatkumāra-Saṁhitā : Sanatkumāra Saṁhitā of the Pāñcarātrāgama ed. V. Krishnamacharya, Adyar, 1969.

Śrīpraśna-Saṁhitā : Ed. Mrs. Seetha Padmanabhan, Kendriya Sanskrit Vidyapitha Series No. 12, Tirupati 1969.

(*d*) Other Works

Hastyāyurveda : Ed. Sivadatta Sharma, Ānandāshrama Sanskrit Series 26, Poona 1894.

B. *Dictionary and Index*

Bloomfield, M. *A Vedic Concordance*, Harvard Oriental Series 10, Camb.-Mass. 1906.

Deva, Raja Radhakanta *Sabdakalpadruma,* Varanasi 1961.

Dowson, J. *A Classical Distionary of Hindu Mythology and Religion, History and Culture*, tenth edn. London 1961.

Hastings, J. *Encyclopaedia of Religion and Ethics*, 12 volumes, Edinburg 1908-26.

Jacob, G. A. — A concordance of the Principal Upanishads and Bhagavadgīta, First reprinted, Delhi 1963.

Macdonell, A. A. and Keith A. B. — *Vedic Index of Names and Subjects*, Oxford 1912.

Sastri, Visvabandhu — *Vaidikapadānukramakoṣa*, Viśveśvarānanda Vedic Research Institute, Lahore-Hoshiarpur 1935-62.

Sharma, H. D. and Sardusai H.G. — *Amarakosa* (Nāmaliṅgānuśāsana of Amara Siṅha) with the commentary of Bhatta Kṣiraswāmin, Poona 1941.

Sorensen, S. — *An Index to the Names* in *the Mahābhārata*, New Delhi, 1963.

C. *Secondary Literature*

1. General Works

Agrawala, V. S. — Matsya Purāṇa—a study, Ist Edn., Varanasi 1963.

Aiyangar, Narayana — Essays on Indo-Aryan Mythology, Part I & II, Madras 1961.

Arthur & Ellen Avalon — Hymns to the Goddess, Madras 1964.

Banerjea, J. N. — P*urānic* and Tantric Religion (Early Phase) Calcutta University, Calcutta 1966.

Development of Hindu Iconography 2nd Edn. University of Calcutta, Calcutta 1956.

Earth, A. — The Religions of India (English Translation by Rev. J. Wood), London 1881.

Belvalkar, S. K. and Ranade, R. D. — History of Indian Philosophy, vol II, Poona 1927.

Bhandarkar, R. G. — *Vaiṣṇavism, Śaivism and Minor Religious System*, Strassburg 1913.

Bhatt, S. R. — *The Philosophy of Pāñcharātra* (An Advaitic Approach) Madras 1968.

Bhattacharya, N. N. — *Indian Mother Goddess*, Calcutta 1971

Bhattacharya, B. C. — *Indian Images* Calcutta 1921.

Bhattacharya, B. T. — *The Indian Buddhist Iconogarphy*, Calcutta 1958.

Bhattasali, N. K. — *Iconography of Buddhist and Brahminical Sculptures in the Dacca Museum*, Dacca 1929.

Bloomfield, M. — *Religion of the Veda*, New York 1908.

Briffault, R. — *The Mothers*, A Study of the Origins of Sentiments and Institutions, 3 volumes, London, 1927.

Chakravarty, Chintaharana — *The Tantras, Studies on their Religion and Literature*, Calcutta 1963.

Chakarvarti, P. C. — *Doctrine of Śakti in Indian Literature*, Calcutta, 1940.

Chatterji, S.K., Atreya, Bhikhanlal and Alain, Denielous — *Indian Culture*, Delhi 1966

Colebrooke, H. T. *Essays on the Religion and Philosophy of the Hindus*, Varanasi 1972,

Coomaraswamy, A. K. *The Yakṣas*, Part I & II, reprinted in Delhi 1971.

Cox, George W. *The Mythology of the Aryan Nations*, 3rd Edn., Varanasi, 1963.

Dange, S. A. *Legends in the Mahāhbārata*, Delhi 1969.

Dasgupta, S. N. *A History of Indian Philosophy*, Vol. III, Cambridge University Press, Cambridge 1940.

Dikshit, S. K. *The Mother Goddess*, Poona, 1941.

Dubois, Abbe, Beauchamp, J. A. and Hery, H. *Hindu Manners, Customs and Ceremonies* 3rd Edn., Oxford, 1953.

Eliot, Charles *Hinduism and Buddhism*, 3 volumes, London, 1954.

Enthoven, R.E. *The Folklore of Bombay*, Oxford, 1924.

Farquhar, J. N. *An Outline of the Religious Literature of India*, First Indian Reprint, Delhi, 1967.

Fausboll, V. *Indian Mythology According to the Mahābhārata in Outline*, London 1903.

Frazer, J. *The Golden Bough*, 3rd Edn., New York, 1955.

Gaity, A. *The Gods of Northern Buddhism*, Japan, 1962.

Gonda, J. *Aspects of Early Viṣṇuism*, Utrecht, 1954.

Change and Continuity in Indian Religion, The Hague, 1965.

Sanskrit in Indonesia, Nagpur, 1952.

Harrison, J. *Prolegomena to the Study of Greek*

Religion, New York, 1957.

Hartmann, Gerda — *Beitrage Zur Geschichte der Gottin Laksmi*, Kiel, 1933.

Hasra, R.C. — *Studies in the Purāṇic Records on Hindu Rites and Customs*, University of Dacca (Bulletin No. XX), Dacca, 1940.

Studies in the Upapurāṇas, Vol. I & II, Calcutta Sanskrit College Research Series 2, 22, Calcutta, 1958-63.

Hopkins, E.W. — *Epic Mythology*, Strassburg, 1915.

Religions of India, 2nd Edn, New Delhi, 1970.

Jacobi, H. — *The Rāmāyaṇa*, Translated from German by S. N. Ghosal, Oriental Institute, Baroda, 1960.

Kakati, B. K. — *The Mother Goddess Kāmākhyā*, Gauhati, 1948.

Kane, P. V. — *History of Dharmaśāstra*, 5 volumes, Bhandarkar Oriental Research Institute, Poona, 1930-62.

Kantawala, S.G. — *Cultural History from the Matsya Purāṇa*, Oriental Institute, Baroda, 1964.

Keith, A.B. — *Religion and Philosophy of the Veda and Upanishads*, 2 volumes, Harvard Oriental Series, 31, 32, Camb-Mass. 1925.

History of Sanskrit Literature, London, 1953.

Kosambi, D.D. — *Introduction to the study of Indian History*, Bombay, 1956.

Myth and Reality, Bombay, 1962.

The Culture and Civilization of Ancient India, London, 1965.

Kumarappa, Bharatan — *Hindu conception of the Deity*, London, 1934.

Levi, Sylvain — *Sanskrit texts from Bali*, Baroda, 1933.

Macdonell, A.A. — *Vedic Mythology*, Strassburg, 1897.

Majumdar, R.C. and Pusalker, A.D. — History and Culture of the Indian People Vol. I—*The Vedic Age*, 5th. impression, Bombay, 1971.
Vol. II—*The Age of Imperial Unity*, 4th. impression, Bombay. 1968.
Vol.III—*The Classical Age*, 3 rd Impression, Bombay, 1970.
Bharatiya Vidya Bhavan, Bombay.

Meyer, J. J. — *Trilogie der altindischen Machte und Feste der Vegetation*, Zurich-Leipzig, 1937.

Morgan, K. W. — *The Basic Belief of Hinduism*, Indian Edition, Calcutta, 1955.

Pai, D.A. — *Monograph on the Religious Sect in India Among the Hindus*, Bombay, 1928.

Pandey, R.B. — *Hindu Saṁskāras*, 2nd Edn., Delhi, 1969.

Pargiter, F.E. — *Ancient Indian Historical Tradition*, Oxford, 1922.

Patil, D.R. — *Cultural History from the Vāyu Purāṇa*, Poona, 1946.

Payne, Ernest A. — *The Śaktas, An introductory and comparative Study*, Calcutta, 1933.

Pischel Richard and Geldner, F. Karl. — *Vedische Studien*, 2 volumes, Stuttgart, 1889.

Pusalker, A.D. — *Studies in Epics and Purāṇas of India*, Bombay, 1963.

Radhakrishnan, S. — *Indian Philosophy*, Vol. II, 8th impression, London, 1966.

Ram Gopal — *India of Vedic Kalpasūtras*, Delhi, 1959.

Rao, T.A.G. — *Elements of Hindu Iconography*, Vol. I, Part II, Second Edn., Delhi, 1968.

Sir Subrahmanya Ayyar Lectures on the History of Śrī Vaiṣṇavas, University of Madras, Madras, 1923.

Raychaudhuri, H. C. — *Materials for the study of the Early History of the Vaishnava Sect*, Calcutta University, Calcutta, 1936.

Ray Govind Chandra — *Prācīna Bhāratmeṅ Lakṣmī Pratimā (eka adhyayana)* (Hindi) Varanasi, 1968.

Ruping, Klaus — *Amṛtamanthana und Kūrma Avatāra*, Ein Beitrag zur Puranischen Mythen und Religions gechichate, Wiesbaden, 1970.

Sastri, H. Krishna — *South Indian Images of Gods and Goddesses*, Madras, 1916.

Sastri, K. A. Nilakantha — *Cultural contacts between Aryans and Dravidians*, Bombay 1967.

Schrader, F. OTTO — *Introduction to the Pāñcarāta and the Ahirbudhnyna Saṁhitā*, Adyar, 1916.

Sen, Asis — *Animal Motifs in Ancient Indian Art*, Calcutta, 1972.

Sengupta, Sankar (Ed.) — *Tree Symbol Worship in India*, Calcutta, 1965.

Sircar, D.C. (Ed.) — *Foreigners in Ancient India and Lakṣmī and Sarasvatī in Art and Literature*, Calcutta University, Calcutta, 1970.

Taimni, I.K. — *An Introduction to Hindu Symbolism*, Adyar, 1965.

Tod, J. — *Annals and Antiquities of Rajasthan*, vol. I, New Delhi, 1971.

Underhill, M.M. *The Hindu Religious Year*, Calcutta, 1921.

Vaidya, C. V. *The Mahābhārata : A Criticism*, Delhi, 1966.

Whitehead, H. *The Village Gods of South India*, Calcutta, 1921.

Wilson, H.H. *Sketch of the Religious Sects of Hindus*, London, 1861.

Winternitz, M. *A History of Indian Literature*, Vol. I & II, Part I, Calcutta University, 1927 and 1933.

Zimmer, H. *Myths and Symbols in Indian Art and Civilisation*, New York, 1953.

2. Select Articles

Agrawala, V.S. 'Padminī Vidyā of the Mārkaṇḍeya Purāṇa', *Purāṇa*', Vol. I, No. 2 (1960), pp. 181-197.

'A difficult passage in the Panchatantra : Lakshmi-Vidambanam', *J. N. Banerjea Volume*, Calcutta University, Calcutta, 1960, pp. 178-189.

Agrawala, P.K. Skanda in the Purāṇas and Classical Literature', *Purāṇa*, Vol. viii, No. 1 (1966), pp. 135-158.

Banerjea, J.N. 'The Representation of Sūrya in Brahmanical Art', *Indian Antiquary* 54 (1925) pp. 161-171.

'Some folk Goddesses of Ancient and medieval India', *Indian Historical Quarterly*, Vol. XIV, (1938) pp. 101-9.

'Padminī Vidyā', *Journal of the Indian Society of Oriental Art*, Vol. IX (1941), pp. 141-146.

Bedekar, V. M. 'The Legend of the Churning of the Ocean in the Epics and the Purāṇas : A comparative Study', *Purāṇa*. Vol. IX, No. 1 (1967), pp.

7-61.

Bhattacharyya, A. 'The cult of Ṣaṣṭhī in Bengal', *Man in India*, Vol. XXVIII, (1948) pp. 152-62.

'The tiger cult and its literature in lower Bengal', *Man in India*, Vol. XXVII, (1947), pp. 44-56.

Chatterji, S. K. 'A Brahminical Deity in Indo-China and Indonesia', *J. N. Banerjea Volume*, Calcutta Univeristy, Calcutta 1960 pp. 86 92

Choudhuri, N. N. 'Goddess Lakṣmī in the Purāṇa and Tantra, *The Poona Orientalist*, Vol. XIII, Nos. 1-2 (1948) pp. 1—6.

'Mother Goddess Durgā', *The Poona Orientalist* Vol. XV (1952).

Coomaraswamy, A. K. 'Early Indian Iconography II, Śrī-Lakṣmī'. Eastern Art, Vol. 1 (1929), pp. 175—89.

'Origin of the Lotus (so-called Bell Capital), *Indian Historical Quarterly* Vol. IV (1930), pp. 373—375.

Dandekar, R. N. 'Some Aspects of the Indo-Mediterranean Contacts,' *Annals of the Bhandarkar Oriental Research Institute* Vol. L, Parts I-V, Poona (1959) pp. 56—74.

Das, S.R. 'A study of the Vrata Rites of Bengal', *Man in India*, vol. XXXII, No. 4, (1952), pp. 207-245.

Dasgupta, Mrinal 'Early Vaiṣṇavism and Nārāyaṇīya Worship', *Indian Historical Quarterly*, Vol. VII (1931) pp. 93-116 ; 343-358; 655-679 ; vol. VIII (1932) pp. 64-84.

Dasgupta, Shashibhusana 'Evolution of Mother-Worship in India', *Great Women of India*, edited by Swamy Madhavananda and R. C. Majumdar, Advaita Ashrama, Almora 1953, pp. 49-86.

Davane, G. V. 'The Goddess Sarasvatī in Sanskrit Literature', *Journal of the University of Bombay* vol. XXXVII No. 73 (1968), pp. 70-77.

Gode, P.K. 'Studies in the History of Hindu Festivals,' *Studies in Indian Cultural History*, Vol. II, Poona, 1960, pp. 186-260.

Gonda, J. 'A Note on Indra in Purāṇic Literature', *Purāṇa*, Vol. IX, No. 2(1967) pp. 222-261.

Gupta, A.S. 'Conception of Sarasvatī in the Purāṇas', *Purāṇa*, Vol. IV No. 1 (1962), pp. 55-95.

Gupta, S. 'The Catur Vyūha and the Viśākhāyupa in the Pancarātra', *Brahma Vidyā*, vol. XXXV, Parts 3—4, December (1071), pp. 189-204,

Gupta, B.A. 'Harvest festivals in honour of Gaurī and Geṇesha', *Indian Antiquary*, vol. XXXv (1906), pp. 60-64.

Hall, Fitz-Edward 'Śrī Sūkta or Litany to fortune; text and commentary with translation,' *Journal of the Asiatic Society of Bengal*, vol. XXv III (1859), pp. 121–135.

Hazra, R.C. 'Compilation of Purāṇic Works or Chapters on Śakti Worship', *Our Heritage*, vol. iv, Part I (1956), pp. 67–88.

Hopkins, E.W. 'Indra as god of fertility', *Journal of the American Oriental Society*, Vol. XXXVI (1917), pp. 242-268.

Macdonell, A.A. 'The Development of Early Hindu Iconography', *Journal of the Royal*

Asiatic Society of Great Britain and Ireland (1916), pp. 125-130.

Menon, C. A. '*Onam*—The Great National festival of Malabar', *Bharat-Kaumudi*, Studies in Indology honour of Radhakumud Mookherji, Part I, 1945, pp. 427-432.

Mitra S.C. 'On the cult of the Tree Goddess in Eastern Bengal', *Man in India*, vol. II, Nos. 1-2 (1972), pp. 228-241.

Motichandra 'Padmā-Śrī—Lady of Beauty and abundance', *Nehru Abhinandan Grantha*, Calcutta, 1949, pp. 497-513

'Yaksha Cult, some aspects of, in ancient India', *Prof. Gurye felicitation Volume*, Bombay, 1955, pp. 245-264

Oldenberg, Hermann 'Die Vedischen Wrote fur "Schon" und "Sehonheit" und das vedische Schonheitsgefuhl,' *Kleine Schriften*, Ed. Klans L. Janert, Wiesbaden, 1967, pp. 830—866.

Palsule, C.B. 'Patanjali's Intepretation of RV 10, 71, 2', *Indian Antiquary*, Vol. III, Nos. 1—4 (1969) reprinted, pp. 1—3.

Rai, G.S. 'Vāmana Legend—In the Vedas, Epics and Purāṇas', *Purāṇa*, Vol. XII No. 1 (1970) pp. 102-140.

Scheftelowitz, I 'Śrī Sūkta ', *ZD.M.G.* 75 (1921). pp. 37-50.

Shembavnekar, K.M. 'The metamorphosis of Uṣas', *Annāls of the Bhandarkar Oriental Research Institute*, Vol. XVII, Part IV (1936), pp. 351-357.

Sivaramamurti, C. 'Goddess Lakṣmī and her Symbols', *Journal of U.P. Historical Society*, Vol. XIV (1941) pp. 21-24.

Srikantaliya, K. 'Notes on South Indian Festivals', *Indian Antiquary*, Vol. XX (1891), p. 430.

Sukthankar, V.S. 'Epic Studies VI', *Annals of the Bhandarkar Oriental Research Institute*. Vol. XVIII (1937), pp, 1-76.

INDEX

W

Y

Z